"双一流"高校建设"十四五"规划系列教材

乒乓球运动双语教程

主　编　杨博文

副主编　屈连朋　任　波　赵柏锜

天津大学出版社
TIANJIN UNIVERSITY PRESS

图书在版编目（CIP）数据

乒乓球运动双语教程 / 杨博文主编. -- 天津 : 天津大学出版社, 2022.6（2025.1 重印）
“双一流”高校建设“十四五”规划系列教材
ISBN 978-7-5618-7214-7

Ⅰ. ①乒… Ⅱ. ①杨… Ⅲ. ①乒乓球运动－双语教学－高等学校－教材 Ⅳ. ①G846

中国版本图书馆CIP数据核字（2022）第098586号

PINGPANGQIU YUNDONG SHUANGYU JIAOCHENG

出版发行 天津大学出版社
地　　址 天津市卫津路92号天津大学内（邮编：300072）
电　　话 发行部：022-27403647
网　　址 www.tjupress.com.cn
印　　刷 北京盛通数码印刷有限公司
经　　销 全国各地新华书店
开　　本 710mm×1010mm　1/16
印　　张 15
字　　数 319千
版　　次 2022年6月第1版
印　　次 2025年1月第2次
定　　价 45.00元

序

从1917年毛泽东同志发出"欲文明其精神，先自野蛮其体魄"的呼喊至今，体育的内涵和外延从未如此丰富和清晰。体育承载着国家强盛、民族振兴的梦想。近些年来，习近平总书记一直强调："体育是提高人民健康水平的重要途径，是满足人民群众对美好生活向往、促进人的全面发展的重要手段，是促进经济社会发展的重要动力，是展示国家文化软实力的重要平台。"（《论把握新发展阶段、贯彻新发展理念、构建新发展格局》，中央文献出版社，2021，第406页）

随着全球化时代的到来，各国政治、经济、文化、社会等领域的交流合作日益紧密。其中，语言是文化的一个重要组成部分，是联通世界的桥梁，会对政治、经济、社会、科技乃至文化本身产生深刻的影响。

一方面，汉语是目前世界上使用人口最多的语言，英语则是当今世界上使用最广泛的语言。因此，掌握这两种语言，充分发挥语言的力量，就拥有了一块进入国际社会的"敲门砖"。鉴于此，我国高等院校和体育院校在体育课上使用汉语教学时有必要将国际通用的英语融入其中，进行体育课双语教学，使学生在两种语言环境下学习、掌握知识和技能。

另一方面，乒乓球作为中国体育"为国争光"以及"全民健身"的典范，已经成为凝聚国家认同的象征符号，并一直在新中国的政治、文化层面广泛地发挥作用。在对外交往中，"国球"乒乓球已经成为一张独特的名片。例如，"小球转动大球"的乒乓外交曾为新中国的外交发展奠定重要基础。当今，中国乒乓球运动的实力已经达到世界顶尖水平。国际乒乓球联合会热切希望中国承担起向全世界推广乒乓球运动的重任，中国乒乓球界也一直承担着乒乓球国际化的推动者这一重要角色，致力于在世界舞台上讲好中国故事，传递中国乒乓文化，积极探索乒乓球运动的可持续发展，积极开展乒乓球国际推广与发展计划。例如，中国国家乒乓球队前往非洲、大洋洲、美洲开展了助力当地青少年乒乓球运动水平提升的"筑梦行动"。如今，大批中国优秀乒乓球教练、运动员走出国门，在世界各国执教、交流；大批外国学生来到北京体育大学等高等体育院校或乒乓球训练基地进行专业乒乓球训练和深造；国家体育总局和上海市人民政府在上海体育学院共建共管的中国乒乓球学院也吸引了众多外国学生来中国学习、交流。在这个过程中，中国乒乓球运动的先进理论被传播到国外，对推进乒乓球运动在世界范围的发展是非常重要的。与此同时，全国大多数高等院校开设了乒乓球必修课、选修课，众多体育院校也在培养全面发展的乒乓球专业人才。为了配合乒乓球国际化的推广进程，拓宽体育和教育结合工作的发展思路，我们需要具备国际交流能力和市场竞争力的高素质、复合型乒乓球人才。在学校中开展乒乓球中英文双语教学，可使学生在掌握专业技能和知识的同时，具备双语表达能力。

因此，为推动乒乓球运动的发展，顺应当前扩大乒乓球对外开放的趋势，满足我国高等院校、体育院校乒乓球专业教学和广大乒乓球爱好者的需求，本书作者编写了《乒乓球运动双语教程》一书。本书汇集了天津大学乒乓球教学团队多年的教学经验和海外执教经验，以中英文对照的方式对乒乓球运动发展史、基本理论、基本技术、基本战术与基本打法、训练方法、教学计划、课程思政教学、竞赛规则等进行讲解，对中国乒乓球运动教学与训练的核心理念做了全新的阐述，并且配置了专业乒乓球运动员张耀文和凌子的连续示范动作图片，图片生动、形象，便于乒乓球教练、运动员和爱好者掌握动作要领。另外，本书介绍了以"国球精神"为代表的乒乓球课程思政教学内容和案例，可向我国学生和海外留学生传递我国乒乓球运动所蕴含的丰富的道德教育元素，有助于培养我国学生的爱国、诚信、友善等社会主义核心价值观。

《乒乓球运动双语教程》一书是对中国乒乓球教学理论国际化的初步探索，既切实可行，又在观念上有所突破。本书能够顺利出版得力于天津大学教务处和体育部的大力支持，天津大学乒乓球教师和天津大学乒乓球队的辛勤付出，以及天津大学出版社的细心工作，在此一并表示诚挚的谢意。

杨博文
2022 年 1 月 7 日于天津大学

图　　示

Diagram

发球者的击球路线

Server’s Path of Ball

接发球者的击球路线

Receiver’s Path of Ball

步法移动之前脚的位置

Initial Position

步法移动之后脚的位置

Finish Position

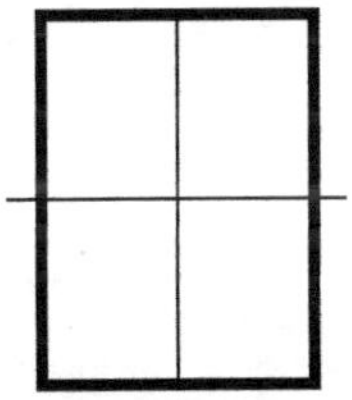

乒乓球台台面

Playing Surface of Table-Tennis Table

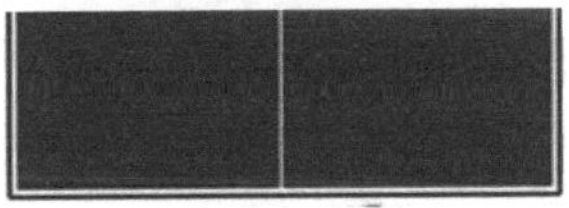

乒乓球台底线区域

End Line Court of Table-Tennis Table

球拍击球的一瞬间

The Moment the Racket Hits the Ball

球被击出后在空中的飞行弧线

Trajectory After thc Ball Is Hit Out

球落桌弹起后的飞行弧线

Ball Bounce Trajectory

目 录

CONTENTS

第一章　乒乓球运动发展史

Chapter 1　Evolutionary History of Table Tennis

第一节　乒乓球运动的起源

Section 1　Origin of Table Tennis

乒乓球是一项有趣且让人感到刺激的运动项目，深受各年龄段、各行各业人们的喜爱。虽然任何人都可以喜欢上乒乓球，但真正要像擅长其他运动一样打好乒乓球，就需要时间和精力的投入、技能指导和训练。它是一项易于上手的运动项目，而且已在世界各地开展得很广泛。乒乓球也被看作一项高精度的运动项目，这意味着，如果一个人想参与其中，那就很可能会比许多其他体育项目投入更长的时间。

Table tennis is an interesting and exciting game enjoyed by people of all ages and from all walks of life. Anyone can enjoy playing table tennis, but to be good at table tennis like any other sport requires dedication, coaching and training. It is a very accessible sport and is widely played throughout the world. Table tennis is regarded as a high-precision sport, which means that once a person wants to get involved, he or she is likely to remain involved for longer than that in many other sports.

乒乓球的历史与其器材的演变发展有着密不可分的关系。乒乓球和其他很多体育运动一样，最初也只是社会中无足轻重的一部分。乒乓球起源于19世纪末的英国，并由网球运动派生而来。由于英国天气多雨，一些英国大学生就尝试着将“草地网球”搬进了室内的餐桌上，进而

The history of table tennis parallels the evolution of its equipment. Like many other sports, table tennis began as a mild social diversion. Table tennis originated in the United Kingdom in the late 19th century and developed from tennis. Some British college students attempted to move the lawn tennis onto the dining table because of its rainy weather.

将其发展成一种叫戈西马(图 1.1.1)或弗利姆—弗拉姆(图 1.1.2)的室内网球运动。由于当时没有统一的规则,乒乓球只是被当作在餐桌上进行的餐后娱乐项目。当时乒乓球器材也和今天的大不一样,球拍用羊皮纸贴成,形状为长柄椭圆形,而球也是用软木或橡胶制成。然而,橡胶球的弹性太大,而软木球的弹性又太小。

They developed the game as an indoor version of tennis, which was originally called Gossima (Figure 1.1.1) or Flim-Flam (Figure 1.1.2). Without any unified rules, the game was played on dining tables as an after-dinner entertainment. The equipment was also much different from what is used today. People played with long handed and oval-shaped rackets covered with parchment and balls of cork or rubber. Nevertheless, the bounce was too wild with rubber balls, and too poor with cork balls.

图 1.1.1　戈西马

Figure 1.1.1　Gossima

图 1.1.2　弗利姆—弗拉姆

Figure 1.1.2　Flim-Flam

大约在 1900 年,有位名叫詹姆斯·吉布的英国人引进了一种用赛璐珞材料制成的球。大家发现这种球很适合用于乒乓球运动,因为赛璐珞球有很好的弹性,它促进了乒乓球运动走向成熟。赛璐珞球的引入使赛璐珞

Circa 1900, James Gibb, a British, introduced into the game a ball that was made from celluloid. The celluloid ball was found to be a perfect ball for the game. The celluloid ball had the perfect bounce, and promoted the maturity of table tennis. The intro-

球代替了橡皮球和软木球。随着20世纪20年代赛璐珞球在全世界的快速传播,乒乓球运动才开始逐渐被人们接受。由于球拍击球后发出“乒乒乓乓”的声音,乒乓球就开始得此绘声之名。

第一次世界大战后,乒乓球运动开始在欧洲的俱乐部中流行起来,欧洲许多国家成立了乒乓球协会。1926年,国际乒乓球联合会(以下简称国际乒联)在柏林成立,被称为“乒乓球之父”的伊沃·蒙塔古(图1.1.3)先生当选为首任主席。同年在伦敦举行了第一届世界乒乓球锦标赛(以下简称世乒赛)。作为最负盛名的乒乓球赛事,截至2021年,世乒赛已经举行了56届比赛。

duced celluloid balls replaced rubber balls and cork balls. With the rapid diffusion of the celluloid ball in the 1920s, table tennis gradually began to be the accepted. The game is named “Ping Pong” by specific sound of celluloid ball bouncing off the racket.

After World War Ⅰ, the game became popular in sport clubs throughout Europe and many table tennis associations were formed in European countries. In 1926, the International Table Tennis Federation (ITTF) was founded in Berlin. Ivor Montagu (Figure 1.1.3), regarded as “the father of table tennis”, was elected the first ITTF president. In the same year, the First World Table Tennis Championships (World Championships) were held in London. As the most reputable table tennis competition around the world, the World Championships have been held 56 sessions by 2021.

图1.1.3　伊沃·蒙塔古

Figure 1.1.3　Ivor Montagu

第二节　乒乓球运动发展的五个时期

Section 2　Five Periods of Development of Table Tennis

一、欧洲统治时期(1926—1951年)

欧洲选手在此期间统治了世界乒坛,他们共获得了109个世界冠军,占全部锦标赛冠军总数的90%以上。除此之外,美国选手获得了其余的所有冠军。这个时期也被称为"硬胶皮"时代,一些运动员开始使用由颗粒胶覆盖的球拍(图1.2.1),从而在一定程度上推动了这项运动的发展。胶皮球拍有一定的摩擦力,可使球旋转,但是速度、力量不足。球拍利守不利攻,使运动员容易控制球和进行防守。因此,削、搓打法是当时的主流,运动强度也不大。

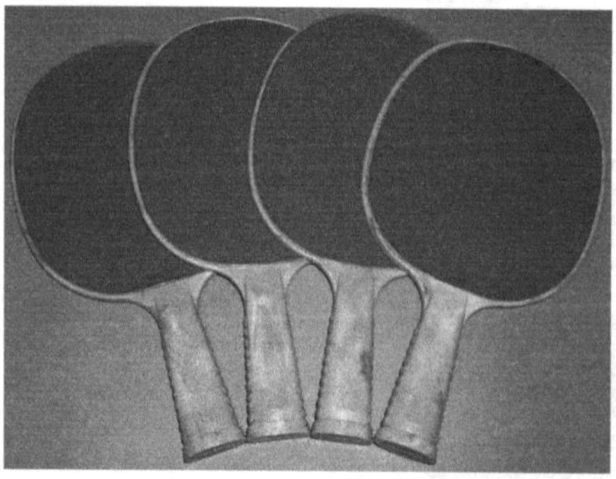

图1.2.1　硬胶皮球拍

Figure 1.2.1　Hard Rubber Rackets

Ⅰ. European Dominance (1926-1951)

European players dominated table tennis competition during this period by obtaining 109 world champion titles. This accounts for over 90% the total number of world champion titles in all the world championships. Besides, the U.S. team won the remaining world champion titles. This period was also known as Hard Rubber Era, the racket covered by pimpled rubber (Figure 1.2.1) began to be used by some players and the game took a major leap forward. The rubber racket had a certain force of friction and could apply a moderate amount of spin to ball in spite of its lack of speed and power. The racket was good for defense and bad for attack, which made it easier for players to control and defend. As a result, it required not much energy and most players just pushed and chopped.

二、日本队称雄世界乒坛（1951—1959年）

日本选手采用直拍打法，以凶狠有力的长抽打法和惊人的步法，在20世纪50年代初至60年代初这段时间成为乒乓球运动的霸主。然而，日本队获得成功最为重要的原因在于创造性地使用了海绵球拍。日本运动员利用该“武器”首次将击球的力量和速度融为一体。佐藤博治成为第一位使用海绵球拍获得男子单打世界冠军的运动员，他也是获得该项荣誉的第一位非欧洲运动员。

然而，海绵球拍的使用曾在当时引起了许多人的反对。

直到1959年，经过国际乒联的一系列实验和商讨后，才通过一项对球拍规格的限制性决定：运动员可以在海绵上覆盖一层颗粒胶（颗粒可朝里或向外），其总厚度不得超过4 mm。从此之后，海绵球拍开始在乒乓球比赛中广泛应用。

Ⅱ. Age of Japanese Dominance (1951-1959)

Japanese, with their pen-hold grip, long and powerful strokes, and excellent footwork, dominated the game from the early 1950s and early 1960s. But their success depended mainly on the creative use of the sponge bat. Japanese players were the first to capitalize on the greatly increased strength and speed of this “weapon”. Hiroji Satoh became the first player to win a world championship when using a sponge bat and was the first non-European winner.

However, the use of sponge bat had aroused a lot of opposition from many people.

Until 1959, after a series of experimentation and repeated discussion by ITTF, the restrictions of rubber over a sponge layer (pimples inward or outward) with a maximum thickness of 4 mm was decided on. Since then, sponge bats has been widely used in table tennis competitions.

三、中国队的崛起（1959—1969年）

中国选手当时多使用正贴胶皮的直拍，以强劲的正手攻球技术和自身“快、狠、准、变”的特点，开始在世界乒坛崭露头角。1959年，中国选手容国团获得世乒赛男子单打冠军，并成为

Ⅲ. The Rise of China (1959-1969)

Chinese players, with their pips-out pen-hold grip, strong forehand strike, and the combination of speed, strength, accuracy and variation, began to be very competitive. In 1959, Rong Guotuan captured the first men’s

中国体育史上第一个世界冠军。

singles champion title in the World Championships and became the world champion in Chinese sports history.

20世纪60年代初，日本人发明了一种足以载入史册的新技术——弧圈球。由于这项技术上旋强烈且弧线多变，因此在当时极具威力。更为重要的是，弧圈球技术对世界乒乓球技术的发展起到了很大的促进作用。

The loop drive, regarded as a revolutionary skill in history, was created by Japanese in the early 1960s. This skill is very forceful with its strong topspin and variable trajectory. More significantly, it had a very big stimulative effect on the development of the skill of world table tennis.

四、欧亚抗衡（1969—1995年）

Ⅳ. Fierce Competition Between Asia and Europe (1969-1995)

随着大量的高科技乒乓球拍的发展和使用，在20世纪70年代后，世界乒乓球技术有了突飞猛进的发展。经过近20年的努力，欧洲选手兼取了中国直拍快攻和日本弧圈球打法的优点，创造了两面弧圈球结合快攻的新打法。采用这种打法的运动员击球力量大、旋转强，左右开弓，能够退至中台用正手对拉弧圈球。瑞典选手斯特兰·本格森在1971年夺得世乒赛男子单打冠军，由此开启了瑞典乒乓球队20年在世界乒坛的重要影响力。另外，迈克尔·阿佩依伦、埃里克·林德、简-诺瓦·瓦尔德内尔和约尔根·佩尔森也为瑞典队立下汗马功劳。中国队也不甘落后，在前南斯拉夫诺维萨德举行的第36届世乒赛上，一举夺得全部7项冠军，令

With the development and usuage of a large number of high-tech rackets, the skill of world table tennis has greatly progressed since the 1970s. After twenty years of efforts, some European players absorbed the strengths of Chinese pen-holders and Japanese loopers to establish a new playing style of fast two-winged looper. Players of this style use longer topspin strokes that carry a lot of power, and are equally strong with both forehand and backhand. They can move back into the middle court and execute counterloops with the forehand. In 1971, Stellan Bengtsson (SWE) won the men's singles champion title in the World Championships and heralded the start of two decades of Swedish influence, with the contributions of top players such as Mikael Appelgren, Erik Lindh, Jan-Ove Waldner,

人称奇。

1988年的汉城奥运会，乒乓球第一次成为正式比赛项目，在这之后乒乓球受到了更广泛的关注。瑞典选手简-诺瓦·瓦尔德内尔在夺得1992年奥运会男子单打冠军后，成为首个乒乓球"大满贯"运动员。

五、中国队统领世界乒坛（1995年至今）

第43届世乒赛在中国天津举行，中国队第二次囊括了全部冠军。该届世乒赛后中国乒乓球队一直统治着世界乒坛。中国乒乓球队的长盛不衰不仅在于运动员采用了领先世界的快攻结合弧圈打法并具备精湛的前三板技术，而且在技术和器材的创新方面，中国乒乓球队也走在了各国的前面。例如直拍横打技术和长齿胶皮的使用都曾为中国乒乓球队的成功发挥了重要作用。在此期间，刘国梁、孔令辉、王楠和张怡宁相继成为乒乓球"大满贯"得主。截至2021年，中国乒乓球队总共获得了252个世界冠军（包括奥运会、世乒赛和世界杯）。在中国有超过6 000万人打乒乓球，其中有一半为注

and Jorgen Persson. Chinese players made a miracle at the 36th World Championships held in Nova Sad, Yugoslavia. People witnessed a total triumph for China, whose athletes won all of the seven championships.

For the very first time, table tennis was featured in the Olympic Games that were held in Seoul in 1988, and after that it gained true worldwide recognition. In 1992, Jan-Ove Waldner (SWE) became Olympic singles champion and the first table tennis millionaire.

V. China's Overlord Position (1995-)

The 43rd World Table Tennis Championships were held in Tianjin, China. It was a total triumph for Chinese teams for the second time, winning all the champion titles. Since then, China has ushered a new era of dominance that continues today. Not only they pioneered the fast attack combined with loop style of play and had the superb technique for the first three strokes, but also they created lots of innovative skills and equipment, such as pen-hold backside hit and long-pip rubber. Liu Guoliang, Kong Linghui, Wang Nan and Zhang Yining became the table tennis millionaire successively. By 2021, the Chinese table tennis teams had won 252 world championships (include Olympic Games, World Cham-

册运动员。由于乒乓球运动出色的战绩、广泛的群众参与度以及较大的社会影响力，乒乓球被誉为中国的“国球”。

pionship and World Cup). More than 60 million people in China play table tennis and half of them are registered athletes. With the outstanding achievements, broad public participation and huge social influence, table tennis has been the national game of China.

虽然近几年中国队依然保持绝对的领先地位，但欧洲和亚洲其他国家的运动员不甘示弱，曾几次获得过世乒赛和奥运会的冠军，力争缩小与中国的差距。

Although China continues to hold its lead in recent years, players from other Asian nations and European players have broken through to gain individual champion title in the World Table Tennis Championships and the Olympic Games titles, and try to narrow the gap.

第三节　奥运会乒乓球运动史

Section 3　History of Table Tennis in the Olympic Games

国际奥委会第84届会议于1981年在巴登举行，会议通过了一项决议：从1988年汉城奥运会开始，乒乓球将被列为夏季奥运会的正式比赛项目。从这以后，乒乓球项目在1992年巴塞罗那奥运会、1996年亚特兰大奥运会、2000年悉尼奥运会、2004年雅典奥运会、2008年北京奥运会、2012年伦敦奥运会、2016年里约奥运会和2020年东京奥运会上脱颖而出，全球电视观众不断增加：在雅典奥运会上，乒乓球比赛在所有奥运会项目的收视率中排名第五。从2008年北京奥运会（图1.3.1）开始，乒乓球比赛项目有所调

The 84th Session of the International Olympic Committee(IOC) was held in Baden in 1981, and passed a resolution: table tennis was listed as the formal event in the Summer Olympic Games, beginning with the 1988 Olympic Games in Seoul, South Korea. Since then table tennis has distinguished itself in the Olympic Games in Barcelona 1992, Atlanta 1996, Sydney 2000, Athens 2004, Beijing 2008, London 2012, Rio 2016 and Tokyo 2020 with ever increasing worldwide television audiences: table tennis ranked number 5 in all sports at the Athens Olympic Games. Starting from the 2008 Olympic Games in Beijing(Figure 1.3.1), the mode

整，团体比赛取代了之前的双打比赛，这项团体赛制类似于网球中的戴维斯杯模式，即 2 个单打、1 个双打，然后是 2 个单打，一个球员只能参加其中的两场比赛。在 2020 年东京奥运会上，乒乓球比赛项目又增设了混双比赛。中国乒乓球男女队在历届奥运会乒乓球比赛上实力超群，共赢得了 37 枚金牌当中的 32 枚。他们在奥运会上最近一次丢掉金牌是在 2020 年东京奥运会，当时日本选手伊藤美诚和水谷隼在混双比赛的决赛中击败了中国队的刘诗雯和许昕。

of the table tennis competition changed. The doubles events were replaced by a team event, similar to the Davis Cup mode in tennis, that is, 2 singles, 1 doubles and then 2 singles, where a single player can only play in two of the contests. In the 2020 Olympic Games in Tokyo, mixed doubles was added to the table tennis events. The Chinese men's and women's teams always distinguished themselves in Olympic table tennis competitions, winning 32 out of 37 gold medals. The latest gold medals they lost in the Olympic Games was in 2020 Tokyo, where Ito Mima and Mizutani Jun(JPN) defeated Chinese players Liu Shiwen and Xu Xin in the mixed doubles final.

图 1.3.1　北京奥运会乒乓球比赛

Figure 1.3.1　Table Tennis Competition at the Beijing Olympic Games

第二章　乒乓球运动基本理论

Chapter 2　Basic Theory of Table Tennis

第一节　乒乓球技术五要素

Section 1　Five Elements of Table Tennis Technique

乒乓球技术有两大基本原则，即一次击球必须同时具备准确性和威胁性。准确性，就是自己击球不失误，即按照比赛规则，当对方合法发球或合法还击后，己方必须击球，使球直接越过（或绕过）球网，然后落到对方的台面上。威胁性，就是合法击过去的球要给对方造成威胁，或让对方失误。准确性和威胁性是对立统一的关系，两者不能孤立地存在。欲提高准确性，击球必须有合理的弧线；欲提高威胁性，就必须将旋转、力量、速度、弧线和落点同时结合在一次击球中。因此，以下就乒乓球技术中的五大要素进行详细介绍。

The table tennis technique has two basic principles. That is to say, to execute a stroke, you have to make it accurate and forceful. Accuracy means making no errors on your own shots. According to the game should rules, the ball, after having been served or returned, should be struck so that it directly passes over (or around) the net assembly and touches the opponent's playing surface. Forcefulness means a good return should do damage to the opponent and, if possible, force him into an error. Accuracy and forcefulness are a kind of unity of two opposites. Neither of the two basic principles can exist in isolation. To increase the accuracy, you must have a proper trajectory on your stroke. To strengthen the forcefulness, you have to combine five elements—spin, power, speed, trajectory and placement on a stroke. Thus, the five elements of the table tennis technique is elaborated as follows.

一、击球旋转

旋转是乒乓球区分于其他体育项目的最重要特征。如果将乒乓球与网球和羽毛球相比较,你会发现乒乓球的旋转变化更加多端,种类更为繁多。一项研究表明,乒乓球击球的最高转速可达 168 r/s。

当击球时,击球力的作用线不通过球心,是球产生旋转的原因。旋转的球体在空气之中飞行时呈一条弧线,由于球体一端的空气阻力大于另外一端,这就使得球体的飞行轨迹朝空气阻力较小的那个方向运动。

击球旋转主要有以下四种:上旋、下旋、侧旋和不转。

上旋球由于其球体上部的空气阻力大于其底部的空气阻力,因此上旋球的旋转方向是向前的,这也导致球体的飞行轨迹是向前下方的。当球落台后,向前拱,前冲力较大。用拍平挡上旋球,球会向上飞,弧线更高。因此,在击打上旋球时,拍形必须保持前倾。

下旋球由于其球体底部的空气阻力大于顶部的阻力,因此下旋球的旋转方向是向后的,这也导致球体的飞行轨迹是向上的。当球落台后前进力

I. Spin

Spin is the most important feature of table tennis in contrast to other sports. Compared to tennis and badminton, you will find that the spin of table tennis is more changeful and can be categorized into many different types. In one study, the highest spin speed of table tennis stroke was calculated at 168 revolutions per second (168 r/s).

When you strike a ball off center, it spins. A spinning ball curves as it travels through the air because the spin creates greater air resistance on one side of the ball than on the other side. This forces the ball to move toward the area of lower resistance.

There are four basic types of spins: topspin, backspin, sidespin, and no spin.

A topspin ball spins toward the direction in which it is traveling. It is because the ball has greater air resistance on the top and smaller on the bottom. This causes the ball to curve downward. When a topspin ball strikes the table, it jumps forward. When a topspin ball strikes your racket, the spin forces the ball into a trajectory that is higher than normal. To strike a topspin ball, you need to hit the center of the ball with a closed racket.

A backspin ball spins backward as it moves forward, for the ball has greater air resistance on the bottom and smaller on the top. This causes the ball to curve upward. When a

较弱。如用拍平挡下旋球，球会向下跑，弧线更低。因此，在击打下旋球时，拍形必须保持后仰。

backspin ball hits the table, the spin causes the ball to bounce up. When a backspin ball hits your racket, the spin forces the ball into a trajectory that is lower than normal. To strike a backspin ball, you should contact the ball below the center with an open racket.

侧旋球分为右侧旋球和左侧旋球。

There are two types of sidespin ball—right sidespin ball and left sidespin ball.

当用球拍击球的右侧时就会产生右侧旋，其在空中飞行的轨迹向击球者的左方偏转。接球者如用拍平挡右侧旋球，球会向左侧飞。因此，回击右侧旋球时，只需将球拍方向朝右侧偏转，击球的左侧。

Right sidespin is produced when the racket strikes the right side of the ball. Right sidespin causes the ball to curve to the server's left while traveling through the air, but bounce to the opponent's left when it hits his racket. To strike a right sidespin ball, angle your racket direction to the right and contact the left side of the ball.

当用球拍击球的左侧时就会产生左侧旋，其在空中飞行时向发球者的右方偏转。接球者如用拍平挡左侧旋球，球会向右飞。因此，回击左侧旋球时，只需将球拍方向朝左侧偏转，击球的右侧。

Left sidespin is produced when the racket strikes the left side of the ball. Left sidespin causes the ball to curve to the server's right while traveling through the air, but bounces to the opponent's right when it strikes his racket. To strike a left sidespin ball, angle your racket direction to the left and contact the right side of the ball.

当以较平的拍形击球的中部就会产生不转球，不转球的飞行方向是向前拱。不转球多被防守球员所采用或偶尔在发球中使用。

No spin is produced when a neutral racket contacts the middle of the ball and the ball travels forward. No-spin balls are primarily used by defensive players or occasionally in the serves.

以下是增加击球旋转的方法：

We can impart spin to the ball by using the following ways.

➢ 使力的作用线远离球心；

➢ 触球一瞬间加大挥拍速度；

➢ 借助来球的旋转；

➢ 用球拍合适的部位触球；

➢ 增加旋转的关键在于手腕和手指的发力。

总而言之，旋转是击球的关键。旋转在现代乒乓球比赛中正扮演着越来越重要的角色。增加旋转不仅能加强击球的威胁性，而且可以增加击球的稳定性。

➢ Strike a ball far off its center.

➢ Increase the racket speed on contact.

➢ Rely on the energy of the incoming ball.

➢ Contact the ball with the proper position of the racket.

➢ The key of imparting spin is the power from the wrist and fingers.

Generally speaking, spin is the key in hitting. Spin plays a more and more important role in modern table tennis competitions. Imparting spin can not only strengthen the forcefulness of hitting, but also increase the stability of hitting.

二、击球速度

乒乓球是一项快速的运动项目，中国人把这项运动形容为“像是在以100千米的时速下象棋”。速度是击球的核心。它是发展乒乓球运动的第一要素。它不仅指击球时球的运行速度，还包括击球时间、击球的突然性、步法移动以及应变的速度等。以下是提高击球速度的几种方法：

➢ 站位更靠近球台；

➢ 缩短引拍距离；

➢ 在球的上升期击球；

➢ 全身肌肉协调用力；

➢ 击球部位尽量靠近球心；

Ⅱ. Speed

Table tennis is a fast game, the Chinese describe the game “as like playing chess at 100 mph”. Speed is the nucleus. It is the first factor for developing the table tennis. It not only refers to the speed of the ball in hitting, but also includes the moment of the stroke, the suddenness of the stroke, footwork and the adjustment speed to changes. There are several ways for greater hitting speed.

➢ Stand closer to the table.

➢ Shorten the distance of backswing.

➢ Contact the ball on the rise of the ball.

➢ The muscles of the whole body coordinate the force.

➢ Striking spot on the ball should be

➢ 触球一瞬间加快挥拍速度；

➢ 挥拍发力方向更加向前以降低击球弧线高度。

closer to the center of the ball.

➢ Increase the racket speed on contact.

➢ Swing your racket more forward to lower the trajectory.

三、击球力量

Ⅲ. Power

力量是击球的基础。球拍对球的冲击力越大，球的移动速度越快；参与挥拍过程的关节和肌肉越多，产生的力就越大，这被称为力的总和。运动员的打法的威胁性、杀伤力都需要通过力量来体现。可以通过以下方法提高击球力量：

Power is the basis. The greater the impact of the racket on the ball, the faster the ball travels; the more joints and muscles involved in the swing process produce the greater of the force, which is known as a summation of forces.To ensure the execution of tactics and forcefulness of playing styles, power is essential. There are several ways for greater hitting power:

➢ 击球前充分引拍，取得足够的击球距离；

➢ 调整到合适的击球位置；

➢ 触球一瞬间加快挥拍速度；

➢ 全身肌肉协调用力；

➢ 击球后肌肉迅速调整、放松；

➢ 加强速度和力量素质训练。

➢ Greater backswing to make an enough space for hitting.

➢ Make a proper position for hitting.

➢ Increase the racket speed on contact.

➢ The muscles of the whole body coordinate the force.

➢ Relax the muscles after executing a stroke.

➢ Strengthen speed and strength training.

四、击球弧线

Ⅳ. Trajectory

击球弧线是指乒乓球被击出后在空中的飞行轨迹。弧线是击球的保证。只有根据不同的来球打出合理的击球弧线，准确性和命中率才会有所

Trajectory is the path that the ball travels through the air after it is hit. Trajectory is the guarantee. If a proper trajectory is produced for different incoming balls, the accuracy and

保障。反之，再好的技术，使用不当，失误过多，就不合理，就不能立足。在击球时，我们可以通过改变球拍运行方向、拍面角度、击球时间和触球部位来调整击球的弧线。

hit ratio of the strokes are ensured. On the other hand, good strokes or skills are nothing if consistency cannot be guaranteed. In actual play, we can adjust the trajectory by changing the racket direction, racket angle, stroke time and striking spot on the ball.

其中，拍面角度的调节对制造出合适的弧线是极为关键的。对于顶尖水平的运动员来说，只要在击球过程中掌握好拍形调节，就没有打不了的球。比如，在攻打台内球和冲杀下旋球时，拍形就需要略微前倾即可。然而，击球时原则上不要过分压低拍形，那是因为压低拍形将会丧失击球中大量的前进力，从而影响力量、速度的发挥。

Among these, the adjustment of racket angle is the most critical for achieving a proper trajectory. For many top players, no stroke is impossible if the racket angle is adjusted properly. For example, the racket should be slightly closed when hitting a short over-the-table ball and a backspin ball. However, the racket angle should never be too closed for in such a case it hinders the ability to produce power and speed in the stroke.

五、击球落点

V. Placement

落点是击球中的保障性元素。乒乓球项目是个体之间技战术的对抗，双方相互制约是其最大的特点。具备较强的变化、应变能力，才能有效地发挥自己的技战术水平。乒乓球的落点指球的触台点。研究乒乓球的落点和击球路线对提高击球质量和战术效果是十分重要的。

Placement is the gurantee element. Table tennis is a sport that pits one individual against another in a contest of skill and strategy. Counteracting against each other is its most intriguing character. Winning the battle of placement enables us to fully realize our technical and tactical objective. The placement refers to the point where the ball touches the table. It is of great significance to study the placement and path of the ball to improve the quality of stroke and tactical effect.

击球落点的作用为：

The effect of placement is as follows.

➢ 扩大对方的跑动范围，最大限

➢ Expand the opponent's running

度地调动对方，使其在前、后、左、右跑动中击球；

range, and maximize the opponent's movement to hit the ball in forward, back, left, and right runs.

➢ 增加对方让位和击球的难度；

➢ Increase the difficulty for the opponent to adjust the position and strike the ball.

➢ 回击对方的弱点和压制对方特长技术的发挥。

➢ Counterattack the opponent's weakness and suppress the opponent's expertise.

提高控制落点和变化落点能力的方法：

Methods to improve the ability to control and change the placement.

➢ 固定落点的练习；

➢ Fixed placement practice.

➢ 按规定击球路线进行变化落点的练习；

➢ Changing placement practice in the fixed paths.

➢ 采用多球练习的方法；

➢ Multi-ball practice.

➢ 提高手腕灵活性，经常进行变化拍形角度和拍面方向的练习。

➢ Improving the flexibility of the wrist: practice changing the racket angle and the racket direction.

总之，五大元素并不是孤立存在的，它们是互相影响、制约、促进、有机结合的。只单纯地掌握速度、旋转技能都不是全面的，都不能达到最高水平。在培养运动员时，要尽量将五大元素融合进去。据研究，一名顶尖运动员，在其身上五大元素一定要占有三项以上，否则他将很难取得突破。（表 2.1.1）

In summary, the five elements are never isolated individual items. They affect, control and push each other. Those who are competent solely in speed or spin will not reach the highest level. In the training of players, all five elements should be integrated. According to a research, an advanced player is good at three of the five at least. Otherwise, he will not make a breakthrough.(Table 2.1.1)

蒂莫·波尔：他的速度、旋转能力十分优秀，弧线、落点意识也不错，只是力量稍差一些。

Timo Boll: His speed and spin abilities are outstanding. His trajectory and placement consciousness are quite good. Only his power is a bit weak.

樊振东：他的速度、旋转、力量能力十分突出，弧线也不错，只是落点意

Fan Zhendong: His speed, spin and power abilities are excellent. His trajectory is

识稍弱。

not bad. His placement consciousness is comparatively weak.

许昕：他的旋转、弧线和落点能力突出，力量也较好，只是速度稍显不足。

Xu Xin: His spin, trajectory and placement abilities are very good. He has a good power but his speed is a bit insufficient.

在当代所有乒乓球运动员当中，马龙的能力是最强的，打法也是最先进的。在他的打法中，速度、力量、旋转三大动力元素完全具备且均高人一筹，高度统一，调节弧线和落点意识也不错。因此，他的击球威胁最大，技术实力也最雄厚。

Among all cotemporary players, Ma Long is the best. His style is also the most advanced. He is good at all dynamic elements of speed, power and spin. He has them well integrated. His ability to adjust trajectory and placement is reasonably good. Thus, his stroke is the most threatening and he has the strongest technical strength.

表 2.1.1　世界优秀男子乒乓球运动员五大竞技要素评价表

姓名	速度	力量	旋转	弧线	落点
蒂莫·波尔	优秀	较弱	优秀	较好	较好
樊振东	优秀	优秀	优秀	较好	较弱
许昕	较弱	较好	优秀	优秀	优秀
马龙	优秀	优秀	优秀	较好	较好

Table 2.1.1　Evaluation Form of Five Competitive Elements of World Elite Male Table Tennis Players

Name	Speed	Power	Spin	Trajectory	Placement
Timo Boll	excellent	fair	excellent	good	good
Fan Zhendong	excellent	excellent	excellent	good	fair
Xu Xin	fair	good	excellent	excellent	excellent
Ma Long	excellent	excellent	excellent	good	good

第二节　乒乓球运动常用术语

Section 2　Common Terms of Table Tennis

一、球台(图 2.2.1)

➢ 端线:沿每个 1.525 m 的比赛台面边缘各有一条 2 cm 宽的白线。

➢ 边线:沿每个 2.74 m 的比赛台面边缘各有一条 2 cm 宽的白线。

➢ 中线:一条与边线平行,将球台划分为两个相等半区的 3 mm 宽的白线。

➢ 左半台和右半台:通常击球范围占半个球台区域,其左右方向是对击球者本身来说的。

Ⅰ. Table(Figure 2.2.1)

➢ End line: A 2 cm-wide white line, along each 1.525 m edge of the playing surface.

➢ Side line: A 2 cm-wide white line, along each 2.74 m edge of the playing surface.

➢ Center line: A 3 mm-wide white line, running parallel with the side lines, dividing the playing surface into 2 equal half courts.

➢ Left half court and right half court: The strike zone is coincident with the half court; its direction is determined from the hitter's point of view.

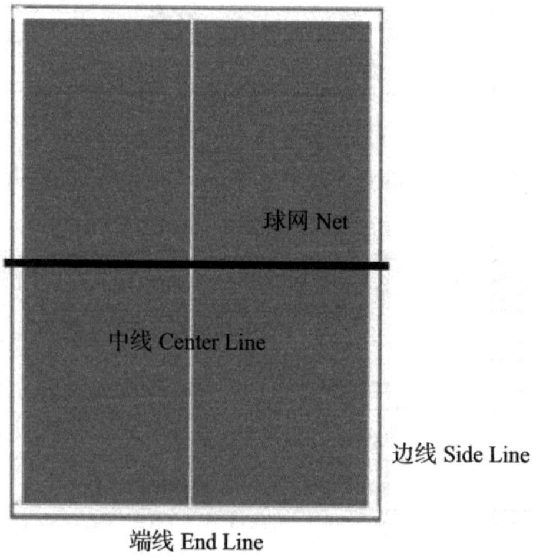

图 2.2.1　球台

Figure 2.2.1　Table

➢ 全台：是指击球范围占整个球台，不限落点和范围。

➢ Full court: The strike zone on the entire table without any placement or zone restriction.

二、站位（图 2.2.2~图 2.2.4）

Ⅱ. Stance（Figure 2.2.2-Figure 2.2.4）

站位就是击球前人与球台之间的位置，以下是三种基本站位方式。

Stance means how one positions himself as regard to the table before hitting. There are three kinds of basic stances as follows.

➢ 近台：指站位在离台端线 50 cm 范围以内。

➢ 中台：指站位在离台端线约 70 cm 处。

➢ 远台：指站位在离台端线 100 cm 范围以外。

➢ Short court: Within 50 cm away off the end line.

➢ Middle court: About 70 cm away off the end line.

➢ Back court: 100 cm or further away off the end line.

图 2.2.2 近台
Figure 2.2.2 Short Court

图 2.2.3 中台
Figure 2.2.3 Middle Court

图 2.2.4 远台
Figure 2.2.4 Back Court

三、击球时间（图 2.2.5）

Ⅲ. Timing（Figure 2.2.5）

击球时间是一个重要的问题。运动员要选择不同的时间段击球，从而获得满意的击球效果。一般打乒乓球存在着五个击球时间段，即上升前期、上升后期、高点期、下降前期和下降后期。

Timing is an important problem. Players need to choose the point of contact with the ball to produce the desired stroke. Generally speaking, there are five time periods for hitting when playing table tennis: early ascending, late ascending, top of the bounce, early descending, and late descending.

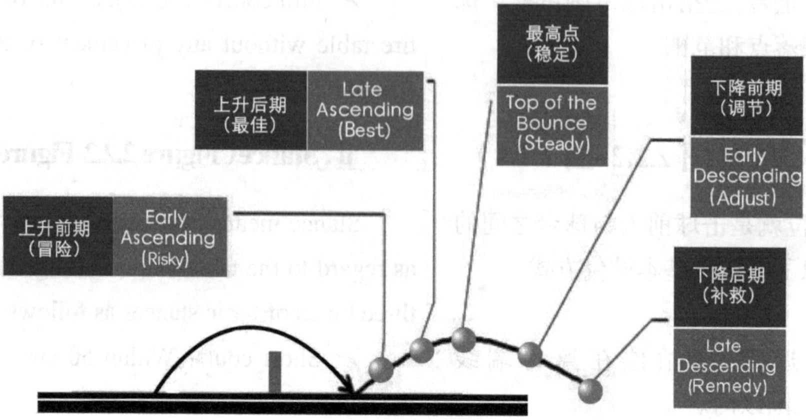

图 2.2.5　击球时间

Figure 2.2.5　Timing

在上升前期击球借力比较容易，然而在这个点球比网低，而且不出台，因此很难发力，很难掌握在该点击球的技术。

It is easy to rely on more energy of the incoming ball at early ascending period. Yet, this point is lower than the net and very short. So it is difficult to put much power into the stroke and mastering the skill is no easy task.

上升后期是最好的击球时间，因为此时球的旋转还没有发出来，而且这个点好发力，也好借力。因此，在这个点发力击球时球速最快，效果最佳，我们就可以将它作为高水平运动员训练、比赛中主要的击球时间，但这个点并不适合初学者。

The period of late ascending is the best time for hitting. The spin has not taken its full effect and the player can hit the shot much faster. It is easy to either put power into the stroke or rely on the energy of incoming ball. Therefore, hitting at this moment will have the fastest speed and obtain the best effect and we should look upon it as the primary timing for the advanced players. However, it is not recommended for the amateurs.

在高点期击球可能是最容易、最稳定的，因为运动员有着充裕的时间击打弧线较高的球，难度较小。然而

Hitting at the top of the bounce is likely to be the easiest and steadiest, because the ball has a high trajectory and the player has a

它的缺点在于：出手速度不快，动作不够隐蔽，击球的威胁性不大。因此，在比赛中不应将其作为主要的击球时间。

lot of time to work with. Nevertheless, there are some disadvantages as well. It is not fast or deceptive. The stroke is not so forceful. Therefore, we can't use it as the primary timing on strokes in the competition.

下降前期和下降后期主要用于防守阶段的击球，因此就不在此赘述。

Early descending and late descending periods are mostly used for thc defensive strokes. Thus, the discussions for these two timings are skipped.

四、球的落点

Ⅳ. The Placement of the Ball

➢ 短球：又称近网球，指球落在对方球台近网区，距网 40 cm 以内。

➢ Short ball: It is also called the near-net ball, which refers to a return landing close to the net (within approximately 40 cm) on the opponent's side.

➢ 长球：指球落在对方球台端线区，距端线 30 cm 以内。

➢ Deep ball: A return lands close to the end line (within approximately 30 cm) on the opponent's side.

➢ 离身球：指将球击到远离对方身体的位置。

➢ Passing shot: A ball to be hit far away from the opponent's body.

➢ 追身球：指将球击到对方中间近身的位置。

➢ Bodyline ball: A ball that hits very close to the opponent's middle position or near his body.

五、击球路线（图 2.2.6）

Ⅴ. Basic Paths (Figure 2.2.6)

五条基本的击球路线分别是左直线、中直线、右直线、右斜线和左斜线。

There are five basic paths along which a player can direct the ball: left down the line, middle down the line, right down the line, right crosscourt and left crosscourt.

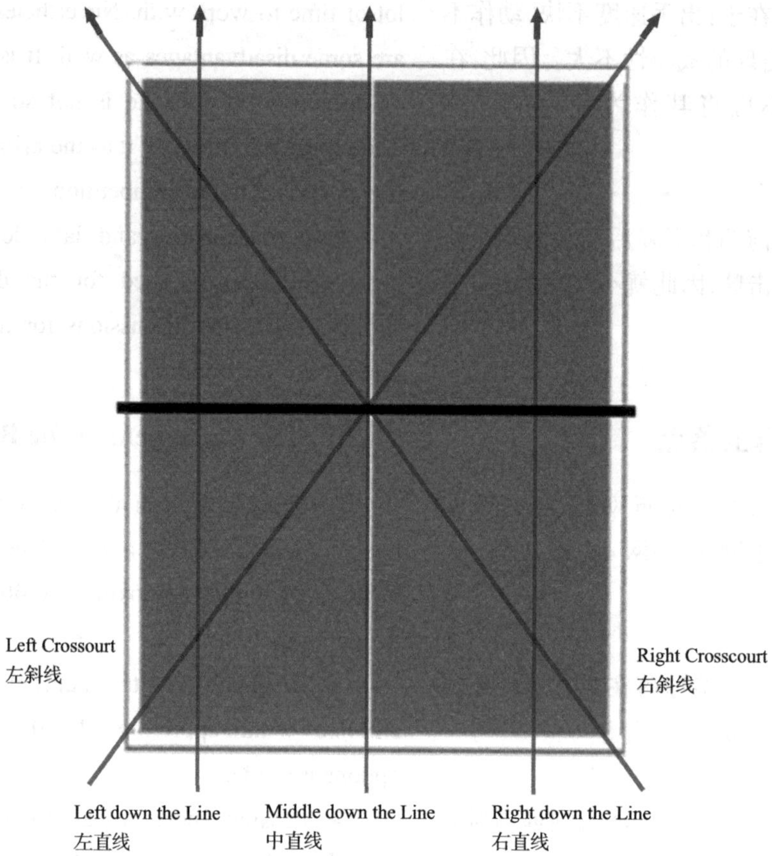

图 2.2.6　击球路线

Figure 2.2.6　Basic Paths

六、拍面角度（拍形）（图 2.2.7）

拍形是指球拍与球台所形成的角度。根据其定义，我们将拍形分为以下五种：前倾、稍前倾、垂直、稍后仰、后仰。

Ⅵ. Racket Angle（Figure 2.2.7）

Racket angle is the angle between the racket and the playing surface of the table. According to its definition, we can divide the racket angle into five categories: racket closed, racket slightly closed, racket in vertical, racket slightly opened and racket opened.

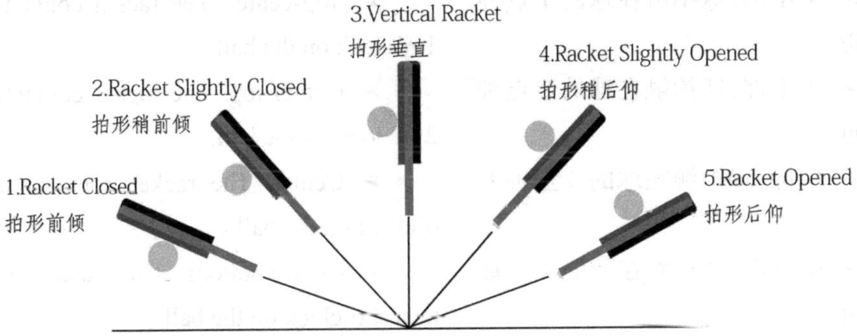

图 2.2.7 拍形

Figure 2.2.7 Racket Angle

七、击球部位

可以把球看成一个钟表。球的表面可以分为以下七个击球部位(图 2.2.8)。

VII. Contact Point on the Ball

The ball can be regarded as a clock. The surface of the ball can be divided into seven contact points (Figure 2.2.8).

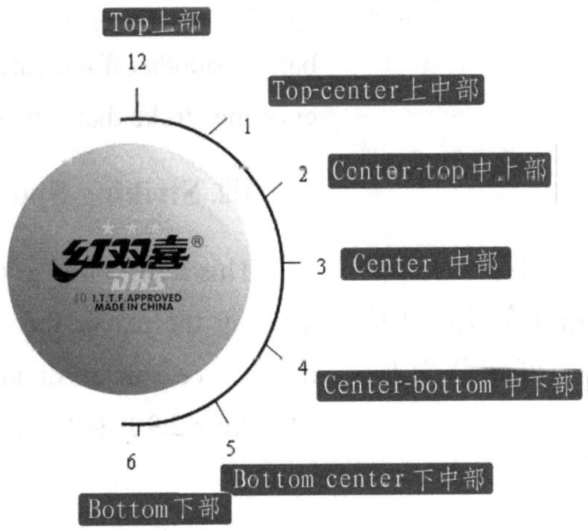

图 2.2.8 击球部位

Figure 2.2.8 Contact Point on the Ball

➢ 上部:球拍触在球的 12 点钟

➢ Top. The racket contacts near 12

处附近。

➢ 上中部：球拍触在球的 1 点钟处附近。

➢ 中上部：球拍触在球的 2 点钟处附近。

➢ 中部：球拍触在球的 3 点钟处附近。

➢ 中下部：球拍触在球的 4 点钟处附近。

➢ 下中部：球拍触在球的 5 点钟处附近。

➢ 下部：球拍触在球的 6 点钟处附近。

球拍的触球点和拍面角度决定了球的旋转强度，而旋转强度又反过来影响球在空中的飞行轨迹和在台面上的弹跳。旋转的类型和转速也会影响球从球拍上反弹的方式，这反过来又会影响下一次击球。

o'clock on the ball.

➢ Top-center. The racket contacts near 1 o'clock on the ball.

➢ Center-top. The racket contacts near 2 o'clock on the ball.

➢ Center. The racket contacts near 3 o'clock on the ball.

➢ Center-bottom. The racket contacts near 4 o'clock on the ball.

➢ Bottom-center. The racket contacts near 5 o'clock on the ball.

➢ Bottom. The racket contacts near 6 o'clock on the ball.

The contact point and angle of the racket determines the spin impact on the ball, which in turn affects the path of the ball through the air and the bounce on the table. The spin type and the rotation speed will also affect how the ball rebounds off the bat, which in turn influence the stroke that can be played next.

八、触拍部位

运动员用球拍上面的哪一个部位击球，这个部位就是触拍部位。球拍的击球拍面（图 2.2.9）可划分为左、右、上、中、下等部位。

Ⅷ. Striking Spot on the Racket

This term refers to the part of the racket used by the player for striking the ball. The racket face can be divided into five regions (Figure 2.2.9): left, right, top, middle, and bottom.

九、拍面方向

在一般情况下，如果你的球拍拍面向左侧挥动，就会击到球的右侧；而

Ⅸ. Racket Direction

Generally, if you swing your racket to the left forward, the right side of the ball will

如果你的球拍拍面向右侧挥动，就会击到球的左侧。

be hit. Conversely, swing to the right forward, the left side of the ball will be hit.

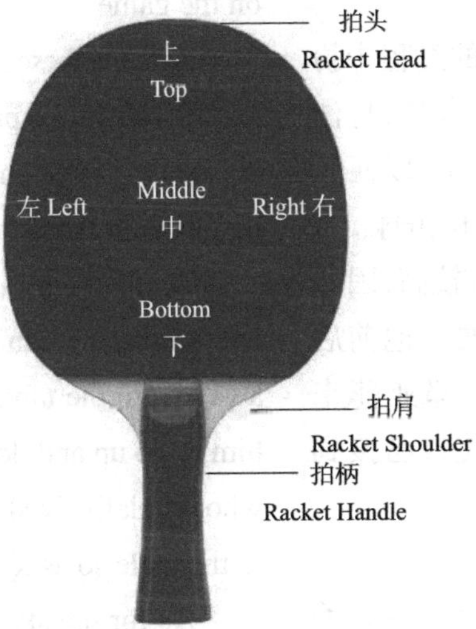

图 2.2.9 球拍拍面
Figure 2.2.9 Racket Face

第三节 击球的基本环节和击球动作的结构

Section 3 Basic Links of Hitting a Shot and Structure of Executing a Stroke

一、击球的基本环节

I. Basic Links of Hitting a Shot

1. 准备

击球的首个环节是准备，运动员在击球之前必须做好充足的准备。这里的准备包含两个方面：一是身体上

1. Preparation

The first link is preparation, which means that players must be prepared before hitting every shot. There are two aspects here.

的准备,包括基本站位和准备姿势;二是心理上的准备,运动员必须盯住球、集中注意力于比赛。

One is the physical preparation including basic stance and ready position. The other is the mental preparation, which means that the player has to watch the ball and concentrate on the game.

基本站位在准备击球的过程中扮演着很重要的角色。不同身高、打法的运动员有着不一样的站位,以便其选择最常使用、最舒服的站位击球。

Among these, basic stance plays an important role in the preparation. It varies depending on the height and style of the player so that he can hit the shots most often and comfortably.

关于身高,王励勤身材较高,因此他的站位能稍远离球台,便于他前后移动。但是对身材较矮的邓亚萍来说,她必须站在近台才能使自己接到短球。

As for height, Wang Liqin is a tall athlete so that he can choose a position slightly away from the table, which is convenient for him to go up and down. But for Deng Yaping, who is relatively short, she has to keep closer to the table so as to hit the short return.

关于打法,如果一名运动员有着很强的反拉能力,他就可以站位稍远;而如果一名运动员发力较弱却善于借助来球的力量击球,则应站在近台附近。

As for the styles, the player with a good strong counterdrive ability should position himself a little further. A player with limited power in stroke and usually relying on more energy of the incoming ball should position himself closer to the table.

2. 判断

2. Judgement

判断是击球过程的基础。在比赛中,运动员如能将对手来球的旋转、落点、弧线判断清楚,就能使自己的动作更加协调、放松和果断。相反,如果他判断不准确,就会在比赛中击球时受到犹豫、紧张等消极情绪的影响。

Judgment is the foundation of hitting the shots. Correct judgement on the ball's spin, placement and trajectory makes the player more coordinated, relaxed and decisive. Conversely, if he fails to do that, it will result in hesitation and tenseness in addressing his strokes in the competition.

提高判断能力的一种方法是预判。预判是指在本方击球质量保证的

One method to improve judgment ability is anticipation. Anticipation is under the

前提下，根据对方的击球习惯做出前期判断。这样对方的回球就基本上在自己的准备、掌控之中，下板球就比较容易按照事先的设想进行，它无疑会对击球的命中率产生积极影响。其中的诀窍有以下三个方面：

premise that one can guarantee the quality of his strokes to make an early judgment on how his opponent is going to play habitually. In that case, the opponent's return is basically under control and his next stroke can be easily executed. This will definitely exert positive impact on hit ratio. There are three ways of doing this trick.

➢ 掌握乒乓球击球的基本规律，这样预判也会变得轻车熟路；

➢ Fully understanding the basic rules of hitting the shots, the anticipation will be more accurate.

➢ 预判需要击球质量作为保证；

➢ Anticipation needs quality strokes as insurance.

➢ 战术套路的运用得当也经常对预判起到至关重要的作用。

➢ The proper use of the tactics usually affects anticipation mostly.

3. 移动

3. Movement

由于来球的落地变化多端，运动员必须迅速移动从而找到一个合适的击球位置。一位中国老教练曾经说过："步法是乒乓球比赛中争取积极主动的重要武器"，"乒乓球比赛靠的是七分脚、三分手"。他的话十分生动形象，而且很有道理。因此，在我们心里必须建立这样一个理念：在击球时先动脚，再挥拍。

Due to the variable placement of incoming ball, players must move quickly to get a proper position to hit a shot. An old Chinese coach once said, "Footwork is a significant weapon for taking initiative", "two thirds of the table tennis is footwork and one-third is hand skill". His words are very clear, vivid and make a lot of sense. Therefore, an idea must be kept in mind that footwork comes first while swinging.

4. 挥拍击球

4. Executing a Stroke

挥拍击球分为四个部分，这四个部分将在下一节详细介绍。我们先来介绍挥拍击球中很重要的一个过程：调节球。调节球有着肉眼难见的内

There are four sections involved in executing a stroke. The detailed discussion of these sections will be the focus of the next section. Here we can read an important

涵。调节是击球过程中最为精华的部分,也可称之为画龙点睛之笔。在比赛中,我们千万不能误认为用一种动作就能打遍所有的球,其中的细微调整变化往往会产生意想不到的结果。顶尖乒乓球运动员一般通过手指、手腕的发力摩擦以及改变击球的弧线和方向来调节球。他们通过手指、手腕带动前臂的收缩得当的击球力量比光用大臂、前臂收缩要大得多。一位著名的中国乒乓球教练曾经说:"用上臂打球的是小学生,用前臂打球的是中学生,用手腕打球的是大学生,用手指打球的那是博士生。"

process during executing a stroke—adjustment, which is something that shows in a subtle way. Adjustment can be the most spectacular part of executing a stroke, or it can be the delicate finishing touch. Particularly, in the competition, it is impossible to make all shots with only one approach. There are always tiny and subtle adjustments which produce different and unexpected results. Top table tennis players adjust by their wrist and fingers to impart power and spin to the ball, and change the direction and trajectory of a return. They get more power by contracting the forearm via fingers and wrist than by contracting arm and forearm alone. A famous Chinese coach once said: "He who plays with his arm is an elementary student. He who plays with his forearm is a secondary student. He who plays with the wrist is an undergraduate and he who plays with his fingers is the PhD."

5. 还原

根据各种不同的情况,运动员应该在击球后还原成准备姿势或调整好重心。这些都有利于下一板击球。

5. Recovery

In accordance with specific situations, the player should recover to the basic stance and position, or slightly adjust his center of gravity after executing a stroke. This will position him favorably for next shot.

二、击球动作的结构

Ⅱ. The Structure of Executing a Stroke

1. 引拍

引拍是击球动作中具有决定性的

1. Backswing

Backswing is a decisive factor in executing

因素,它是发力和使球产生旋转的前提条件。在挥拍击球之前,运动员要根据不同的来球情况进行引拍。如来球较长,引拍幅度就要更大;如来球较短,就要适当地引拍。

a stroke; it is the prerequisite to impart power and spin to the ball. Before making a stroke, the player executes different styles of backswing in different situations. For the deep incoming ball, a long backswing is needed. For the short return, we need a limited backswing.

2. 挥拍迎球

挥拍迎球是介于引拍和触球两者之间的动作过程,这个过程包括挥拍方向、挥拍速度、顺序、挥拍方法以及运动员的肌肉等元素。其中,挥拍方向会对球的旋转产生很重要的影响,而挥拍速度更多地影响击球的力量。在大多数情况下,球拍挥动的轨迹必须成一条直线,除非对球的落点和旋转判断有误,而需要你纠正准备执行的错误动作。

2. Swinging Toward the Ball

Swinging toward the ball is a process between the backswing and the contact, which includes the direction, speed, sequence, method of swing, and the working muscles. Among these, the direction of swing will exert many impacts on the spin of the ball, while the speed of swing mostly affects the power of the stroke. The track of the racket for most forward swings should be straight, except when you need to correct a wrong action for a misjudgment in placement or spin.

3. 球拍触球

球拍触球是击球动作中的核心和最关键的一步。它是提高击球质量的主要因素,包括拍面角度(拍形)、拍面方向、击球时间和触球位置四个方面的内容。而这几个方面的因素就决定了击球的旋转、力量的大小、弧线的高低、速度的快慢、击球的落点。

3. Contact

Contact is the nucleus and the most critical step of every stroke. It is the primary factor for quality strokes and includes four aspects: the racket angle, the racket direction, timing and striking point on the ball. All of these factors determine the spin, power, trajectory, speed and placement.

4. 随势挥拍

由于惯性的作用,在球被击出之后,球拍仍然会继续向前上方挥动一段距离,这就是随势挥拍。如果没有

4. Follow-through

Due to the force of inertia, the racket will go on swinging forward and upward for a short distance, even if the ball has been hit out. This

足够的随挥动作，就会导致击球力量过轻，质量不高。然而，也应该避免不必要的过度随挥动作，因为这会使你失去重心，在击下一板球时难以还原。

is commonly referred to as follow-through. Lack of sufficient follow-through will results in weak shots. However, it's also important to avoid overextending follow-through, because you will lose your balance and take long to recover for the next stroke.

第四节　器材
Section 4　Equipment

打乒乓球，必须有球拍（粘贴有海绵胶的底板）、球桌、球网装置、球和球鞋。这一节将介绍乒乓球器材，帮助乒乓球爱好者选择一款适合自己的器材。

To play table tennis, you need a racket (a blade covered with sponge rubber), a table, a net set, a ball and a pair of gym shoes. This section will introduce the table tennis equipment, and help the table tennis lovers to select suitable equipment.

一、底板（表 2.4.1）

乒乓球底板必须由 85%的天然木料制成，另外也可以含有碳素、钛、纤维等复合材料。底板的形状是多种多样的，其因运动员的打法特点而有所不同。例如，防守型运动员一般采用拍面较大的底板；中国快攻型运动员大多喜欢使用椭圆形的拍子，这有利于提高他们动作转换的速度；而日本、韩国直拍弧圈打法的运动员喜欢使用长方形的拍子，这样的球拍有利于增

Ⅰ. Blade (Table 2.4.1)

Table tennis blades must be composed of 85 percent wood and composite materials such as carbon, titanium and fiber. The shape of blade varies somewhat by the playing style of the player. For example, defensive players often use blades with slightly large head size; Chinese fast attackers often prefer oval blades for quicker movement; many Japanese and Korean loopers prefer rectangular blades for more power and spin; the two-winged loopers

大击球的力量和旋转;两面弧圈球打法的运动员一般使用标准形状的底板。球拍拍柄的形状也是不同的。要根据自己手握的舒适程度选择适合自己的拍柄。拍柄按形状一般分为收腰柄、直柄和葫芦柄。在不计海绵胶的情况下,运动员所用底板的质量为80~90 g,厚度一般为6~7 mm。选择乒乓球底板时,应考虑底板的拍柄形状、重量、板层结构、材料、厚度、长宽、速度等指标。

like to use the normal-shape blades. Blades come with a variety of handle shapes. When selecting a blade, make sure the handle shape is comfortable in your hand. The widely used handle shapes are flared, straight, and anatomic. Most blades weigh 80 to 90 g and the thickness is about 6 to 7 mm without sponge rubber. When selecting table tennis blades, the indexes of the blade should be considered, such as racket handle shape, weight, structure, material, thickness, length, width, and speed, etc.

表 2.4.1 乒乓球底板指标中英文对照表

Table 2.4.1 Chinese-English Comparison Table of the Indexes of Table Tennis Blade

	英文 English	中文 Chinese
拍柄形状 Handle Shape	ST=STRAIGHT	直柄
	FL=FLARED	收腰柄
	AN=ANATOMIC	葫芦柄
底板指标 Index of Blade	WT=WEIGHT	重量
	THICKNESS	厚度
	LENGTH/WIDTH	长/宽
底板材料 Material of Blade	W=WOOD	木质
	A=ARYLATE	芳基纤维
	C=CARBON	碳素纤维
	G=GLASS FIBRE	玻璃纤维
底板速度 Speed of Blade	OFF=OFFENSIVE	攻击型
	ALL=ALLROUND	全能型
	DEF=DEFENSIVE	防守型

二、海绵胶

海绵胶是由一层胶皮覆盖物及其下面的一层海绵组成的。海绵的使用能加大击球的速度和旋转。海绵胶的总厚度不能超过 4 mm。根据乒乓球规则,在正式比赛中,运动员使用的球拍两面必须一面为鲜红色,另一面为黑色。

海绵胶的胶皮可分为以下四种:短齿胶皮、长齿胶皮、防弧胶皮和反贴胶皮。

短齿胶皮的颗粒朝外且排列紧密,其颗粒较短、较宽,高度一般为 0.8 ~ 1 mm。直拍推挡和快攻型运动员大多喜欢使用这种胶皮。另外,短齿胶皮也能制造出一定的旋转。

长齿胶皮的颗粒也是朝外的,其颗粒更细、更长(1.5 ~ 1.7 mm),故在击球瞬间容易倒斜。用长齿胶皮击出的球的旋转通常和对手的来球旋转相反,而且对方来球越转,回球的反向旋转也越大。因此,长齿胶皮一般多用于防御型击球。初学者一般不采用长齿胶皮。

防弧胶皮的表面比较光滑且胶齿较短,其特点是能消除弧圈球的强烈上旋,但该胶皮自身很难制造出旋转,因而缺少进攻能力。防守型运动员多在球拍的一面使用防弧胶皮来阻止对

Ⅱ. Sponge Rubber

The sponge rubber is composed of a rubber covering and a sponge layer underneath to provide more speed and spin. The total thickness of the sponge rubber cannot exceed 4 mm. According to the rules of table tennis, all rackets used in any official tournament play must have black rubber on one side and red on the other.

The four general types of rubber surfaces are short-pip rubber, long-pip rubber, antispin rubber, and inverted rubber.

Short-pip rubber has short, wide pips (0.8 to 1 mm high) that face outward and are closely spaced together. This rubber is mostly used by blocking and fast attacking players. Moreover, short-pip rubber can produce a moderate spin on the ball.

Long-pip rubber has thinner and longer (1.5 to 1.7 mm) pips that face outward and bend easily on contact with the ball. Long-pip rubber will produce the opposite type of spin when returning the opponent's spin to him. The more spin the incoming ball has, the more reverse spin will the long-pip rubber produces. Therefore, long-pip rubber is mainly a kind of defensive rubber. It is not recommended for beginners.

Antispin rubber has a slick, smooth surface that removes most of the spin from the ball. Its lack of ability to produce spin makes attacking very difficult. It is used most often by defensive players on one side of the

方的进攻。

racket only to provide steady returns for the opponent's attack.

反贴胶皮是最常用的一种胶皮。这种胶皮的表面非常光滑,黏性大,其颗粒朝下与海绵粘在一起。反胶能制造出最强烈的旋转和最快的速度,是两面弧圈球打法运动员的必备武器。

Inverted rubber is the most popular type of rubber. It features a smooth and sticky top surface with the pips facing downward and attached to a layer of sponge rubber. Inverted rubber can produce the most intense spin and the fastest speed and is used by all two-wing loopers.

三、怎么把套胶粘牢在乒乓球底板上

Ⅲ. How to Glue the Rubber on a Table Tennis Blade

粘球拍(图 2.4.1)所需的装备如下:

- 剪刀;
- 乒乓球拍专用胶水;
- 海绵擦;
- 滚胶棒——用于滚动并压紧套胶,使其能粘牢在底板上;
- 乒乓球底板;

The required equipment for gluing (Figure 2.4.1) is as follows.

- The scissors.
- Special glue for table tennis rubber and blade.
- Sponge.
- Roll stick—We need to use it to roll on the rubber and apply pressure on the rubber to make it stick to the blade.
- The blade.

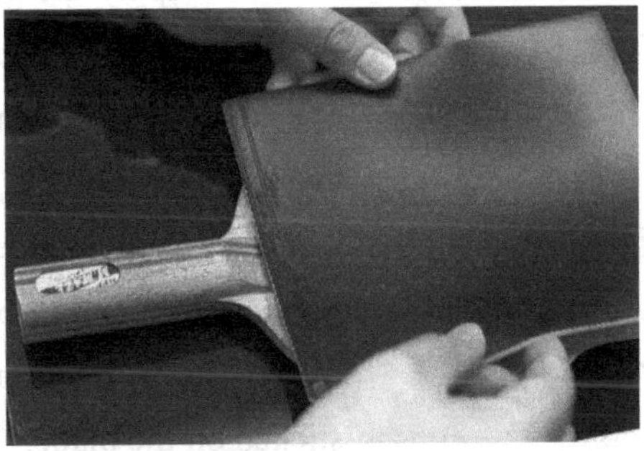

图 2.4.1 粘球拍
Figure 2.4.1 Gluing

➢ 适合你的套胶。

粘球拍的步骤(图 2.4.2~图 2.4.6)如下。

(1)注意套胶的面上有一个品牌标志,确保在粘球拍时套胶的标识和拍柄上的标识在同一侧,不要贴反了。

(2)注意在涂胶水时,要把胶水刷在套胶的海绵上。

(3)当涂上足够的胶水时,要用海绵擦把胶水按一个方向刷在套胶上,并把胶水在套胶上涂抹均匀。

➢ The rubber of your choice.

The steps of gluing (Figure 2.4.2-Figure 2.4.6) are as follows.

(1) Note that there is a logo on the rubber. Make sure it is on the same side with that of the racket handle and don't reverse it.

(2) Make sure to apply the glue on the sponge side of the rubber.

(3) When enough glue has been applied to the rubber, use the sponge to rub the rubber evenly in one direction, and balance the glue out on the rubber.

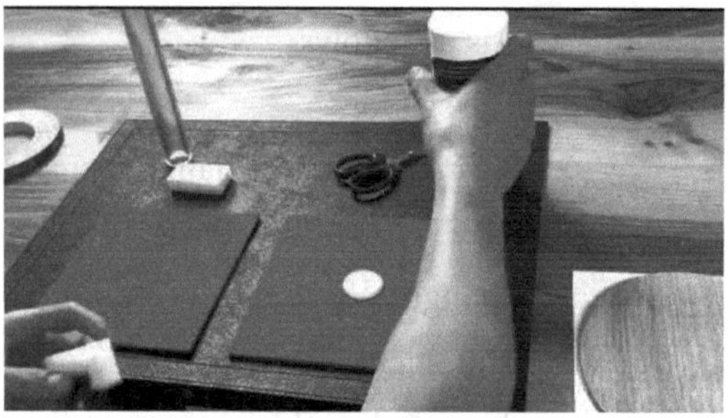

图 2.4.2 步骤(1)

Figure 2.4.2 Step (1)

图 2.4.3 步骤(2)~(3)

Figure 2.4.3 Step (2)-(3)

(4)把胶水涂在底板上,按照刷套胶的方式,把胶水均匀地覆盖在底板上。

(5)均匀地涂抹胶水在粘球拍的过程中是非常关键的。否则,在把套胶粘在底板上后套胶会变得不平整。

(6)在套胶和底板上涂好胶水后,

(4) Apply the glue to the blade. Just do the same as the rubber by applying the glue in one direction. Cover the blade with glue evenly.

(5) Applying the glue evenly is very important during this process. Otherwise, the rubber surface will not be flat after being sticked on the blade.

(6) Once the glue is applied to the rub-

可以让它们自然风干一段时间(15~20 min)。之后,你会发现在套胶和底板上的胶水从白色变成了透明状,这就意味着胶水现在已经完全干燥了。如果想让胶水干得更快,可以用电风扇来吹一吹它们。

ber and blade, leave them to dry for some time (15-20 minutes naturally). After that, you will notice the glue on both rubber and blade has changed from white to transparency. This means the glue is completely dry by now. If you want to dry them quicker, you may use a fan to blow them.

图 2.4.4 步骤(4)

Figure 2.4.4 Step(4)

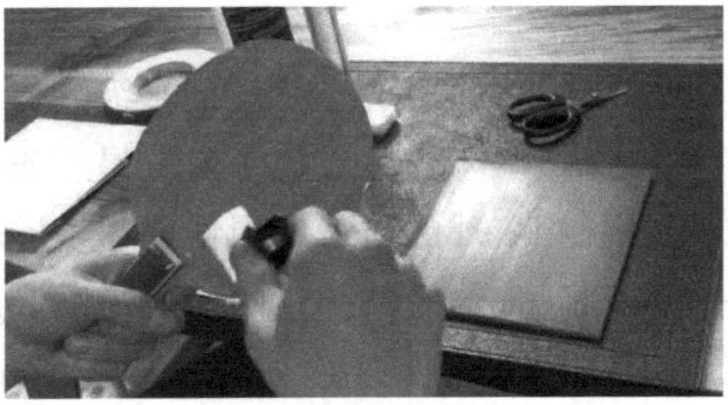

图 2.4.5 步骤(5)~(6)

Figure 2.4.5 Step(5)-(6)

(7)把套胶粘牢在乒乓球底板上。缓慢地将套胶边缘和拍柄对齐,用手指轻轻按压球拍边缘,拿滚胶棒在套胶上轻柔地向一个方向滚动,让套胶粘牢在底板上。

(7)Stick the rubber on the blade. Slowly align the edge of the rubber to the racket handle. Apply a little pressure on the edge with your fingers. Get the roll stick to roll on the rubber gently and lightly in one direction. This is to stable the rubber on the blade.

图 2.4.6 步骤(7)

Figure 2.4.6 Step(7)

四、球、球桌和球网

2000年国际乒联对乒乓球比赛用球进行了一项重要改革，用直径为40 mm的大球替代直径为38 mm的小球。该项改革的目的在于提高乒乓球运动的观赏性。乒乓球重2.7 g，颜色一般为白色或橙色，且为不反光饰面。

乒乓球的质量由球表面上的星级界定，一般为一星球、二星球和三星球。星级越高，球的质量和弹性就越好。拥有良好、稳定的弹性的球更易于掌控并能提高击球稳定性。

所有乒乓球比赛用台长2.74 m、宽1.525 m、高76 cm。乒乓球台分别有两条白色的底线和边线，以及一条较细的白色的中线，一般球台是蓝色的。球台表面顶层的厚度是很重要的，因为它影响着球的弹性。球台表面顶层一般厚17~24 mm，正式比赛球台推荐厚度为22 mm，但19 mm厚的球台也能让球拥有较好的弹性。球网通过金属网柱系附于球桌上。绑紧后，球网高15.25 cm，网柱外缘距球桌边线外缘15.25 cm。

Ⅳ. Ball, Table and Net

ITTF made a major change in 2000 by increasing the size of the ball from 38 mm to 40 mm. The purpose for this change was to improve the ball visibility. The ball weighs 2.7 g and it is usually white or orange and must have a matt finish.

The quality of a table tennis ball is indicated by a star rating found on the ball, which may be one-star, two-star, or three-star. The higher the star rating is, the higher the quality and the better bounce of the ball will be. A ball with good, consistent bounce makes it easier to control and improve the consistency.

All regulation tables are 274 cm × 152 cm and 76 cm high. All tables have two white side and end lines as well as a white center line, and they are often colored blue. The thickness of the table top is important as it has an effect on the bounce of the ball. It varies from about 17 mm to 24 mm with the recommended match-play thickness of 22 mm, but 19 mm will still provide a good bounce. The net is attached to the table by the use of the metal net posts. When attached, the net is 15.25 cm high and the net posts extend 15.25 cm to the side of the table.

五、鞋、袜

乒乓球选手应始终穿着合适的

Ⅴ. Footwear

Suitable footwear should always be worn

鞋，任何球鞋都需要有纹路的鞋底，以防止滑倒并避免受伤。鞋底也要采用无痕橡胶，这是使用许多乒乓球场地设施的基本要求。提供良好支撑（尤其是在脚跟和脚背周围）的轻质鞋是必不可少的。球鞋的灵活性也很重要，因为打乒乓球需要快速的步法、大量的转身和转向。一旦球鞋过了最佳状态，更换它也是很重要的。磨损的鞋底可能会导致滑倒和受伤，鞋支撑减弱可能会导致大量脚部受伤的情况发生。有许多专门的乒乓球器材供货商出售专门开发的鞋类。

and any footwear needs to have a well-defined tread to prevent slipping and avoid injury. The sole should also be non-marking, an essential requirement for using many table tennis courts and facilities. Lightweight footwear that offers good support, particularly around the heel and instep, is essential. Flexibility is also desirable as table tennis requires fast footwork with a lot of turning and changing of direction. It is also important to replace your footwear as soon as it is past its best. Worn soles may result in slipping and injury and weakened support can cause a number of foot injuries. There are a number of specialist stockists of table tennis equipment, who sell specially developed footwear.

乒乓球袜子的选择也很重要。运动袜通常比普通袜子厚，所以当试穿任何鞋子时都要注意这一点。另外，在买鞋的时候一定要选择适合的袜子。无缝袜子通常更舒适，而且有助于减小摩擦。

The choice of socks is also important. Sports socks are often thicker than normal socks, so bear this in mind when you try on any footwear. In addition, make sure you have chosen the right socks when buying your footwear. Seamless socks are usually more comfortable and will reduce rubbing.

第三章　乒乓球基本技术

Chapter 3　Basic Techniques of Table Tennis

本章将介绍乒乓球的基本技术，包括正手攻球、反手攻球、搓球、削球技术和步法。掌握这些技术将为更快地提高技术水平打下坚实的基础。在开始上台训练之前，必须先掌握好乒乓球的握拍法、准备姿势等基本要素，以培养良好的控球感觉。

This chapter covers a series of basic techniques including forehand and backhand attacks, push shots, chop strokes and footworks. Mastery of these techniques will lay a solid foundation for further improvement. Before beginning on-the-table training, you must learn basic elements of the game, such as grip and ready position, so as to control the ball well.

第一节　握拍法、准备姿势与重心交换

Section 1　Grip, Ready Position and Weight Transfer

一、握拍法

Ⅰ. Grip

每名运动员在开始学习乒乓球之前必须为自己确定好一种握拍法。目前乒乓球握拍法主要有直握法和横握法两大类。人们为握拍法命名，给它们作了生动形象的诠释。直握法因很像手拿钢笔或筷子，所以多为亚洲运动员所采用；而西方人更喜欢横握球拍，因其如同手执刀叉。

The primary decision every player has to make is what grip to use on the racket. There are two main grip styles: shake-hands grip and pen-hold grip. Their names describe them very visually. For the pen-hold grip, it has always been the predominant choice in many Asian countries and is formed by holding a pen or a pair of chopsticks. Most Western players prefer the shake-hands grip, which looks like holding the knife and fork.

1. 横握法

1.Shake-hands Grip

● 传统优缺点

运动员横握球拍的优点是其正反手进攻能力威胁大且较均衡,能拉出速度快、旋转强的弧圈球,在中远台有较强的相持能力。然而,其弱点在于处理台内小球的能力以及回击近身中路球的能力较弱。

● Traditional strengths and weaknesses

The shake-hands grip allows for the development of equally powerful backhand and forehand strokes. Players who usc this grip have fast and spin loop and good counerdrives when far from the table. However, it is weak in short game that uses drop shots and provides limited ability to return shots on the center line of the table.

● 深握和浅握

横握球拍有深握和浅握之分。一般而言,握得越深,控制球和稳定性就越好;握得越浅,越能增加旋转变化和手腕的灵活性。近年来,进攻型运动员多将球拍握得较原先浅而松了。

● High and low grips

Shake-hands grip is divided into high grip and low grip. Generally speaking, the higher up toward the blade you grip, the more control and stability you have. The lower you grip, the more spin variation and wrist flexibility you have. In recent years, offensive players have tended to use the low shake-hands grip.

● 基本握拍法(图 3.1.1)

(1)拇指轻贴于球拍的正面中间位置;

(2)食指自然伸直横贴在球拍的背面;

(3)中指、无名指和小指自然地握住拍柄。

● Basic grip(Figure 3.1.1)

(1)The thumb should be placed in the middle on the forehand side of the racket.

(2)Thc index finger should be straight and placed on the backhand side of the racket.

(3)The other fingers should hold the handle naturally.

● 关键点

(1)正手攻球时,食指压拍传递击球力量,中指控制拍形;

● Key points

(1)The index finger is used in forehand attack to deliver power while middle finger is used to adjust the racket angle.

(2)反手攻球时，拇指压拍控制击球弧线，并传递击球力量。

(2)Thumb is used in backhand attack to adjust the trajectory of the ball and to transfer energy to the ball.

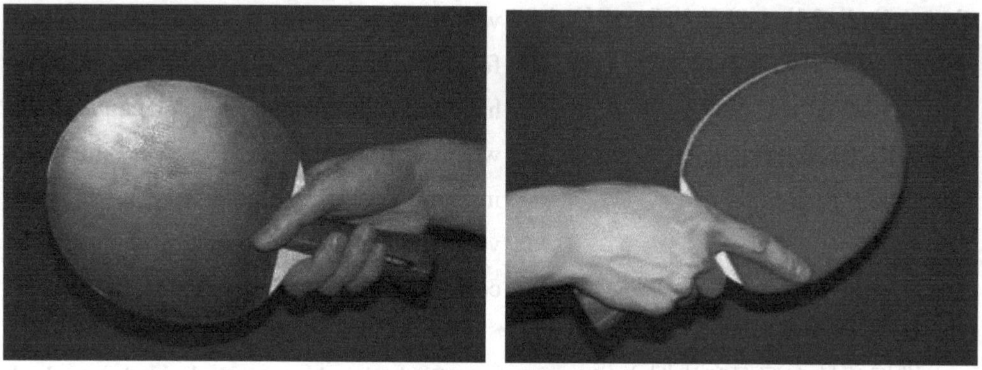

图 3.1.1 横握法

Figure 3.1.1 Shake-hands Grip

● 易犯错误和纠正方法

(1)易犯错误：两个手指贴于球拍背面。

纠正方法：中指握拍，只留食指横贴于球拍上。

(2)易犯错误：将球拍握得太紧。

纠正方法：将球拍握得较松。

(3)易犯错误：食指翘到球拍中间。

纠正方法：食指横贴于球拍边缘。

● Mistakes and corrections

(1)Mistake: Two fingers are on the back of the racket.

Correction: Move the middle finger to the handle, leaving only the forefinger on the blade.

(2)Mistake: The grip is too tight.

Correction: Hold the racket a little looser.

(3)Mistake: The forefinger is up the middle of the blade.

Correction: Move the forefinger down to the edge of the blade.

2. 直握法

● 传统优缺点

直握球拍选手的发球和接发球能力强，正手杀伤力大，出手速度快。然

2.Pen-hold Grip

● Traditional strengths and weaknesses

The pen-hold grip player has excellent serve-return ability, strong forehand damage,

而，其弱点是中台对攻能力较弱；反手进攻和防守能力较弱。

● 基本握拍法

（1）大拇指和食指握在球拍前面，自然弯曲，两指之间的距离大约是2 cm；

（2）中指、无名指和小指自然弯曲，放置在球拍的后面。

● 中式和日式直握法

中式直握法（图3.1.2）拍面背后的三指较为弯曲，这种握法在正手和反手攻球时手腕比较灵活，更加有利于使用直拍背面进攻技术。

and fast hand speed. However, the pen-hold grip has difficulty on counterdrives when stepping back from the table. Additionally, it provides weak backhand attacks and defenses.

● Basic grip

(1)The thumb and index fingers should be placed in front of the racket and curled naturally. The distance between the two fingers is about 2 cm.

(2)Middle, ring and small fingers should be placed in the back of the racket and curled naturally.

● Chinese and Japanese pen-hold grip

In the Chinese pen-hold grip (Figure 3.1.2), the three fingers on the reverse side are curled. This grip allows for much more use of the wrist on both backhand and forehand strokes. Moreover, it is especially convenient to use reverse backhand techniques.

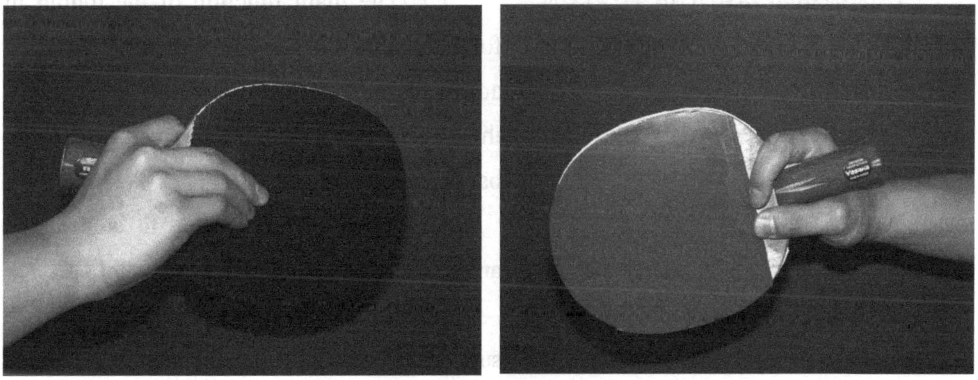

图3.1.2 中式直握法

Figure 3.1.2 Chinese Pen-hold Grip

日式直握法(图 3.1.3)与中式直握法较为类似。区别在于其拍面背后三指略微伸直。这种握拍法的正手杀伤力巨大,但其弱点是手腕不够灵活,处理反手位的台内球较为困难。

The Japanese pen-hold grip (Figure 3.1.3) resembles the Chinese pen-hold grip. The difference is that the three fingers on the reverse side are slightly straight. This grip supports strong forehand play, but makes it difficult to use the wrist and return the short ball on the backhand.

图 3.1.3　日式直握法

Figure 3.1.3　Japanese Pen-hold Grip

- 关键点

(1)大拇指主要用于正手攻球时控制拍形、调节弧线,在使用直拍反面横打时控制拍形;

(2)食指在推挡时控制拍形;

(3)中指、无名指用于支撑及决定发力的方向;

(4)弧圈型打法的运动员可伸直其中指和无名指,以利于发力。

- Key points

(1)The main function of the thumb in forehand attack is to control the racket angle, adjust the trajectory of the ball and to control the angle of the racket when using reversed backhand techniques.

(2)Index finger is used to control the angle of the racket when blocking.

(3)Middle and ring fingers are used to support and determine the direction of the force.

(4)Looping style player can straighten out the middle and ring fingers in order to deliver more power.

二、准备姿势(图 3.1.4)

➢ 上体前倾,收腹;

➢ 两手臂自然弯曲置于身体前方;

➢ 膝盖微屈;

➢ 两脚开立略比肩宽,左脚稍在前(右手运动员);

➢ 提踵,重心迁移到两个前脚掌上。

Ⅱ. Ready Position (Figure 3.1.4)

➢ Upper body should lean slightly forward with stomach tucked in.

➢ Two arms are bent naturally and placed in front of the body.

➢ Knees should be bent naturally.

➢ Stand with feet apart, a bit wider than shoulder length, and left foot slightly forward (for the right-handed player).

➢ The heel off the ground and the weight move forward toward the balls of feet.

图 3.1.4　准备姿势

Figure 3.1.4　Ready Position

三、重心交换

重心交换是运动员在击球过程中通过腰部、膝关节、前脚掌等部位协调配合而完成的动作。重心交换应贯穿整个击球过程的始终。例如我们在正手攻球的动作过程中,身体重心需从靠后的脚转到稍靠前的脚。较好的重

Ⅲ. Weight Transfer

Weight transfer is the process of utilizing the coordinated body movements of hips, knees and balls of the feet when striking the ball. It should be carried out during the entire process of hitting a shot. For forehand drive, we transfer our weight from back foot to the

心交换有助于：

➢ 增加击球的力量；
➢ 控制合理的击球距离；
➢ 保持身体平衡；
➢ 击球后以更快的速度还原；
➢ 为下一板击球做更充分的准备。

forward foot. The advantages of good weight transfer are as follows.

➢ Impart more power to the shot.
➢ Control proper space for hitting.
➢ Keep balance.
➢ Recovery is quicker.
➢ Preparation for the next shot is quicker.

第二节　熟悉球性

Section 2　Ball Control Drill

做以下 10 个有关控球能力的训练。记录每一次练习的击球板数。前 3 个训练当中,你必须在每项练习中连续颠球 100 次;后 7 个训练当中,你需要在每项练习中完成连续颠球 20 次。在进行以下练习时请注意正确的握拍方法。

（1）用正手连续颠球；

（2）用反手连续颠球；

（3）用正、反手交替连续颠球；

（4）用正手和球拍边缘交替连续颠球；

（5）用正手对墙击球；

Practice each of the following ten ball control exercises. For each exercise, record the number of bounces. For the first three drills you are required to bounce the ball 100 times on the racket and for the other drills bounce the ball 20 times. Be sure to use the correct grip while completing these exercises.

（1）Bounce the ball using the forehand side of the racket.

（2）Bounce the ball using the backhand side of the racket.

（3）Alternatively bounce the ball once on the backhand side of the racket and once on the forehand side.

（4）Bounce the ball once on the forehand side of the racket and once on the edge of the racket.

（5）Volley the ball against a wall using

the forehand side of the racket.

（6）用反手对墙击球；

（6）Volley the ball against a wall using the backhand side of the racket.

（7）用正、反手交替连续对墙击球；

（7）Alternatively volley the ball against a wall using the forehand side of the racket and the backhand side.

（8）用正手朝地面拍球；

（8）Bounce the ball on the floor using the forehand side of the racket.

（9）用反手朝地面拍球；

（9）Bounce the ball on the floor using the backhand side of the racket.

（10）用正、反手交替连续朝地面拍球。

（10）Alternatively bounce the ball on the floor using the forehand side of the racket and the backhand side.

第三节　发球与接发球
Section 3　Serve and Receive

发球、接发球和发球抢攻技术统称前三板技术，该技术在现代乒乓球运动中扮演着十分重要的角色。前三板技术是中国乒乓球队取得成功的关键因素。

The skills of serving, receiving and attacking after serve are known as the first three shots, which is particularly important in the modern table tennis game. The skill of the first three shots is a key to success for the Chinese table tennis team.

一、发球

Ⅰ. Serve

在所有执拍类运动项目中，发球是每一分的开始。发球员有很大的优势，能赢下更多的分数。这是因为接发球员在球发出之前并不知道球的落点、旋转类型和速度。以下是发球的

In all racket sports, serve is the beginning of every point. The server has a huge advantage and should be able to win the majority of points on the serve. It is because the receiver does not know where the ball is going,

主要作用。

➢ 限制对方进攻，破坏对方的战术。

➢ 使对方回球质量较差，为自己进攻创造条件。

➢ 通过发球的旋转变化，使对方回球失误，直接得分。

➢ 增强自己获胜的信心，造成对方的心理恐惧。

1. 发球的种类

根据发球旋转和发球动作，发球可分为上旋发球、下旋发球、不转发球、左侧旋发球、右侧旋发球、高抛发球和下蹲式发球等。下面介绍不同种类的发球技术。

1）正手下旋发球

● 动作要领（图 3.3.1 和图 3.3.2）

（1）向上抛球约 15 cm，同时向右侧转腰，带动球拍向后方引拍，拍面保持后仰。

（2）当球下落至腹部时，向左回转腰并带动前臂向前下方挥拍。

（3）在球拍触球的一瞬间，手腕快速抖动。

（4）用拍头部分摩擦球的底部。

the type of spin and speed the ball will have. Following are the main effects of serve.

➢ Restrict opponent's attack or damage his tactics.

➢ Force a passive return or a weak medium-speed topspin return from opponent so that you can attack.

➢ Win the point outright by deceiving opponent about the type or amount of spin you are using.

➢ Make yourself confident and disrupt opponent's mentality.

1. The Type of Serves

Serves are classified according to spin and stroke motion by topspin serve, backspin serve, little spin serve, left sidespin serve, right sidespin serve, high-toss serve and squatting serve. The introduction of different kinds of serves is as follows.

1)Forehand Backspin Serve

● Movement essentials（Figure 3.3.1 and Figure 3.3.2）

（1）Toss the ball at 15 cm high, at the same time, rotate your waist to the right, bringing your bat back with an open racket angle.

（2）As the ball drops to your belly level, rotate left to get your forearm swinging forward and downward.

（3）Wrist shakes quickly when racket contacting the ball.

（4）Graze the bottom of the ball with the

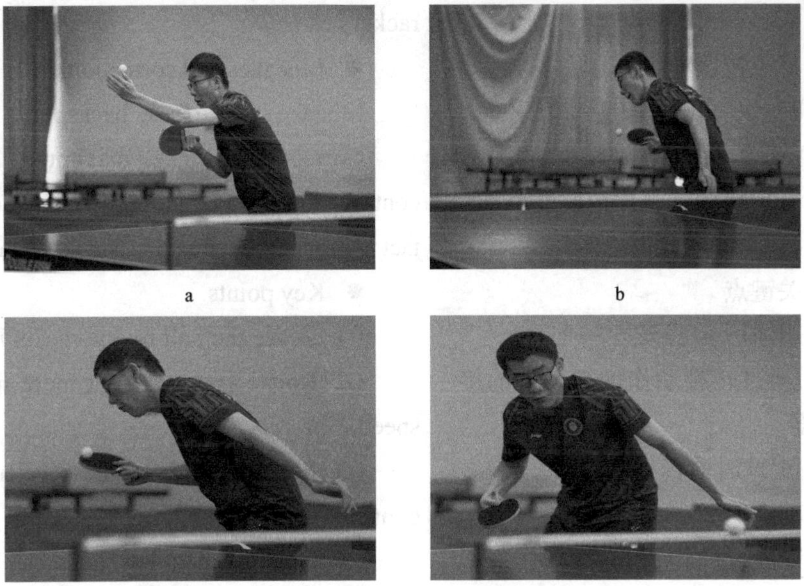

a　b　c　d

图 3.3.1　横拍正手下旋发球

Figure 3.3.1　Forehand Backspin Serve with Shake-hands Grip

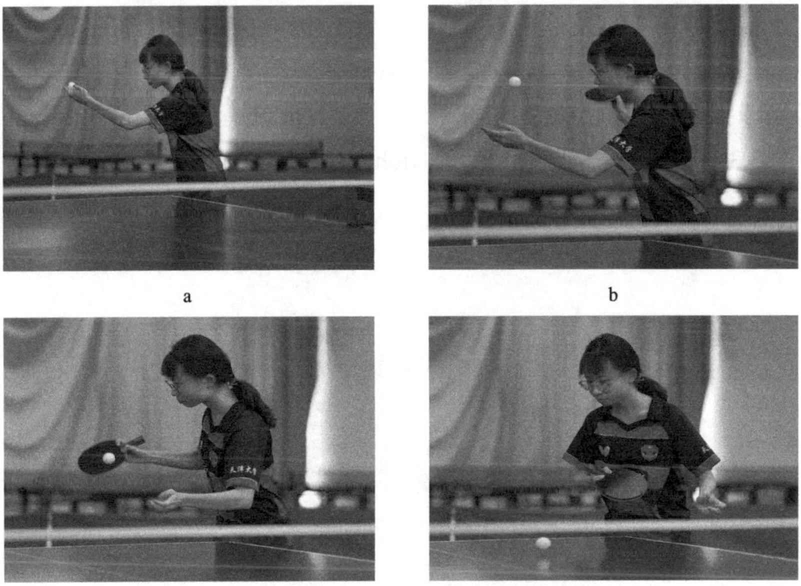

a　b　c　d

图 3.3.2　直拍正手下旋发球

Figure 3.3.2　Forehand Backspin Serve with Pen-hold Grip

racket head.

● 易犯错误和纠正方法

易犯错误:发球不转。

纠正方法:在触球的一瞬间充分摩擦球,并加快挥臂和挥拍速度。

● Mistakes and corrections

Mistake: Serve lacks backspin.

Correction: Make maximum friction contact, forearm and racket accelerate on contact to produce maximum racket acceleration.

● 关键点

(1)用拍头摩擦球。

(2)通过转腰动作增加发球的旋转和速度。

(3)触球时前臂加速挥拍。

(4)可通过高抛和跺脚动作来迷惑对方。

● Key points

(1)Graze the ball by the racket head.

(2)Rotate your waist for more spin and speed.

(3)Forearm and racket accelerate on contact.

(4)High toss and foot stamp can be used to prevent opponent from reading the spin.

2)不转发球

2)Little Spin Serve

● 动作要领

(1)不转发球与下旋发球的动作类似。

(2)用球拍的偏右侧位置触击球的中部(图 3.3.3)。

● Movement essentials

(1)Its movement is similar to backspin serve.

(2)Hit the middle of the ball by the right part of the racket(Figure 3.3.3).

图 3.3.3　正手不转发球时的球触拍部位

Figure 3.3.3　The Striking Spot on the Racket in Little Spin Serve

（3）在球拍触球的一瞬间增加撞击、减小摩擦。

● 易犯错误和纠正方法

易犯错误：发球弧线较高。

纠正方法：击球点不能太高，应接近球台水平高度。

3）反手右侧旋发球

● 动作要领（图 3.3.4 和图 3.3.5）

（1）向左侧身 45° 站立，右脚稍前、左脚稍后。

（3）Increase strike and decrease friction when racket contacting the ball.

● Mistakes and corrections

Mistake: The ball bounces too high on the table.

Correction: Contact the ball close to table height.

3）Backhand Right Sidespin Serve

● Movement essentials（Figure 3.3.4 and Figure 3.3.5）

（1）Stand at a 45-degree angle to the left with the right foot slightly forward of the left foot.

a b c

d. 右侧下旋（Right Side Backspin） e. 右侧上旋（Right Side Topspin）

图 3.3.4 横拍反手右侧旋发球

Figure 3.3.4 Backhand Right Sidespin Serve with Shake-hands Grip

a b c d

图 3.3.5 直拍反手右侧旋发球

Figure 3.3.5 Backhand Right Sidespin Serve with Pen-hold Grip

（2）在向上抛球的同时稍向左转腰，并带动前臂向后上方引拍，屈腕。

（2）Toss the ball into the air and slightly rotate your waist to the left, bringing your forearm back and upward while bending your wrist.

（3）当球下落至与网同高时，迅速以前臂挥拍击球。右侧上旋发球，球拍向右上方挥动，摩擦球的中部；右侧下旋发球，球拍向右下方挥动，摩擦球的底部。

（3）When the ball drops to the net level, quickly swing your forearm to hit the ball with racket. For right side topspin serve, graze the middle of the ball with a left to right upward motion. For right side backspin serve, graze the bottom of the ball with a left to right downward motion.

4)正手左侧旋发球

● 动作要领(图 3.3.6 和图 3.3.7)

(1)为了使球的旋转更强烈,在发球时需要调整握拍法,只用拇指和食指轻轻握住球拍即可。这样的握拍法有利于手腕转动。

4)Forehand Left Sidespin Serve

● Movement essentials (Figure 3.3.6 and Figure 3.3.7)

(1)In order to generate stronger spin, we need to adjust the grip. Hold the racket a little looser just by your thumb and index finger. This type of grip allows for greater movement of the wrist.

a

b

c. 左侧上旋(Left Side Topspin)

d. 左侧下旋(Left Side Backspin)

图 3.3.6 横拍正手左侧旋发球

Figure 3.3.6 Forehand Left Sidespin Serve with Shake-hands Grip

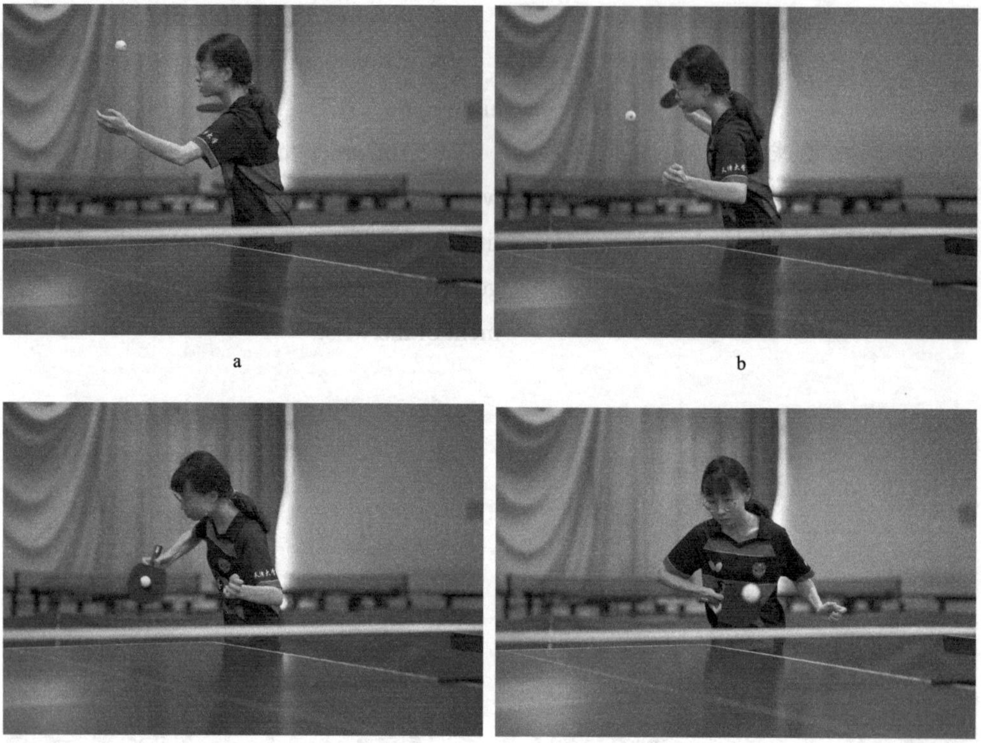

a b c d

图 3.3.7　直拍正手左侧旋发球

Figure 3.3.7　Forehand Left Sidespin Serve with Pen-hold Grip

（2）在向上抛球的同时向右转腰，并带动前臂和手腕向后上方引拍。

（3）以肘为轴带动前臂挥动。

（4）左侧上旋发球，球拍从右向左上方挥动，摩擦球的中部；左侧下旋发球，球拍从右向左下方挥动，摩擦球的底部。

（5）在球拍触球的一瞬间，手腕快速抖动。

（2）Toss the ball into the air and rotate your waist to the right, binging your forearm and wrist back and upward.

（3）Pivot forearm around your elbow.

（4）For left side topspin serve, graze the middle of the ball with a right to left upward motion. For left side backspin, graze the bottom of the ball with a right to left downward motion.

（5）Wrist quickly shakes when racket contacting the ball.

● 关键点

（1）前臂挥拍的动作类似于钟摆的动作。

（2）触球时前臂加速挥拍。

（3）发球后迅速还原成正常握拍动作。

5）高抛发球

通过高抛，可增强发球的旋转，增大发球的速度，并使对手在接发球时遇到困难。把球高抛过头顶，球下落时会获得更大的加速度，所以有助于在球拍触球的一瞬间产生更强的旋转和更快的速度。然而，要掌握高抛发球需要多加练习。因为按照规则的规定，发球时必须将球竖直地向上抛起。

● 动作要领（图 3.3.8）

（1）站位为左脚稍前、右脚稍后，上半身几乎平行于边线。

● Key points

（1）Forearm swing resembles pendulum's motion.

（2）Forearm accelerates on contact.

（3）After serve, transfer from special grip to normal grip.

5）High-toss Serve

One way to increase spin and speed to your serve and make it difficult for your opponent to read is to use high-toss serve. By tossing the ball over your head, you can utilize a greater ball acceleration generated as the ball descends to increase spin and speed to the serve. But you need a lot of training to control high-toss serve, because by rule the ball must be tossed straight up.

● Movement essentials（Figure 3.3.8）

（1）Stand with your left foot slightly forward of the right foot and upper body should be nearly parallel to the side line.

a　　b　　c

图 3.3.8　正手高抛发球

Figure 3.3.8　Forehand High-toss Serve

（2）往上方抛球 30~80 cm，同时执拍手与非执拍手向上引拍。

（2）Toss the ball at 30 to 80 cm high, meanwhile, your racket hand and free hand are in high backswing position.

（3）当球下落至球网高度时，向左转腰挥拍击球。

（3）As the ball descends to the net level, rotate your waist to the left, swing at the ball.

（4）整个动作是自右向左前方呈弧形挥拍，摩擦球的左侧面。

（4）Graze the left side of the ball with a right to left forward motion.

（5）在触球的一瞬间抖动手腕，产生更强的旋转。

（5）Wrist shakes at contact to generate stronger spin.

6）下蹲式发球

6）Squatting Serve

另一种增强发球的旋转、增大发球的速度的发球方式是下蹲式发球。在触球的一瞬间下蹲可以产生向下的加速度和更充分的引拍空间。另外，下蹲式发球不受“无遮挡发球”规则的限制。

Another way to increase spin and speed to your serve is to execute squatting serve. By squatting at contact, you can acquire downward acceleration and more backswing space. Moreover, this kind of serve is not covered by the rule of no-hiding serve.

- 动作要领（图 3.3.9）

- Movement essentials（Figure 3.3.9）

（1）膝盖弯曲呈半蹲状。

（1）Bend your knees.

（2）右侧旋发球时，左脚稍前，上半身略向右偏，当球下降至与头同高时，从左后方向右前方挥拍，摩擦球的中部。

（2）For right sidespin serve, stand with your left foot slightly forward of the right foot and upper body should be sideways to your right. When the ball drops to your head level, graze the middle of the ball with a left backward to right forward motion.

（3）左侧旋发球时，上半身几乎平行于端线，当球下降至与头同高时，从右后方向左前方挥拍，摩擦球的中部。

（3）For left sidespin serve, stand with your upper body nearly parallel to the end line. When the ball drops to your head level, graze the middle of the ball with a right backward to left forward motion.

（4）在触球的一瞬间手腕快速抖动，并完成下蹲动作。

（4）Wrist quickly shakes, and execute a squatting motion at contact.

a b c

图 3.3.9 正手下蹲式发球

Figure 3.3.9 Forehand Squatting Serve

7)正手右侧旋发球

● 动作要领(图 3.3.10)

(1)向右侧身 45° 站立,左脚稍前、右脚稍后。

(2)在向上抛球的同时稍向内屈腕,前臂向后上方引拍。

7)Forehand Right Sidespin Serve

● Movement essentials(Figure 3.3.10)

(1)Stand at a 45-degree angle to the right with the left foot slightly forward of the right foot.

(2)Toss the ball into the air and bend your wrist back, swing your forearm back and upward.

a b c

图 3.3.10 正手右侧旋发球

Figure 3.3.10 Forehand Right Sidespin Serve

(3)当球下落至与网同高时,以前臂挥拍。右侧上旋发球,球拍向右前方挥动,摩擦球的中部;右侧下旋发

(3)When the ball drops to the net level, quickly swing your forearm to hit the ball. For right side topspin serve, graze the middle of

球，球拍向右下方挥动，摩擦球的底部。

the ball in a left to right forward motion. For right side backspin serve, graze the bottom of the ball with a left to right downward motion.

2. 发球的长短

● 发短球

要想发出高质量的短球，首先在击球时需要更强的摩擦。在触球的一瞬间，通过手腕和手指的制动控制击球的力量。另外，发球过程中的随势挥拍动作应较小。最重要的是，球的第一跳应靠近本方球台的球网。高质量的短球在第二跳后会向球网回退。

● 发长球

要想发出高质量的长球，在击球时应以前臂发力为主，手腕发力为辅，以撞击为主，摩擦为辅。另外，在发长球时，引拍和随势挥拍动作更大。在发球时通过转腰可以增强球的旋转，增大球的速度。发长球的最关键之处在于球的第一跳须靠近本方球台的端线。高质量的长球的落点应紧逼对方底线大角，从而增加其回球的困难。

● 发半出台球

发短球可以防止对方进攻，而发半出台球可以为自己提供进攻机会。半出台球第二跳的落点通常在对方台面的中间区域，在这个落点，对方既难

2. Depth of Serves

● Short serve

To produce a high-quality short serve, you need to hit the ball with more friction. When contacting, control the power with your wrist and fingers and keep the follow-through short. Above all, the first bounce should close to the net of your side. For high-quality short serve, the ball will back up toward the net after the second bounce.

● Long serve

To produce a high-quality long serve, you need to hit the ball with your forearm more and wrist less. Contact is primarily strike, not friction. Longer backswing and follow-through are necessary to guarantee a long serve. Rotate your waist during the serve for more spin and speed. For the serve to be successful, the first bounce should close to the end line of your side. For high-quality long serve, the ball must be placed deep into the corner on the table of opponent's side to jam his return.

● Mid-depth serve

Short serves are used to stop opponent's attack, mid-depth serves are used to facilitate your own attack. Mid-depth serve has the second bounce on opponent's side that the ball

以摆短，也不能轻易抢攻，回球往往质量不高，从而有利于发球者抢攻。在发半出台球时，可以加入一些侧旋。因为一方面，接发球员在回球时不仅要考虑球半出台的落点，而且要应付球落桌后侧拐的弧线；另一方面，发至中路的侧旋球会让接发球员感到左右为难。

lands around the middle of the table. This serve is too long to easily return back short, but not long enough to easily attack. Often, the result is a weak return that allows the server to attack first. Mid-depth serve can be more effective by imparting sidespin to the ball. For one thing, when against a sidespin serve, the receiver has to deal with not only the uncomfortable mid-distance of the serve but also the fact that the ball jumps sideways on the contact with the table. For another thing, a serve that curves sideways across the center line can confuse the receiver as whether to use a backhand or forehand return.

3. 发球的落点(图 3.3.11)

3. Placement of Serves (Figure 3.3.11)

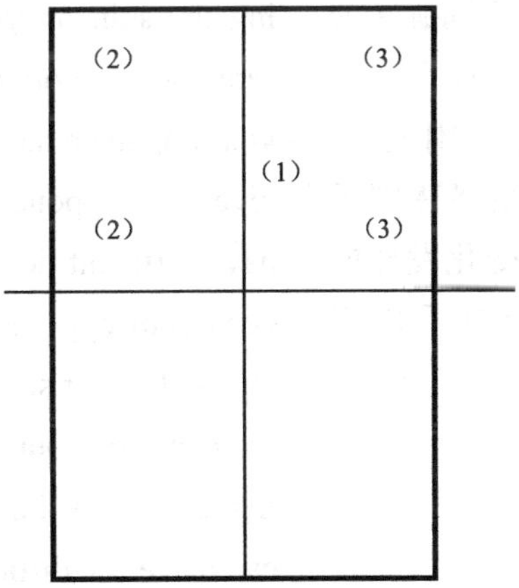

图 3.3.11 发球的落点

Figure 3.3.11 Placement of Serves

(1)对方的中路近网区域；

(2)对方的正手位近网和底线

(1)Opponent's center line net zone.

(2)Opponent's forehand net and end

区域；

（3）对方的反手位近网和底线区域。

4. 基本发球策略

● 应尽快发现对手接发球的弱点

和一个陌生的对手比赛时，可在比赛开始阶段多变化发球的落点。所有运动员都有其接发球的漏洞，一旦发现对手的弱点，就要不断在发球时向其施加压力。

● 要使对手被你的发球所迷惑

在发球时可以通过以下两种策略使对手忙中出错：第一种策略是以尽可能相似的发球动作发出不同旋转的球，从而使对手被相同的发球动作产生的不同旋转所迷惑而陷入困境，目的是让对手对你的发球始终琢磨不透；另外一种策略是不断变化发球的落点，发球时长时短，让对手措手不及。

● 等待对手在接发球时做出被动调整

当找到一种对付对手最有效的发球方式时，一定要以这种发球对其穷追猛打，直至对手做出接发球调整或

line zone.

(3)Opponent's backhand net and end line zone.

4. Basic Serve Strategy

● Find out opponent's serve return weaknesses early

If you are playing with an opponent you do not know, serve to a variety of locations early in the match. All players have serve return weaknesses. Once you find opponent's weakness, direct the majority of your serves to that area.

● Keep opponent guessing about what serve is coming

There are two ways to keep opponent off balance using your serves. One way is changing the spin on your serves while using the same serve motion. Try to find a serve that your opponent has problem receiving and then give your opponent serves look the same but have different degrees of spin. The goal is to keep your opponent guessing and uncomfortable with your serves. Another way is varying the depth of your serves. By constantly varying short, medium and long placement, you can make life difficult for your opponent.

● Wait for opponent's adjustments during receiving

When you find an effective serve pattern, continue to use it until your opponent makes an adjustment and begins to make

放手一搏。当对手做出调整时，你也要使自己的发球落点稍加变化，对对方进行干扰。在对手适应后，再重新使用那种最有效的发球方式。

stronger returns. When this happens, try changing the location of your serves for a while, and then use the effective serve pattern again.

二、接发球

Ⅱ. Receive

1. 合理的接发球站位

1. Be in the Correct Receive Position

● 根据对方发球的位置决定自己的站位

在大多数情况下，接发球员应站在反手位接发球。如果对方站在中路发球或者对方是一名左手运动员，接发球时应站在球台中路附近。

● Choose your position according to the server's position

Generally, the receive position should be the backhand corner. However, if your opponent serves from the middle of the table or your opponent is a left-handed player, shift your ready position at the center of the table.

● 根据自己的打法决定自己的站位

进攻型运动员常站在反手位接发球，以便直接用正手进攻。削球打法的运动员往往站在中台接发球，以利于控制旋转和落点。

● Choose your position according to your playing style

Offensive players usually stand at the backhand corner so that they can execute attacking strokes with the forehand during receiving. While choppers prefer to receive at the mid-range of the table to easily control spin and placement.

● 与球台保持适当的距离

在任何情况下，接发球都要避免站得离球台太近，因为这样不利于回接长而快的发球。由于向前移动接短球比向后退接长球容易，因此接发球时应站在离球台约一个手臂距离的位置。

● Keep a proper distance from the table

Wherever you stand to receive, make sure you are not too close to the table to return deep and fast serve. Moving forward to return a short serve is easier than moving backward to return a long serve. Therefore, try to set up at least an arm's length away from the table.

2. 判断对方发球的旋转种类和强弱

● 根据来球的运行路径和弧线判断来球的旋转性能

上旋球在空中飞行时前段较慢，球落台后向前冲；下旋球在空中飞行时前段较快，球落台后下沉。

● 根据对方发球时的挥拍方向判断来球的旋转性能

在一般情况下，发球时球拍从上向下挥动，来球下旋；球拍从下向上挥动，来球上旋；球拍从右向左挥动，来球右侧旋；球拍从左向右挥动，来球左侧旋。

● 根据对方发球时在触球的一瞬间前臂和手腕加速的快慢判断来球的旋转性能

发球时在触球的一瞬间，前臂和手腕挥动的速度越快，球的旋转越强，这是因为发球者通过增大触球一瞬间的挥拍速度加强了球的旋转；相反，前臂和手腕挥动的速度越慢，球的旋转越弱。

● 根据触球一瞬间的球拍角度判断来球的旋转性能

如果对方发球时球拍前倾，来球

2. Read the Type and Amount of Spin the Server Puts on the Ball

● Watch the path and the trajectory of the ball to read the spin

If the ball is a little slow in the early phase and tends to jump forward after it hits the table, the serve has topspin. If the ball is a little fast in the early phase and dips downward after it hits the table, the serve has backspin.

● Watch the racket direction to read the spin

In general, if he swings the racket with an upward to downward motion, the serve has backspin. If it is a downward to upward motion, the serve has topspin. If he swings the racket from right to left, then right sidespin will occur. Conversely, left sidespin will occur with a left to right motion.

● Watch the amount of forearm and wrist acceleration on contact with the ball to read the spin

The greater the forearm and wrist acceleration is, the more spin there will be on the ball. This is because the server imparts more spin to the ball by increasing the racket speed on contact. Conversely, the ball will have less spin.

● Watch the racket angle at contact to read the spin

If the racket angle is closed, the serve

可能是上旋球;如果球拍后仰,则可能是下旋球。但是该方法只能用于业余比赛当中,而不能在顶尖水平的比赛中采用,这是因为优秀的选手通常会在发球时使用假动作来迷惑对方。

will have topspin. If it is open, the serve will have backspin. This principle only can be used in the amateur competition but not in the advanced, for the advanced players always make some deceptive motions to disguise the type of spin.

3. 合理回接

3. Return the Serve Properly

● 回接上旋球

一般采用推挡、挑打和正手攻回接。在回接时应注意球拍前倾,以压住球的弧线。

● Return a topspin serve

You can use block, flip and forehand drive to return. Pay attention to keep the racket slightly closed to lower the trajectory.

● 回接下旋球

一般采用搓球和拉弧圈球回接。当用搓球回接时,球拍要更加后仰,以增大向上方的力。

● Return a backspin serve

You can use push and loop drive to return. When you push, the racket angle should be more open and swing upward a little.

● 回接左侧旋球

一般采用搓球、推挡和挑打回接。在回接时,拍面要朝左,触击球的右侧,以抵消来球的左侧旋。

● Return a left sidespin serve

You can use push, block and flip to return. But angle blade of the racket to the left side, and contact the right side of the ball, so as to counteract left sidespin.

● 回接右侧旋球

反手侧旋发球和下蹲式发球属于右侧旋发球。一般采用搓球、推挡和挑打回接。在回接时拍面要朝右,触击球的左侧,以抵消来球的右侧旋。

● Return a right sidespin serve

Backhand sidespin serve and squatting serve belong to right sidespin serve. You can use push, block and flip to return. But angle blade of the racket to the right side, and contact the left side of the ball, so as to counteract right sidespin.

● 回接短球

回接时可用摆短技术或者用手腕挥拍摩擦球进行挑打。在接短球时,挥拍动作要小,并确保在击球时向前

● Return a short serve

Drop shot, or flip racket with your wrist to graze the ball to return. You just need a little bat movement. Be sure to move your fore-

移动前臂和上身,以靠近来球。同时,注意保持身体平衡。接发球后迅速还原,准备下一板击球。

arm and upper body forward to close to the ball when execute the stroke, but keep your balance at the same time and recover quickly.

第四节 基础类技术
Section 4 Basic Techniques

一、正手攻球

正手攻球技术是乒乓球基本技术,也是最重要的技术之一。在现代比赛当中,运动员经常用正手攻球来回击上旋球。正手攻球具有力量大、速度快、落点变化多的特点。下面对正手攻球动作进行详细介绍。

● 动作要领(图 3.4.1 和图 3.4.2)

(1)正手攻球的准备姿势与本章前面介绍的准备姿势一样。

(2)当正手位来球时,向后转腰带动前臂向右后方引拍;拍面稍前倾,手臂自然弯曲使肘关节成 120°。

Ⅰ. Forehand Drive

Forehand drive is one of the basic techniques of table tennis and clearly one of the most important techniques. In the modern games, forehand drive is often executed against opponent's topspin return. It is characterized by having great power, high speed and changeful placement. Detailed introduction of forehand drive is as follows.

● Movement essentials (Figure 3.4.1 and Figure 3.4.2)

(1)The ready position is the same as mentioned in this chapter.

(2)As the ball approaches to your forehand, rotate your waist backward to bring your forearm backswing to the lower right. The racket should be closed slightly, and keep your elbow joint at a 120-degree angle.

a　　b　　c

图 3.4.1　横拍正手攻球

Figure 3.4.1　Forehand Drive with Shake-hands Grip

a　　b　　c

图 3.4.2　直拍正手攻球

Figure 3.4.2　Forehand Drive with Pen-hold Grip

（3）当球跳至最高点时，向前转腰带动前臂向前上方挥拍击球；前臂击球应以肘为轴挥动。

（3）When the ball is at the peak of its bounce, rotate your waist forward to bring your forearm and racket swing mostly forward and slightly upward to hit the ball. Your forearm should pivot around the elbow.

（4）在触球的一瞬间加快挥拍速度。

（4）Increase the racket speed on contact.

（5）随势挥拍至左眼处。

（5）Follow through to left eye level.

（6）重心由右脚转至左脚。

（6）Transfer your weight from right foot to left foot.

● 易犯错误和纠正方法

● Mistakes and corrections

（1）易犯错误：以肩为轴挥拍。

（1）Mistake：Swing with your shoulder as axis.

纠正方法：以肘为轴挥拍。

Correction：Swing with your elbow as

axis.

（2）易犯错误：击球时肩和肘关节上抬。

（2）Mistake：Your shoulder and elbow lift up when you strike.

纠正方法：肩和肘关节自然放松。

Correction：Keep your shoulder and elbow relaxed.

（3）易犯错误：球拍后仰过多。

（3）Mistake：The racket opens too much.

纠正方法：球拍稍前倾。

Correction：Make the racket closed slightly.

（4）易犯错误：在击球过程中没有转腰和重心转换。

（4）Mistake：You don't rotate your waist and transfer your weight.

纠正方法：在训练中强调转腰和重心转换的重要性。

Correction：Emphasize the importance of rotating your waist and transfering your weight during the practice.

（5）易犯错误：手腕上翘。

（5）Mistake：Your wrist turns up.

纠正方法：手腕略微弯曲。

Correction：Keep your wrist bent slightly.

● 关键点

● Key points

（1）在整个挥拍过程中，肘关节的角度由 120° 变成约 90°。

（1）During swing，your elbow should move from 120-degree angle to 90-degree angle.

（2）击球过程就像敬军礼。

（2）Imagine you are giving a salute during striking.

（3）肩膀放松，前臂挥拍。

（3）Relax your shoulder and swing with your forearm.

（4）正手击斜线球时，在触球的一瞬间肩膀朝向斜线方向，站位较平；正手击直线球时，站位向右侧偏转，肩膀在击球时朝向直线方向。

（4）To direct the ball crosscourt，point your shoulder in that direction（with an open stance）when racket contact the ball. To direct the ball down the line，turn sideways more so that your shoulder points down the line.

二、反手攻球

反手攻球是一项乒乓球运动员必须熟练掌握的基本技术，一般应在初学阶段进行学习。根据握拍方式的不同，反手攻球可分为以下三种：横拍反手拨、直拍推挡、直拍横打。下面依次介绍这三种技术。

1）横拍反手拨

● 动作要领（图 3.4.3）

（1）反手攻球的准备姿势与正手攻球的准备姿势相同。

（2）手臂自然弯曲，球拍稍前倾，引拍至腹部使拍头几乎与球台平行。

（3）当球跳至最高点时，以肘为轴，前臂外旋向前上方挥拍击球。

（4）在身体前方击球，击球的中上部。

Ⅱ. Backhand Drive

Backhand drive is a basic skill that all the table tennis players must proficiently master. This skill should be learned at the beginning of training process. It can be divided into three categories by grips: shake-hands backhand drive, pen-hold block, and pen-hold reverse backhand stroke. The following will introduce these three techniques in turn.

1）Shake-hands Backhand Drive

● Movement essentials（Figure 3.4.3）

（1）Backhand drive is executed from the same ready position as forehand drive.

（2）Your arm bends naturally and the racket should be closed slightly. Back swing to the belly level with the racket head nearly parallel to the table.

（3）When the ball is at the peak of its bounce, your forearm swings forward and up to hit the ball by pivoting around your elbow.

（4）The stroke is done in front of your body. The contact point is slightly above the center of the ball.

a　　b　　c

图 3.4.3　横拍反手拨

Figure 3.4.3　Shake-hands Backhand Drive

（5）随势挥拍动作较小，球拍挥至身体右侧。

（5）Use short follow through, the racket finishes forward and slightly to the right of your body.

● 易犯错误和纠正方法

● Mistakes and corrections

（1）易犯错误：击球时前臂伸展不充分。

（1）Mistake: Your forearm is not fully extended when executing the stoke.

纠正方法：击球时前臂放松并展开。

Correction: Keep your forearm relaxed and push it out when executing the stoke.

（2）易犯错误：拍头上翘。

（2）Mistake: Racket head is elevated.

纠正方法：使拍头几乎平行于球台。

Correction: Keep racket head nearly parallel to the table.

（3）易犯错误：站位错误，右脚靠前。

（3）Mistake: You are in a wrong posture, your right foot moves forward.

纠正方法：左脚稍靠前。

Correction: Left foot moves slightly forward.

（4）易犯错误：击球缺少引拍动作。

（4）Mistake: Stroke without an enough backswing.

纠正方法：引拍至腹前。

Correction: Back swing to the belly level.

（5）易犯错误：手腕动得太多。

（5）Mistake: You get too much wrist movement.

纠正方法：只需在发力弹击时更多地用到手腕。

Correction: Use your wrist only for full kill stroke.

（6）易犯错误：抬肘。

（6）Mistake: Your elbow lifts up.

纠正方法：收拢肘关节并放松。

Correction: Drop down your elbow and keep it relaxed.

● 关键点

● Key points

（1）做动作时想象你正在扔飞盘。

（1）Imagine you are throwing a frisbee when executing the motion.

（2）向前挥的动力来自肘关节外展动作，旋转源于手腕的动作。

（2）The forward motion is produced by your elbow, while the rotational effect comes from your wrist action.

2)直拍推挡

● 动作要领(图 3.4.4)

(1)手臂自然弯曲,球拍稍前倾,将球拍稍引至身体前方使其与台面基本垂直,球拍与来球同高,前臂和肘关节尽量靠近身体右侧。

(2)在球的上升后期击球,上臂带动前臂向前发力挥拍迎球,在触球的一瞬间手腕外旋。

(3)击球的中上部。

(4)随势挥拍时手臂几近伸直,然后迅速还原。

2)Pen-hold Block

● Movement essentials(Figure 3.4.4)

(1)Your arm bends naturally and the racket should be closed slightly. Use a short backswing toward your body to make the racket nearly vertical to the table and parallel to the oncoming ball. Your forearm and elbow should be close to the right side of your body.

(2)Move your upper arm to swing your forearm quickly forward to contact the ball as it rises. Roll your wrist outward at contact.

(3)The contact point is above the center of the ball.

(4)Follow through with your arm almost straight and recover quickly.

a　b　c

图 3.4.4　直拍推挡

Figure 3.4.4　Pen-hold Block

● 易犯错误和纠正方法

(1)易犯错误:手腕上翘或下垂。

纠正方法:使拍头几乎平行于球台。

● Mistakes and corrections

(1)Mistake: Your wrist is elevated or comes down.

Correction: Keep racket head nearly parallel to the table.

(2)易犯错误:抬肘,肘关节远离身体。

纠正方法:收拢肘关节并使其靠近身体。

(3)易犯错误:球拍过于后仰。

纠正方法:球拍稍前倾。

● 关键点

(1)推挡的击球力量主要来自食指、中指发力和身体转动的力量。

(2)推挡时应多借助来球的力量。

3)直拍横打

● 动作要领(图 3.4.5)

(1)击球前的姿势与反手推挡一样。

(2)手臂自然弯曲,手腕内扣形成接近垂直的角度,引拍至腹前,球拍略微前倾。

(2)Mistake: Your elbow lifts up and is far away from your body.

Correction: Drop down your elbow and keep it close to your body.

(3)Mistake: The racket opens too much.

Correction: Keep the racket closed slightly.

● Key points

(1)Deliver power to stroke mostly by index finger and middle finger, and the rotation of your body.

(2)Block should rely on more energy of the oncoming ball.

3)Pen-hold Reverse Backhand Stroke

● Movement essentials (Figure 3.4.5)

(1)Begin the stroke the same way as backhand block.

(2)Your arm bends naturally while wrist bends inside to form a nearly vertical angle. Back swing to the belly level with the racket slightly closed.

a b c

图 3.4.5 直拍横打

Figure 3.4.5 Pen-hold Reverse Backhand Stroke

(3)当球跳至最高点时,前臂以肘为轴向前上方挥动。在触球的一瞬间手腕略微外旋。

(3)When the ball is at the peak of its bounce, your forearm swings forward and up by pivoting around your elbow. Slightly roll your wrist outward at contact.

(4)击球的中上部。

(4)The contact point is above the center of the ball.

(5)与直拍推挡不同,直拍横打击球时主要用拇指与中指发力,食指放松。

(5)In contrary to pen-hold block, the power of pen-hold reverse backhand stroke comes from your thumb and middle finger, and your index finger should be relaxed.

● 易犯错误和纠正方法

● Mistakes and corrections

(1)易犯错误:球拍过于前倾,使回球下网。

(1)Mistake: The racket closes too much, resulting in the ball consistently goes into the net.

纠正方法:球拍略微前倾。

Correction: Keep the racket closed slightly.

(2)易犯错误:在体侧击球。

(2)Mistake: Hit the ball at the side of your body.

纠正方法:一定要在身前击球。

Correction: Be sure to hit the ball in front of your body.

三、搓球

Ⅲ. Push Stroke

搓球是每名乒乓球运动员都必须掌握的一项基本技术,其回球具有下旋的性质,能用来回击对方的下旋发球或下旋球。因此,搓球主要是一项防守控制性技术。在业余比赛中,可以通过搓球的旋转和落点变化迫使对方失误而得分。搓球技术可分为以下四类:慢搓、快搓(摆短)、劈长和搓不转球。这一节介绍慢搓,其他三种较

Push stroke is a basic technique for every table tennis player. It is a backspin stroke used against opponent's backspin serve or return. Therefore, push stroke is mainly a defensive skill used to control the ball. In amateurish match, you can win a point with push stroke by changing the amount of spin and the placement to force your opponent to make an error. There are four types of push stroke: slow

高级的搓球技术在下一节中介绍。

push, fast push (drop shot), long heavy-spin push and no-spin push. This section introduces slow push, while the rest three skills will be introduced in the upcoming section.

慢搓

Slow Push

● 动作要领(图 3.4.6~图 3.4.9)

● Movement essentials (Figure 3.4.6-Figure 3.4.9)

(1)引拍时拍面后仰约45°。反手搓球时,向后引拍至身体中部;正手搓球时,稍向后上方引拍。

(1)The racket should be opened 45 degree. For backhand push stroke, swing the racket back to the center of your body. For forehand push stroke, slightly swing the racket backward and upward.

(2)当球处于下降前期时,前臂向前伸展挥拍迎球;在触球的一瞬间手腕抖动发力。

(2)When the ball is at the early stage of the descending phase, extend your forearm to swing the racket to hit the ball, and shake your wrist forward at contact.

(3)向前下方挥拍,摩擦球的底部。

(3)Graze the bottom of the ball with a forward and downward stroke.

(4)在身体前方击球。

(4)Hit the ball in front of your body.

● 易犯错误和纠正方法

● Mistakes and corrections

(1)易犯错误:手腕动得过多,前臂前伸不够。

(1)Mistake: You get too much wrist and too little forearm.

纠正方法:用前臂挥拍击球,手腕略微发力。

Correction: Execute stroke with your forearm and slightly shake your wrist.

(2)易犯错误:缺少引拍。

(2)Mistake: You lack backswing.

纠正方法:在徒手挥拍时强调引拍动作。

Correction: Emphasize the importance of backswing during the shadow strike.

(3)易犯错误:击球时间过早。

(3)Mistake: Hitting point is too early.

纠正方法:在下降期击球,确保充分的挥拍动作。

Correction: Hit the ball at the descending phase to have an enough swing movement.

(4)易犯错误:球拍过于前倾。

(4)Mistake: The racket closes too

a　b　c　d

图 3.4.6　横拍反手搓球

Figure 3.4.6　Backhand Push Stroke with Shake-hands Grip

a　b　c

图 3.4.7　横拍正手搓球

Figure 3.4.7　Forehand Push Stroke with Shake-hands Grip

a b c

图 3.4.8　直拍反手搓球

Figure 3.4.8　Backhand Push Stroke with Pen-hold Grip

a b c

图 3.4.9　直拍正手搓球

Figure 3.4.9　Forehand Push Stroke with Pen-hold Grip

纠正方法:球拍略微后仰。

● 关键点

(1)挥拍击球的拍形取决于来球的旋转:球的下旋越强烈,球拍越要后仰,球的上旋越强烈,球拍越要前倾。

(2)手腕略微抖动,以增大速度,增强旋转。

much.

Correction: Keep the racket open slightly.

● Key points

(1)The racket angle depends on the spin of the oncoming ball. Heavier backspin requires more open racket; the more topspin there is, the more you should close the racket.

(2)Slightly shake your wrist for more speed and spin.

四、削球

削球是一项站位靠后、远离球台的防守型技术，运动员利用不同旋转的削球迫使对方直接失误或者使对方回球质量不高而为自己的进攻创造条件。为了使削球具有威胁性，削过去的球必须又低又转。下面分别介绍正手削球与反手削球。

Ⅳ. Chop Stroke

Chop stroke is a defensive technique which is executed from a deep position, away from the table. Chopping players use chop strokes with different spins to force their opponents to commit outright errors or weak returns that they can attack to finish the point. To be effective, chop returns must land low and revolving on opponent's side. A separate discussion of forehand chop stroke and backhand chop stroke is elaborated as follows.

1. 正手削球

● 动作要领（图 3.4.10）

（1）右脚稍后，身体偏向于右侧，与此同时肘关节略微弯曲使球拍向上竖立，引拍至肩高附近。

（2）在来球的下降期，上臂带动前臂向前下方挥动。

1. Forehand Chop Stroke

● Movement essentials（Figure 3.4.10）

（1）Step your right foot back and rotate your waist to the right so that your body is sideways to your right. At the same time, bend your elbow and make the racket upward, then back swing to your shoulder height.

（2）Move your upper arm to swing your forearm forward and downward to contact the ball as it descends.

a　　b　　c

图 3.4.10　正手削球

Figure 3.4.10　Forehand Chop Stroke

（3）摩擦球的底部，在触球的一瞬间手腕有一定的摩擦球的动作。

（3）Graze the bottom of the ball. Slightly shake your wrist at contact to increase the amount of backspin.

（4）向回球的方向随势挥拍，并快速还原。

（4）Follow through to the target and quickly recover.

2. 反手削球

2. Backhand Chop Stroke

● 动作要领（图 3.4.11）

● Movement essentials（Figure 3.4.11）

（1）左脚稍后，身体偏向于左侧，与此同时肘关节略微弯曲使球拍向上竖立，引拍至肩高附近。

（1）Step your left foot back and rotate your waist to the left so that your body is sideways to your left. At the same time, bend your elbow and make the racket upward, then back swing to your shoulder height.

（2）在来球的下降期，上臂带动前臂向前下方挥动。

（2）Move your upper arm to swing your forearm forward and downward to contact the ball as it descends.

（3）摩擦球的底部，在触球的一瞬间手腕有一定的摩擦球的动作。

（3）Graze the bottom of the ball. Slightly shake your wrist at contact to increase the amount of backspin.

（4）向回球的方向随势挥拍，并快速还原。

（4）Follow through to the target and quickly recover.

a b c

图 3.4.11 反手削球

Figure 3.4.11 Backhand Chop Stroke

● 易犯错误和纠正方法

(1)易犯错误:球拍后仰过多。

纠正方法:在引拍时球拍要稍竖立。

(2)易犯错误:站得太直,重心太高。

纠正方法:削球时重心必须更低,膝盖必须更弯曲。

(3)易犯错误:削过去的球太高、太长而出界。

纠正方法:多向下摩擦球。

● 关键点

(1)从挥拍击球到还原的整个过程呈现出一个画圆的动作。

(2)向上引拍至肩膀高度,而不是向后引拍。

(3)在削球的过程中注意重心转换并快速移动。

● Mistakes and corrections

(1)Mistake: The racket opens too much.

Correction: Make the racket upward during backswing.

(2)Mistake: Your posture is straight up too much.

Correction: During chopping, you should place yourself at lower center of gravity with knees bent more.

(3)Mistake: Returns go high and long against heavy topspin.

Correction: Chop downward more at contact.

● Key points

(1)From swing to recover, the stroke has a circular feel.

(2)Back swing upward to your shoulder level but not backward.

(3)Pay attention to weight transfer during chop stroke, and move quickly.

第五节　提高类技术
Section 5　Advanced Techniques

这一节将介绍一系列乒乓球提高类技术。提高类技术以上一节介绍的基础类技术为基础。学习和掌握提高类技术有助于取得更明显的

This section will introduce a number of advanced techniques of table tennis. Advanced techniques are based on basic techniques introduced in last section. Learning and master-

进步。

ing advanced techniques will help you make significant progress.

一、正手提高类技术

I. Advanced Forehand Techniques

1. 正手扣杀

扣杀是一项极富攻击力的进攻技术，当面对较高的来球，特别是来球从球台上弹起至高于自己肩膀的位置时，运动员通常会用扣杀技术结束战斗。扣杀可分为正手扣杀和反手扣杀。下面介绍正手扣杀，反手扣杀将在反手提高类技术中介绍。

● 动作要领（图 3.5.1）

（1）正手扣杀动作与正手攻球动作类似。

（2）正手扣杀的要点在于引拍和随挥动作位置更高、幅度更大。

（3）击球时上臂带动前臂向前下方快速用力挥动。

（4）注意在挥拍击球时转腰和重心转换的幅度更大，充分利用转腰来加大击球的力量。

（5）为下一板击球快速还原。

● 易犯错误和纠正方法

（1）易犯错误：扣杀下旋球时球下网。

纠正方法：球拍更加后仰，以击打

1. Forehand Smash

Smash is an effective offensive skill. Players usually execute a point-winning smash against a high return, especially the ball bounces higher than their shoulders. Smash is usually classified as forehand and backhand. The former will be introduced as follows, while the latter is to be introduced in advanced backhand techniques.

● Movement essentials (Figure 3.5.1)

(1) The motions of forehand drive and forehand smash are basically the same.

(2) The main point of forehand smash is that backswing and follow-through should be higher and longer.

(3) Forcefully swing your upper arm and forearm forward and downward to hit the ball.

(4) Pay attention to greater rotation of waist and weight transfer during swing. Add power by rotating your waist.

(5) Recover quickly for next shot.

● Mistakes and corrections

(1) Mistake: When smashing against backspin ball, the ball goes into the net.

Correction: Open the racket more to hit

a b c

图 3.5.1 正手扣杀

Figure 3.5.1 Forehand Smash

球的中下部,略微向上提拉发力。

(2)易犯错误:扣杀上旋球时球出界。

纠正方法:球拍更加前倾,以击打球的中上部,以向下发力扣杀为主。

2. 正手弧圈球

弧圈球是一种具有弧线高、速度快等特征的强烈上旋球,已经成为比赛中使用最多、对对方威胁性最大的进攻技术。弧圈球可分为加转高吊弧圈球、前冲弧圈球和侧拐弧圈球。加转高吊弧圈球具有十分强烈的上旋,而且稳定性较好,因此当来球又转又低时,可用加转高吊弧圈球回击。前冲弧圈球的力量更大、速度更快,球在落台后会急速往前下方坠落。当右手选手拉出正手侧拐弧圈球时,击出的球具有很强的右侧旋,球在落台后会急速向左侧拐弯。反手弧圈球将在反手提高类技术中予以介绍。下面介绍

the ball further below its center. Push up more at contact.

(2)Mistake: When smashing against topspin ball, the ball flies out of the table.

Correction: Close the racket more to hit the ball further above its center. Press down more at contact.

2. Forehand Loop Drive

Loop drive has high trajectory, high speed and strong topspin. It has been the most used stroke in the competition and is a formidable offensive skill for the defender. Loop drive can be divided into three categories: high-spin loop (slow topspin), fast loop (fast topspin) and loop with sidespin. High-spin loop, which has strong topspin and high hitting ratio, can be used against strong backspin ball. Fast loop has heavier impact and higher speed that violently kicks forward and downward after hitting the table. When right-handed player uses forehand loop with sidespin, this stroke carries strong right side-

正手弧圈球。

spin and breaks sharply to the left after hitting the table. Backhand loop drive will be introduced in advanced backhand techniques. Detailed introduction of forehand loop drive is as follows.

1)正手加转高吊弧圈球

● 动作要领(图 3.5.2)

(1)屈膝,向后转体使右肩下沉,并引拍至膝盖处。

(2)当球跳至最高点时,蹬腿并向前转腰、转髋以增加击球力量,从而带动前臂向前上方挥拍。

(3)以肘关节为轴挥动前臂,在触球的一瞬间前臂迅速收缩,手腕稍抖动摩擦球。

(4)随势挥拍方向更靠上。

(5)击球后重心转至左脚。

1)Forehand High-spin Loop

● Movement essentials (Figure 3.5.2)

(1)Knees should be bent. Turn your upper body back to drop down your right shoulder and back swing to your knee level.

(2)When the ball drops from the peak of its bounce, start the stroke by straightening your legs and rotating your waist and hip forward to add force, bringing your forearm swing upward and forward.

(3)Your forearm should pivot about your elbow. When contacting the ball, your forearm should quickly contract and your wrist should shake slightly to graze the ball.

(4)Follow through upward more.

(5)Transfer your weight to the left foot after hitting the ball.

2)正手前冲弧圈球

● 动作要领(图 3.5.3)

(1)动作与高吊弧圈球类似。

(2)要点是前臂向前挥多于向上挥,并增大撞击、减少摩擦。

(3)在击球过程中转腰和重心转换异常重要。

2)Forehand Fast Loop

● Movement essentials (Figure 3.5.3)

(1)The motion is similar to the high-spin loop.

(2)The main point is that the forearm swings forward more than upward and increasing strength and decreasing friction.

(3)It is also important to rotate your waist and weight transfer should be greater.

a b c

图 3.5.2 正手加转高吊弧圈球

Figure 3.5.2 Forehand High-spin Loop

a b c

图 3.5.3 正手前冲弧圈球

Figure 3.5.3 Forehand Fast Loop

● 怎样拉正手加转弧圈球?

我们先从下半身谈起,即腿的位置或者可以说步法。当然,完美的站位很重要,距离球不能太近,也不能太远,腿的站位稍微侧开。要想把击球

● How to play the forehand topspin with a lot of rotation?

Let’s start at bottom, the leg position or the footwork. Obviously, it is important to stand perfectly to the ball. The distanc to the ball should not be too closed, but also not too

的质量提到最高，利用好腿的力量是关键因素之一。首先，你需要把重心放得非常低，你的膝盖有时甚至会碰到地面。其次，你需要从腿部爆发出来力量，正如利用胳膊和手腕的张力，对于腿的力量也是一样的。当腿和胳膊甚至是手腕刚好同时发力时，你会获得击球最高的质量。保持核心稳定绷紧也很重要，能让你把力量传递到球上，因为你如果核心不稳定，就会失去具有决定性的力量。

far away, and the leg position is slightly offside. One of the crucial points for the maximum quality of the stroke is the use of the power of the leg. Firstly you have to go very low, you even touch the ground with your knee. Secondly you have to use your legs explosively similar creating tension with the arm or wrist, you have to create the same with the legs. You will get the most quality out of it, if the input is made at exactly the same time with the legs and the arm or even the wrist. The abdominal tension is also important, so that you can transfer the power into the stroke. Because if you are unstable, you'll lose the decisive percentages.

尽量全身收紧，这能提升你对球的敏感度。在这方面，对弧圈球这项技术，如果摩擦得很薄就容易得到高质量的球，使球旋转获得最大的加速度。不像大多数技术那样在最高点击球，加转弧圈球要在低一些的击球点击球，大概和球台一样高或者更低一点，这一般取决于你的站位。如果有足够的时间做到最好的选位，我喜欢把我的加转弧圈球拉得比较短而且弧线低，这样它的第二跳也会比较低平，对手就不得不在球的下降点推挡或反拉，而且我有足够的时间移动到位打下一板相持球。如果对手把球打回来了，我会时刻准备着。如你所见，这不是一项容易的技术，你需要培养爆发

Try to be very compact overall, so that you can also develop the necessary sensitivity. In this area it is the easiest to hit the ball very thinly, that is to stroke but still generate maximum acceleration in this case not in speed but in rotation. Instead of hitting at the highest point like most other techniques, but hitting at a later and lower point, perhaps at the same height as the table or a little lower. It always depends on how you position yourself. If there is enough time to the optimal position, I like to play my super spin a little bit shorter very low over the net, so that it also bounces very flight and the opponent actually has to hit it in a falling face to block or counter.In addition, I then have enough time to position

力和薄摩擦的感觉。

for the follow-up ball. If the opponent plays it on table at all, but I'm always ready.As you can see, it is not an easy stroke, you have to develop this feeling of explosiveness and thin hitting.

3)侧拐弧圈球

● 动作要领

(1)拉侧拐弧圈球的准备姿势与拉一般弧圈球的准备姿势相同。

(2)拉侧拐弧圈球的引拍动作与拉一般弧圈球的引拍动作相比更靠近背后,引拍时手腕内扣。

(3)击球时,挥拍轨迹是一个先向右、再向左的正手拉球动作,触球时摩擦球的右侧。

(4)击球后继续向目标方向随势挥拍。

● 易犯错误和纠正方法

(1)易犯错误:前臂挥拍速度太慢。

纠正方法:触球一瞬间加快挥拍速度。

(2)易犯错误:右肩和引拍位置过高。

纠正方法:引拍位置应较低。

(3)易犯错误:撞击过多缺少摩擦。

纠正方法:打、摩结合。

(4)易犯错误:没有转腰。

3)Forehand Loop with Sidespin

● Movement essentials

(1)Begin the forehand loop with side-spin as you did a normal forehand loop drive.

(2)During the backswing phase, put your racket more behind your back. Have your wrist laid back.

(3)Swing your racket with a right to left motion and brush the right edge of the ball.

(4)Stroke continues toward target.

● Mistakes and corrections

(1)Mistake: Your forearm swing is too slow.

Correction: Quickly swing at contact.

(2)Mistake: Your shoulder and back-swing are elevated too much.

Correction: The backswing should be low.

(3)Mistake: More contact and less friction.

Correction: Mixed friction and force at contact.

(4)Mistake: You do not rotate your

纠正方法:拉球时必须转腰并注意重心交换。

waist.

Correction: Be sure to rotate your waist and transfer your weight.

● 关键点

(1)先沉肩,迅速向上挥臂,并尽可能薄地摩擦球。

(2)摩擦时间更久以便产生更多旋转。

(3)通过屈膝、转腰和重心交换所产生的力量制造出更多旋转和速度。

● Key points

(1)Firstly drop down your right shoulder for an enough backswing; bring the arm up quickly and then brush the ball as lightly as possible.

(2)It is important to start the contact slowly so that you can properly spin the ball.

(3)Generate more speed and spin by bending of the knee, rotation of the waist and weight transfer.

3. 正手挑打

在现代乒乓球比赛中,进攻短球的能力变得异常重要。挑打技术就能以上旋球的方式进攻下旋短球,从而争取积极主动。挑打技术可分为正手挑打和反手挑打。反手挑打技术将在反手提高类技术中学习,以下为正手挑打技术的介绍。

3. Forehand Flip

In the modern game, the ability to attack a short return is becoming more important. The flip can be executed to play against the short return by a topspin stroke, which helps you take initiatives. The flip can be divided into two categories: forehand flip and backhand flip. The backhand flip will be introduced in the advanced backhand skills. The introduction of forehand flip is as follows.

● 动作要领(图 3.5.4)

(1)向前迈一步的同时身体和前臂一起向前迎球。

(2)肘部和手腕微屈,拍形稍微后仰。

(3)当球至最高点时,挥动前臂,触球一瞬间手腕挥动摩擦球。

● Movement essentials(Figure 3.5.4)

(1)Step in with the right foot to move your upper body and forearm forward at the same time.

(2)Bend your elbow and wrist back; the racket angle should be opened slightly.

(3)When the ball is at the peak of its bounce, snap your forearm forward and flip the racket with wrist to graze ball.

（4）击球后继续向目标方向随势挥拍。

（4）Stroke continues toward target.

（5）击球后迅速还原至准备姿势。

（5）Recover to ready position quickly.

a　　　b　　　c

图 3.5.4　正手挑打

Figure 3.5.4　Forehand Flip

● 关键点

（1）步法快速向前移动。

（2）执拍手放松朝向来球。

（3）击球时手腕较灵活。

● Key points

（1）Quickly move forward.

（2）The racket hand is loosely described as pointing to the ball.

（3）Stroke with a flexible wrist movement.

4. 反拉弧圈球

反拉弧圈球是指本方运动员用拉球技术将对手的弧圈球反拉过去。在专业运动员比赛当中，反拉弧圈球已经成为一项必不可少的重要技术。运动员既可以在近台进行反拉，也可以退到远台反拉，从而在防守过程中争取积极主动。反拉技术可分为正手反拉和反手反拉。这一节先介绍正手反拉技术，反手反拉将在反手高级技术中作详细介绍。

4. Counterloop

Executing a loop stroke against your opponent's loop return is referred to as counterloop. At the professional level, it is a highly utilized skill. Players can execute the counterloop both close to the table and away from the table, which will help them take the initiative. The counterloop can be divided into two categories: forehand counterloop and backhand counterloop. The backhand counterloop will be introduced in the advanced backhand skills. The forehand counterloop is as follows.

正手反拉弧圈球

Forehand Counterloop

● 动作要领(图 3.5.5)

● Movement essentials(Figure 3.5.5)

(1)拍形更前倾,引拍时球拍要低于来球,但是引拍位置不必像拉下旋球那样低。

(1)Use a more closed racket and it should be back and a little lower than the oncoming ball, but your racket does not need to be as low as it was when against a backspin return.

(2)通过蹬腿、伸膝、转腰的动作来带动你向前上方挥拍。

(2)Begin the counterloop stroke by straightening your knees and rotating your waist to bring your racket forward and upward.

(3)挥拍动作幅度稍大,并且动作轨迹要高于拉下旋球的动作。

(3)Your swing movement should be much greater and more horizontal than it was when returning a backspin ball.

(4)在来球的高点期触球的中部,增加摩擦,减少击打。

(4)Contact the center of the ball at top of its bounce. More friction and less hitting.

(5)借来球的力量和旋转向前击球。

(5)Rely on more energy and spin of the oncoming ball to stroke forward.

a b c

图 3.5.5 正手反拉弧圈球

Figure 3.5.5 Forehand Counterloop

二、反手提高类技术

1. 反手扣杀

● 动作要领(图 3.5.6)

(1)右脚稍靠前,站位离球台约 60 cm。

(2)腰、髋向左转动,带动球拍向左后方引拍,以便拉开充足的击球空间。

(3)当来球跳至高点期时,腰、髋向右转动,带动前臂迅速向前下方加速挥动。

(4)球拍稍前倾击球的中上部。

(5)随势挥拍距离较长。

Ⅱ. Advanced Backhand Techniques

1. Backhand Smash

● Movement essentials(Figure 3.5.6)

(1)Stand with right foot slightly forward, about 60 centimeters away from the table.

(2)Rotate your waist and hip to the left, bringing the racket to the left backward to make an enough space for hitting.

(3)Rotate your waist to the right and move your upper arm to bring your forearm quickly swing forward and downward to contact the ball at the peak.

(4)The slightly closed racket contacts the ball above the center of the ball.

(5)Finish in a long follow-through.

a b c

图 3.5.6 反手扣杀

Figure 3.5.6 Backhand Smash

● 关键点

(1)击球时手腕弹击发力。

● Key points

(1)Snap the wrist more as you contact the ball.

(2)引拍的距离取决于来球的高度和长短位置。

(2)The distance of backswing depends on the ball's height and position.

2. 反手弧圈球

2. Backhand Loop Drive

● 动作要领(图 3.5.7)

● Movement essentials (Figure 3.5.7)

(1)向左转腰使执拍手的肩部前探,并引拍至膝盖。

(1)Rotate your waist to the left so that your racket side shoulder is closer to table than nonracket side shoulder, and backswing to the knee level.

(2)使前臂自然弯曲、手腕内屈。

(2)Bend your forearm and wrist laid back.

(3)通过脚蹬地、伸膝、转腰的动作带动前臂向前上方挥动。

(3)Straighten your knees and rotate your waist to bring your forearm swing upward and forward.

(4)前臂以肘为轴挥动并充分展开。

(4)The forearm pivots around the elbow and fully extends.

(5)当触球时,手腕外旋。

(5)When contact is made, snap your wrist.

a　　b　　c

图 3.5.7　反手弧圈球

Figure 3.5.7　Backhand Loop Drive

● 易犯错误和纠正方法

● Mistakes and corrections

(1)易犯错误:挥拍过于向上导致失去重心。

(1)Mistake: Your upward swing is so great that you lose your balance.

纠正方法:注意挥拍动作不要过

Correction: Pay attention to have a lim-

大并保持身体平衡。

(2)易犯错误:撞击过多,摩擦过少。

纠正方法:拉球时注意"打、摩"结合。

3. 直拍横拉

作为一项新兴技术,直拍反手反面拉球技术已经帮助直拍运动员克服了传统的反手位弱点,并且使直拍打法焕然一新。奥运冠军王皓,就以直拍横拉技术闻名于天下,并向世界展示了该项技术的独特魅力。

● 动作要领(图 3.5.8)

(1)其击球原理与直拍横打类似。

(2)两脚几乎平行站位,屈膝。

(3)向身体左侧转腰并向下引拍至膝关节处。

(4)前臂自然弯曲,手腕自然内扣下垂。

ited swing and keep balanced.

(2)Mistake: More contact and less friction.

Correction: Mixed friction and force at contact.

3. Pen-hold Backside Loop Drive

As a new-born skill, the development of pen-hold backside loop drive has revitalized this style of play and successfully eliminated the traditional backhand weaknesses of this style. Wang Hao, Olympic champion, is famous for his pen-hold backside loop drive and shows the glamour of this skill to the world.

● Movement essentials(Figure 3.5.8)

(1)Its stroke mechanism is similar to the pen-hold backside hitting.

(2)Place feet parallel to the table and dccply bend your knees.

(3)Rotate your waist to the left and bring the racket below the table to the knee lovel.

(4)Bend your forearm; wrist laid back and down.

a b c

图 3.5.8 直拍横拉

Figure 3.5.8 Pen-hold Backside Loop Drive

（5）通过伸膝蹬地、转腰的动作带动前臂和手腕向前上方挥动，触球一瞬间手腕发力摩擦。

（6）前臂以肘为轴挥拍并充分展开。

● 关键点

（1）触球时手腕用力更多。

（2）打、摩结合。

4. 反手挑打

● 动作要领（图 3.5.9）

（1）向前迈一步的同时身体和前臂一起向前迎球。

（2）引拍时肘部微屈，手腕稍内扣；拍形稍微前倾。

（3）当球至最高点时，挥动前臂，触球一瞬间手腕外旋摩擦球。

（4）击球后继续向目标方向随势挥拍。

（5）Straighten your knees and rotate your waist to bring your forearm and wrist swing forward and upward. When making contact, snap your wrist.

（6）The forearm pivots around the elbow and fully extends.

● Key points

（1）Snap your wrist more at contact.

（2）Mixed friction and force at contact.

4. Backhand Flip

● Movement essentials（Figure 3.5.9）

（1）Step forward to get your upper body and forearm close to the ball.

（2）Bend your elbow; wrist is laid back slightly. The racket angle should be closed a little.

（3）When the ball is at the peak of its bounce, swing forearm forward a little, with the external rotation of wrist to graze ball.

（4）Stroke continues toward target.

a　　b　　c

图 3.5.9　反手挑打

Figure 3.5.9　Backhand Flip

● 关键点

（1）主要依靠前臂和手腕的动作击球。

（2）击球时一定要使前臂和上身靠近来球；除了回击反手位大角度的来球，在回接其他大多数短球时均上右脚。

（3）击完球后迅速还原。

● Key points

(1) Execute the stroke mainly with forearm and wrist.

(2) Be sure to move your forearm and upper body forward to close to the ball when executing the stroke. For most short return, except those to the wide backhand, step in with your right foot.

(3) Recover your ready position quickly.

5. 反手弹击

反手弹击是一项横板反手位特有的技术。反手弹击动作较小、击球速度较快，常被用于回击质量较差、速度较慢的上旋球，因此具有一定的速度和力量。

● 动作要领（图 3.5.10）

（1）引拍动作较大，在引拍时手腕向后屈。

（2）向前打开肘部和前臂，击球动作较大。

（3）触球一瞬间，手腕用力外旋。

● 关键点

（1）肘部前顶并充分展开。

（2）引拍位置比较高。

5. Backhand Trampoline

Trampoline is a unique backhand skill for the shake-hands player. It can be used to attack the weak topspin and slow return with a short and fast stroke. Therefore, its return has speed and power.

● Movement essentials (Figure 3.5.10)

(1) The backswing is longer, with the wrist laid back toward the body during backswing.

(2) Push your elbow and forearm forward more.

(3) Snap wrist hard and forward at contact.

● Key points

(1) Fully extend your elbow.

(2) Utilize a higher backswing position.

6. 反手拉台内短球（拧拉）

反手拧拉是一项创新技术，专门用来进攻台内短球。它具有速度较快、动作小且有一定的旋转的特点。因此，这项技术有助于运动员主动上手占据主动。

6. Backhand Twist-drive

Backhand twist-drive is a creative skill to be executed against the short oncoming ball. It is characterized by having a number of spin, high speed and small stroke movement. Therefore, it helps players take the initiative.

a　b　c

图 3.5.10　反手弹打

Figure 3.5.10　Backhand Trampoline

● 动作要领(图 3.5.11)

(1)向前迈步使上体和前臂靠近来球。

(2)压低身体重心,前臂和手腕内收幅度更大。引拍至腹部位置,使拍形前倾。

(3)当球至最高点时,前臂以肘为轴充分展开,触球一瞬间手腕外旋摩擦球的左侧。

(4)向后退并为下一板击球迅速还原。

● 关键点

(1)在引拍过程中要使球拍始终保持台面之上。

(2)击球动作主要依靠前臂和手腕共同发力。

7. 加力推

直拍运动员多采用加力推技术。加力推具有回球上旋力量大、速度快、弧线低的特点,能有效地抑制对方的进攻,并使对方回球质量不高。加力

● Movement essentials (Figure 3.5.11)

(1) Step forward to get your upper body and forearm close to the ball.

(2) Lower your gravity and bend your elbow and wrist back more. Backswing to the belly level with the closed racket.

(3) When the ball is at the peak of its bounce, the forearm pivots around the elbow and fully extends, with the external rotation of wrist to graze the left side of the ball.

(4) Move back and recover quickly for next stroke.

● Key points

(1) Keep the racket above the table during the backswing.

(2) Produce stroke primarily with forearm and wrist.

7. Punch Block

The punch block is a staple backhand offensive stroke for the penholder. This stroke produces a strong, fast, and very flat return with topspin to stop opponent's attack and

a　b　c　d

图 3.5.11　反手拧拉

Figure 3.5.11　Backhand Twist-drive

推在用于对付速度较慢、旋转较弱的上旋球时效果最佳。

force him to make a poor shot. The punch block is best against a slower, little topspin return.

● 动作要领(图 3.5.12)

(1)开始击球的姿势和推挡技术相同。

(2)稍向右后方转腰使引拍幅度更大,引拍至腹部位置,拍形稍前倾。

● Movement essentials(Figure 3.5.12)

(1)Begin the stroke the same as you did the basic block.

(2)Slightly rotate your waist right backward to have a longer backswing to bring the

a　　　　　　　　b

图 3.5.12　加力推

Figure 3.5.12　Punch Block

（3）当来球处于高点期时，在大臂的带动下，前臂向前挥拍迎球。

（4）触球的一瞬间，前臂快速推出，手腕用力，向前下方击球。

（5）球拍击球的中上部。

（6）随挥动作更长使肘部充分展开。

● 关键点

（1）引拍和随时挥拍动作更长。

（2）引拍位置较高。

（3）通过转腰产生更大的力量。

racket toward the belly level; the racket face is slightly closed.

（3）Move your upper arm to quickly swing your forearm forward to contact the ball at the peak.

（4）At contact, the forearm pushes quickly and wrist adds force to the ball forward and down.

（5）The racket contacts the ball above the center of the ball's face.

（6）The follow-through should be longer to extend your elbow fully.

● Key points

（1）Longer backswing and follow-through.

（2）Higher backswing position.

（3）Get more power by rotating your waist.

8. 反手减力挡

反手减力挡是一项专门用来防守对方扣杀和弧圈球的技术，直拍或横拍运动员都可以使用。

● 动作要领（图 3.5.13）

（1）拍形应前倾压住来球。

（2）当球处于上升期时，开始挥动前臂击球，击球时手腕和肩膀较为固定。

（3）注意借助来球的力量。

8. Backhand Cushion Block

Backhand cushion block, which is a defensive skill to be used against the opponent's smash and loop drive, can be executed with any grip.

● Movement essentials（Figure 3.5.13）

（1）The racket should be closed more to trap the ball.

（2）When the ball is at the ascending phase, hit the ball with forearm swing maintaining a fixed shoulder and wrist.

（3）Pay attention to rely on more energy of the oncoming ball.

a

b

图 3.5.13 反手减力挡

Figure 3.5.13 Backhand Cushion Block

● 关键点

（1）引拍和挥拍动作距离较小。

（2）击球的上升期。

（3）被动击球以缓冲球的旋转。

● Key points

（1）Limited backswing and movement.

（2）Meet the ball as soon as it bounces.

（3）Cushion the spin by letting the ball hit the bat.

9. 侧切(推侧旋)

侧切(推侧旋)技术常被用于回击对方的弧圈球,其回球具有侧旋、弧线较低的特点,可迫使对方失误,然而其回球速度较慢,因此只能在比赛中偶尔使用侧切技术。不仅直拍运动员较多运用侧切技术,而且一些横拍运动员,如奥运冠军马龙,也经常在比赛中将左侧旋侧切作为一项重要的防守武器。

● 动作要领(图 3.5.14)

(1)首先略向身体右侧引拍。

(2)拍形前倾以便压住强烈的上旋球。

(3)触球的左侧中上部,整个动作由右侧向左侧下方用力。

(4)触球时摩擦、击打相结合。

9. Sidespin Block

Sidespin block is always used against loop drives. Its return can produce a great deal of sidespin and lower trajectory so that often forces errors from an opponent. But accounting for its slow speed, you should use the sidespin block stroke only as the occasion demands. Players who use pen-hold backhand more often use sidespin block, but some shake-hands players, like Ma Long, Olympic Games winner, also used to execute the left sidespin block in competition.

● Movement essentials (Figure 3.5.14)

(1)At first, slightly backswing to the right of the upper body.

(2)Keep your racket closed to against the strong topspin.

(3)The racket contacts the center top of the ball's face and toward the left side of the ball with a right to left downward motion.

(4)Use mixed friction and force contact.

a b c

图 3.5.14 推侧旋

Figure 3.5.14 Sidespin Block

● 关键点

（1）稍向右侧引拍，留出足够的挥拍击球的空间。

（2）触球时注意撞、摩结合。

● Key points

(1)Backswing to the right to ensure an enough striking path.

(2)Mixed friction and force contact.

10. 推下旋

推下旋技术常被用于减慢对方的击球节奏。其回球带有一定的下旋，经常能迫使对方击球失误。传统直拍运动员常在比赛中使用推下旋技术。

10. Chop Block

The chop block is used to slow down your return to an opponent. Its return can produce an amount of backspin, which can often force errors from an opponent. Usually, the traditional pen-hold players execute this skill in the competition.

● 动作要领（图 3.5.15）

（1）引拍动作较小。

（2）击球时间为高点期。

（3）触球时拍面稍后仰，击球的中下部，前臂和手腕向前下方用力推切。

（4）以前臂发力摩擦为主。

● Movement essentials (Figure 3.5.15)

(1)It should be a limited backswing.

(2)Contact the ball at its peak.

(3)Keep your racket slightly opened to contact the ball below the center of the ball's face with a mostly downward and slightly forward motion of the forearm and wrist.

(4)Use more friction contact with mostly your forearm.

a

b

图 3.5.15　推下旋

Figure 3.5.15　Chop Block

11. 反手反拉弧圈球

● 动作要领（图 3.5.16）

（1）拍形更前倾，引拍时球拍要低于来球，引拍位置靠近你非执拍手的髋关节处，手腕内扣。

（2）通过重心转换的动作来带动向前上方挥拍。

（3）在来球的高点期触球的中部。

（4）挥拍动作幅度稍大，随势挥拍至与肩高位置。

（5）借来球的力量和旋转向前击球。

11. Backhand Counterloop

● Movement essentials（Figure 3.5.16）

（1）Use a more closed racket and it should be back and lower than the oncoming ball. Bring your racket close to hip on non-racket side. Wrist should be laid back.

（2）Transfer weight to move your racket forward and upward.

（3）Contact the center of the ball at top of its bounce.

（4）Your swing movement should be much greater and finish about shoulder height.

（5）Rely on more energy and the spin of the oncoming ball to stroke forward.

a　　b　　c

图 3.5.16　反手反拉弧圈球

Figure 3.5.16　Backhand Counterloop

三、搓球提高类技术

1. 快搓与摆短

摆短技术是乒乓球运动员控制对方进攻得分的关键。一个高质量的摆短球在落台后必须又短又低。摆短技术虽然看似比较简单，但实际上运动

Ⅲ. Advanced Push Techniques

1. Fast Push and Drop Shot（Short Heavy-spin Push）

Making a short return, also called drop shot, is always the key to being able to control and win a point. An effective drop shot must be very short and also stay low after bouncing.

员需要大量的练习和时间才能熟练掌握。

This stroke seems to be very simple, but in fact, it takes a lot of skill and time to master.

● 动作要领(图 3.5.17 和图 3.5.18)

● Movement essentials (Figure 3.5.17 and Figure 3.5.18)

(1)右脚向前一步,身体靠近球台。

(1)Step forward with right foot to close to the ball.

(2)拍形后仰更多。

(2)The racket angle should be opened more.

(3)在球的上升期触球。

(3)The contact should be made at the ascending phase.

(4)击球动作较小,更多是用较小的向下的手腕动作。

(4)Stroke is very short; just make a little downward motion with your wrist.

a b c

图 3.5.17 反手摆短

Figure 3.5.17 Backhand Drop Shot

a b c

图 3.5.18 正手摆短

Figure 3.5.18 Forehand Drop Shot

（5）摆短要借助来球的力量。

（5）Drop shot should rely on the energy of incoming ball.

● 关键点

引拍时肘部尽量靠近身体。

● Key points

Keep your elbow close to your body during the backswing.

2. 劈长

2. Long Heavy-spin Push

● 动作要领

（1）引拍幅度较长，在高点期击球。

（2）摩擦球的底部。

（3）随势挥拍的幅度要大。

● Movement essentials

（1）The backswing should be longer and push the incoming ball at the peak.

（2）Friction should be applied at the bottom of the ball.

（3）The long follow through is necessary to guarantee longer push.

3. 搓不转

3. No Spin Push

在对搓过程中变化搓球的旋转，可使对手分不清来球的旋转，导致回球质量不高，从而给你提供一个轻松进攻的机会。

By applying the variation of spin to the ball during the push stroke, your opponent will fail to read the spin and would be forced to make a weak return which provides an easy kill for you.

● 动作要领

（1）与搓转球动作略有不同。

（2）减少拍形后仰，稍立起。

（3）击球的中部，增多撞击，减少摩擦。

● Movement essentials

（1）The motion is a little different from heavy spin push.

（2）The racket angle should open less.

（3）The main point is to hit the middle of the ball, increase contact and decrease friction.

第六节 步法

Section 6 Footwork

在比赛双方之间是一张长约2.7 m的球台。乒乓球击球后的球速可达100 km/h，你必须在短时间内判断出对手回球的方向、速度、旋转，并移动到位，做出合理的击球动作。因此，步法是现代乒乓球运动的一个重要组成部分。随着乒乓球技术的发展，步法的重要性日益突出。比赛中，运动员为了在合理的位置和最佳的时间击球，就必须快速移动到位。步法不仅是衔接每一次击球的枢纽，而且是执行各种战术的有力保证。而且，快速地向来球移动并为下次击球保持最佳的身体平衡对于成功击球而言非常重要。因此，不论是初学者还是专业选手，在打球时必须强化“先动脚、再动手”的意识。

Between you and your opponent, there is only a 2.7 m table. With the ball speeds that can reach more than 100 km/h, you have only a fraction of a second to judge the direction, speed, and amount of spin on your opponent's return; move into position; and execute your stroke. Therefore, the footwork is an instrumental aspect of today's game. Footwork becomes increasingly important as the development of the techniques of table tennis. In the competition, players must move quickly in order to get a proper position and optimal timing to hit a shot. It is not only a hinge of using and linking every stroke, but also a guarantee for executing the tactics. Moreover, the ability to get to the ball as quickly as possible and maintain balance for the next stroke is crucial for a successful stroke. Therefore, whether you are a beginner or a professional player, you must establish an idea of moving into position before executing a stroke.

一、单步

单步通常在对方回球速度很快、击打近距离来球时使用，如运动员回击追身球和近网短球。随着乒乓球运动的速度越来越快，使用单步更频繁。

Ⅰ. One-step Footwork

One-step movement is used to cover a short distance when a ball is played quickly by an opponent and there is not enough time to get into the ideal position. Players most often use it to hit the bodyline ball and the near-net ball. As the speed of the game has increased, single step has been used more frequently.

使用单步时,若向右移动,左脚保持不动,右脚向来球方向移一小步(图3.6.1);若向左移动,右脚保持不动,左脚向来球方向移一小步。

To move to your right, use your right foot to move to the ball and leave your left foot in place (Figure 3.6.1). To move to your left, move your left foot to the ball and leave your right foot in place.

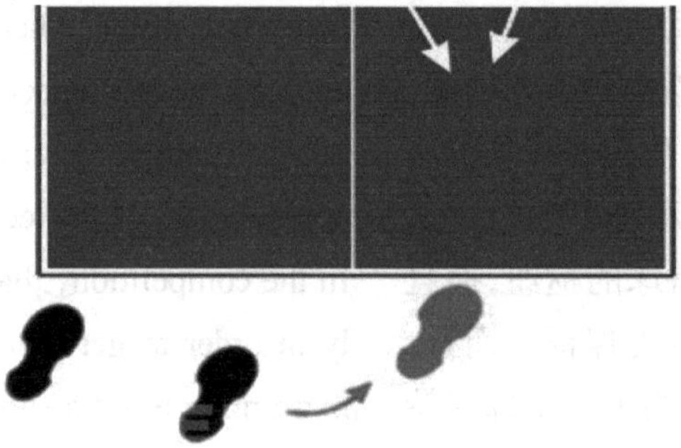

图 3.6.1 单步

Figure 3.6.1 Single Step

练习方法:搓接长、短球练习

该练习的具体方法将在第五章乒乓球训练方法——长、短球训练法中详细介绍。

Drill: Mixed short and long pushes drill

The detailed information for this drill will be covered in short and deep ball drills in Chapter 5.

二、侧滑步

Ⅱ. Side-to-side Footwork

侧滑步多在击中等距离来球时使用。在使用侧滑步向左右移动时,都是靠你的前脚掌进行滑行。在使用侧滑步向右移动时,左脚先启动滑向右脚,然后右脚向来球方向移动(图

The side-to-side step is used to cover short to medium distances. It can be used to move right and left by the balls of feet. To move to your right, first slide your left foot close to your right foot and then step to the

3.6.2);向左移动时的步法动作相同,方向相反。通常侧滑步也可称为并步。

ball using your right foot (Figure 3.6.2). To move to your left, reverse the movement. Often, this step may also be referred to as the level step.

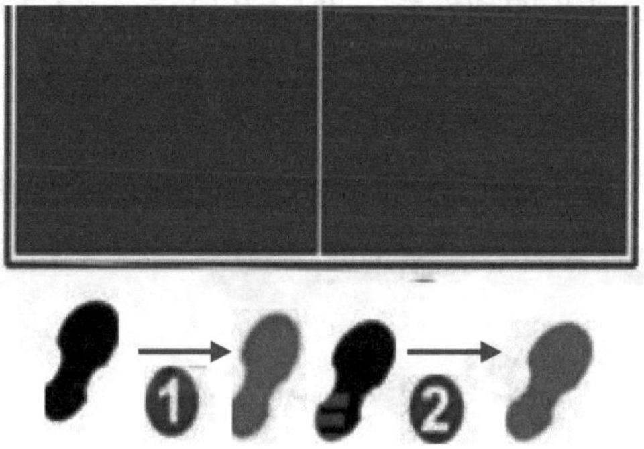

图 3.6.2 侧滑步

Figure 3.6.2 Side-to-side Footwork

侧滑步多年来一直是乒乓球比赛中运用最广泛的步法。因为侧滑步可以使你处于最佳的击球位置,从而有利于保持身体的平衡,并能通过充分的重心转换加大击球的力量和旋转。

The side-to-side step has been the primary form of footwork used in the table tennis for many years. For it will put you in the best location to maintain your balance and help you transfer full weight to develop more power and spin on your strokes.

练习方法:正手三点攻

该练习的具体方法将在第五章乒乓球训练方法——复线训练法中详细介绍。

Drill: Three-position forehand drives

The detailed information for this drill will be covered in multiple position drills in Chapter 5.

三、交叉步

Ⅲ. Crossover Step Footwork

交叉步移动范围大,多用于攻打对方大角度来球。

The crossover step is a footwork for covering a large distance when moving to the wide forehand.

在使用交叉步时，右脚先向右颠一小步并用力蹬地启动，然后左脚向右跨出一大步，使左脚与右脚形成前交叉，在左脚落地的同时击球，最后右脚随之落在左脚的侧后方（图 3.6.3）。如果是左手运动员，交叉步的动作相同、方向相反。

At first, take a small step to the right and push off with your right foot, and then step across with left leg in front of the right leg and strike the ball. After this stroke, right foot finishes in a wide position to keep it back to the left (Figure 3.6.3). If you are left-handed, reverse the instructions.

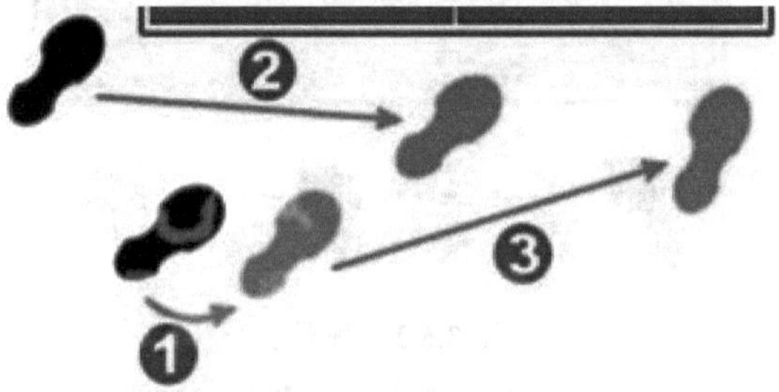

图 3.6.3　交叉步

Figure 3.6.3　Cross Step

使用交叉步有利于在击球时获得充分的重心交换，从而可以产生极大的击球力量。然而，交叉步是最难学习的一种步法，因此需要勤加练习。

The crossover step will help you transfer full weight to develop maximum power when you are striking. However, it is the most difficult type of footwork and requires much practice.

练习方法：推挡侧身扑正手

该练习的具体方法将在第五章乒乓球训练方法——复线训练法中详细介绍。

Drill: Falkenberg drill with cross step

The detailed information for this drill will be covered in multiple position drills in Chapter 5.

四、侧身步

Ⅳ. Pivot Step Footwork

侧身步是在侧身攻时使用。运动员在侧身攻球时，先向右转体至反手位，然后在反手位完成一次正手击球

The pivot step is used for pivot attacking. During the pivot attacking, players firstly pivot the body into the backhand corner, and

动作。

then execute a forehand drive from the backhand corner.

在使用侧身步时，右脚先蹬地发力，然后左脚和右脚同时向左跳出一大步，落地时使左脚在右脚的前面，最后使身体完全移动到球台边线外侧（图 3.6.4）。如果是左手运动员，其侧身步的动作相同、方向相反。

Start by pushing off with right foot. The left and right feet take a large jump to the left, keep right foot behind left. At last, the player is completely off the left sideline（Figure 3.6.4）. If you are left-handed, reverse the instructions.

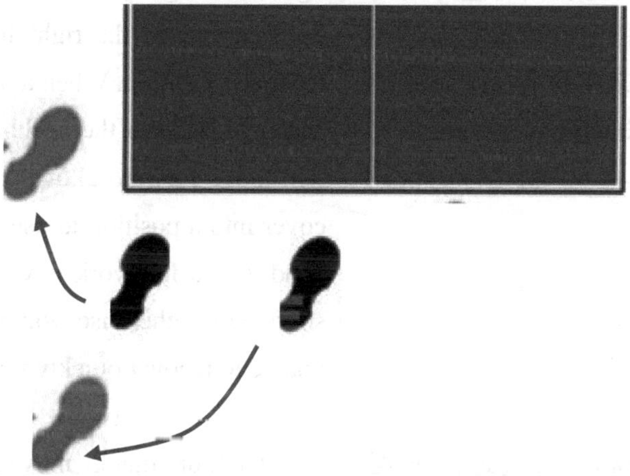

图 3.6.4　侧身步
Figure 3.6.4　Pivot Step

练习方法：正手三点攻

该练习的具体方法将在第五章乒乓球训练方法——单线训练法中详细介绍。

Drill: Pivot drill

The detailed information for this drill will be covered in one-position drills in Chapter 5.

五、前后步法（接台内短球）

V. In and Out Footwork（for returning a short ball）

另一种在乒乓球运动中需要的移动方式是向台内移动回击短球，然后

Another movement pattern required in table tennis is the movement in for returning a

再向后回到之前的准备位置上，以便在下一板长球到来时进攻。这种步法现在被大量使用，因为台内短发球是一种用来阻止对手获得优势的战术。对于右手球员回击短球时，右脚向前移动到球桌下，身体前倾，右臂略微弯曲。在完成短球击球后，运动员右脚先回到准备位置。当来球比较短且在反手位小三角时，运动员的左脚先向前移动，这样有利于击球者能迅速还原到利于正手进攻的位置上。良好的步法在回击短球时至关重要，否则你会发现自己无法在下一次击球时快速还原。

short ball, and then out again into a ready position in order to attack the longer ball if it comes. This type of footwork is used quite a lot because the short serve is a tactic used to stop an opponent gaining the advantage. For right-handed player returning a short ball requires the right foot to move under the table with the body angled forward and with the right arm slightly bent. After the stroke has been completed the right foot will return to the ready position. When a ball is played short and very wide to the backhand, the left foot will move forward allowing the player to recover into a position to use an attacking forehand. Good footwork is vital when returning short balls otherwise you will find yourself unable to recover quickly for next stroke.

● 关键点

(1)为了在场上更快速地移动，必须使身体重心落在前脚掌上，并稍提踵。

(2)移动时重心越低，速度就越快、身体也更加平衡。

(3)屈膝可以使移动更快、更灵活。

(4)在移动的一瞬间脚蹬地发力。

(5)运动员应学会用小碎步调整。小碎步对调整位置、调整重心和预先

● Key points

(1)For quick movement, you must keep your body weight resting on the front part of your feet with your heels off the ground.

(2)The lower your center of gravity is, the quicker you will be able to turn and the better your balance will be.

(3)Bend you knees for more accelerated speed and flexibility.

(4)Strongly push off with your feet as soon as you move.

(5)One should try to master the small step (skipping). Skipping is very important

启动都是十分有益的。

（6）在击球动作完成后，应迅速还原成准备姿势。

in adjusting position and ‘pre-hit’ moving.

(6)After finishing your stroke, always try to return to the ready position.

第四章　乒乓球基本战术与基本打法

Chapter 4　Basic Tactics and Basic Playing Styles of Table Tennis

第一节　基本战术

Section 1　Basic Tactics

乒乓球基本战术用于迫使对手失误或回球质量较差以赢得分数。在乒乓球战术中,计谋的使用是很重要的,这是通过从发球开始到每个连续来回击球的旋转、速度和落点的变化来实现的。任何战术都必须建立在球员的技术能力之上。换句话说,技术和战术之间总是有联系的。一个好的技术将给你更多的战术可能性,因为你将有更全面的击球技术可依靠。

Basic tactics are used to force an error or weak shot from your opponent in order to win the point. The use of deception is important in table tennis tactics and this is achieved by variation of spin, speed and placement at every stage of a rally starting with the serve. Any tactic has to build on the player's technical ability. In other words there is always a connection between technique and tactic. A good technique will give you many more tactical possibilities because you will have a greater repertoire of strokes to rely on.

在乒乓球比赛中,拥有良好的战术意识是至关重要的。你必须清楚你想用一种特定的战术取得什么样的成绩,并且这基于你对比赛对手的弱点和优势的认知。如果你以前从未与该对手交手,那么在开始比赛时就需要分析该球员,并根据你在比赛中遇到的情况调整战术。如果你以前和这个

Having a good tactical awareness is vital in table tennis and it is important that you understand what you are trying to achieve with a particular tactic, and that it is based on what you perceive the weaknesses and strengths of your opponent to be. If you have never played this opponent before you will need to analyse the player as you begin to play the match and

对手交过手，那么你应该已经知道他（或她）的弱点了，记下这名球员的强项和弱项总是一个好方法，这样你就可以为下次比赛做好准备。

adjust tactics in response to what you learn as the match proceeds. If you have played this opponent before then you should already have some idea of his or her weaknesses. It's always a good idea to make notes about a player's strengths and weaknesses so you can prepared for when you next play them.

在乒乓球比赛中，旋转和速度的变化经常被用作战术来误导对手，并迫使对方打出微弱的回击球或出现失误。使用假动作和变化的重要性已经在各种各样的击球技术中涉及。

Variation of spin and speed in a rally is used regularly as a tactic in table tennis to deceive an opponent and force a weak stroke or error. The importance of using disguise and variation has already been mentioned in relation to the various strokes and its importance as a tactic can not be emphasized enough.

一、发球抢攻战术

Ⅰ. Attack after Serve

发球抢攻战术是现代乒乓球比赛中重要的战术之一。各种类型打法的运动员普遍希望在比赛中采用这种战术迅速解决战斗。要想成为一名高水平的运动员，必须拥有很强的前三板的进攻能力。

Attack after serve is one of the most important tactics in modern table tennis games. Players of various styles are all expected to end points as quickly as possible with this aggressive tactics. To become a competitive player, you must have the ability to make strong attacks on the first three strokes.

在运用发球抢攻战术时，应注意以下几点：

- 注意发球与抢攻的配合；
- 注意提高发球质量，通过发球时的旋转、落点的变化来迷惑对手；
- 判断清楚对方回接的深度和

Following points should be noted for the tactic of attacking after serve.

- Pay attention to the coordination of serve and attacking.
- Develop the ability to produce the high quality serves. Try to vary the placement and spin on each serve to confuse your opponent.
- Make the correct judgement on the

旋转；

➢ 明确自己抢攻的方式；

➢ 注意发球抢攻战术和其他战术的协调配合。

发球抢攻战术有下列几套。

● 发转与不转球抢攻(图 4.1.1)

一般以发至对方正手位短球和反手位大角度长球为主,然后在第三板抢拉弧圈球,进攻对方的左右两大角。欧洲横板运动员经常采用这种战术对付直拍运动员。

depth and spin of the opponent's return.

➢ Choose the way of your attacking.

➢ Coordinate this tactic with others.

Specifically, attack after serve can be implemented in following ways.

● Attack after heavy backspin or no-spin serve (Figure 4.1.1)

Generally, serve to the short forehand or to the wide backhand. Then execute a loop to attack the return to opponent's either corner. This tactic is often used by Europeans to play against the penholders.

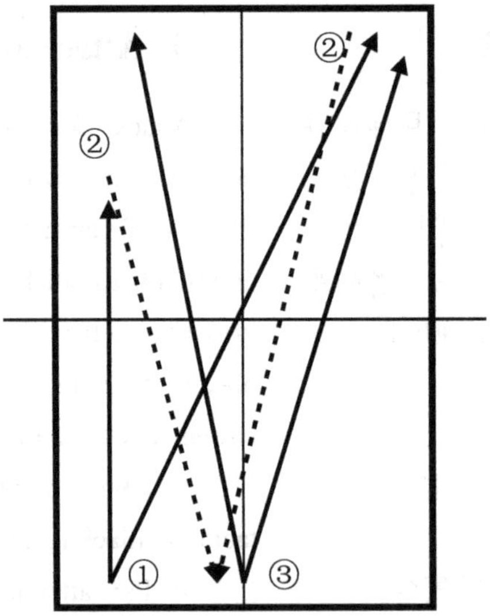

图 4.1.1　发转与不转球抢攻

Figure 4.1.1　Attack after heavy backspin or nospin serve

● 发正手侧旋球抢攻

一般发正手侧旋球至对方的反手

● Attack after a forehand sidespin serve

Serve sidespin to the wide backhand or,

大角度、正手短球或发至中路偏右（向侧拐弯正好至对方怀中），然后用弧圈球或扣杀抢攻。这是比赛中最常用的一种战术。

- 发反手侧旋球抢攻（图 4.1.2）

反手侧旋球通常发至对方的正手近网或中路半出台，然后在第三板进攻对方的左右两个大角。具有很强的正反手进攻能力的运动员经常采用这种战术。另外，这种战术在对付削球运动员时也很奏效。

the short forehand, or try serving mid-depth serves into his right elbow. Then execute a loop or a smash. This tactic is the most frequently used in table tennis competition.

- Attack after a backhand sidespin serve (Figure 4.1.2)

Use mostly serves to the short forehand or mid-depth serves into his right elbow. This tactic is always used by the players who have the ability of strong first attacking strokes from either backhand or forehand. Moreover, it is often used to play against the chopper.

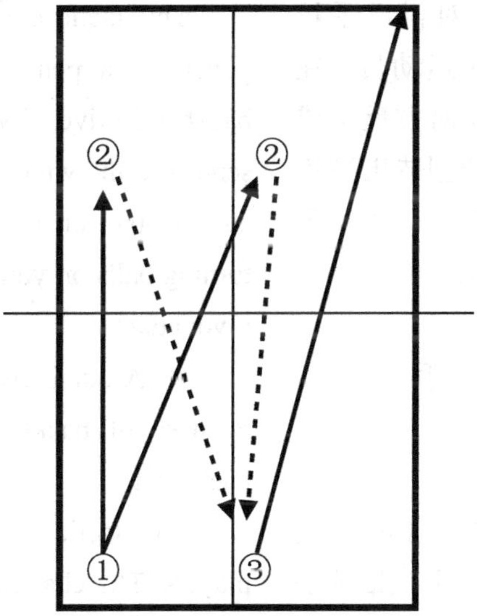

图 4.1.2　发反手侧旋球抢攻

Figure 4.1.2　Attack after a backhand sidespin serve

- 发下蹲球抢攻

发下蹲球时，可以将左侧旋和右侧旋结合运用。落点以中路偏反手为

- Attacking after squatting serve

Execute a combination of right sidespin and left sidespin on your squatting serve. Use

主，结合偷袭发对方的左右两大角。但是在发完球后，发球员必须从下蹲姿势中迅速还原，以调整重心便于下一板击球。

mostly mid-depth serves to the backhand, mixed with an occasional long wide serve to either corner. To use squatting serve, it is essential to stand up right after the serve and get ready for the third ball attack.

二、对攻战术

Ⅱ. Counter Attack

两名进攻型选手相遇时，常形成攻对攻的局面，常采用下列战术。

There used to be a situation that a drive made against a drive occurs in two offensive players' games. Following tactics are useful in the case of counter attacking.

● 连续压对方反手位，伺机正手侧身攻

● Pivot attack after sequences of backhand drives to opponent's backhand

这种战术一般用于对付反手较弱、进攻能力不强的直拍运动员。在准备侧身攻之前，应狠压对方反手或压一板反手大角度，主动创造出进攻机会。在侧身攻后应防范下一板正手位的来球。

This tactic is mostly used when the opponent is a penholder who lacks a strong backhand drive. Try to hit the ball harder or send it to the wide backhand before you execute a pivot attack. Get ready to receive returning balls on your forehand open side after pivot attack.

● 连续压反手再变正手

● A quick switch to forehand after sequences of backhand drives to opponent's backhand

左手执拍的运动员用此战术较多，因变线的角度大，使右手执拍选手往往很被动；另外，运动员常采用此战术对付对方正手位攻击力不强的选手。如自己反手位进攻能力强，可在变对方正手位时直接得分。

This tactic is often used by left-handed players. The change of direction often forces weak returns from a right-handed player. The tactic is especially effective when the opponent is weak in forehand attacks. With strong backhand drive, you can score outright when changing direction to his forehand.

● 先打对方正手大角度，再进攻

● Hit to opponent's wide forehand,

对方反手位(调右压左)

运动员常采用此战术对付有着较好步法且擅长侧身攻的直拍运动员。在反手位用正手侧身攻是直拍运动员的主要得分手段。当你将他调到正手位,使他被迫离台时,再攻其反手位,会让他措手不及。应注意,去往对方正手位的击球要凶且出其不意。

and then attack the return to his backhand

This tactic is useful when playing against the penholder who has the excellent footwork and quick pivot attack. This style of player is anxious to step around and use her forehand from her backhand side to get a point. When forced wide to the forehand, she may have difficulty in recovering and protecting the backhand side. Note: the ball to the wide forehand side should be unexpected to your opponent. protecting the

● 连压对方中路或偏正手,伺机抢攻

这是对付横拍两面弧圈球打法对手的重要对攻战术。压住对方的执拍手或球台中间位置,然后伺机抢攻对方的两大角度。

● Attack after sequences of drives to your opponent's middle

This tactic is widely used when the opponent is two-winged looper who uses the shake-hands grip. Try keeping pressure on your opponent's playing elbow (the middle), and then attacking wide to either corner.

三、拉攻战术

Ⅲ. Driving Attack

拉攻战术是进攻型打法对付削球的主要战术,即先用拉弧圈球找机会迫使对方回球质量低,然后伺机大力突击得分(包括扣杀和抢冲)。根据在比赛中的具体运用情况,这种战术有如下几种。

Driving attack is a tactic that is mainly used in the game against the chopper. To execute this tactic, you should use loop drives to force the opponent to make a passive return, and then give a powerful shot (smash and powerful loop drive) to score. As for different situations in the game, this tactic can be implemented through one of following ways.

● 拉一角杀中路战术

拉一角至对方削球旋转较弱的一

● Smash to the middle after driving to a corner

You can execute sequences of loop drive

面寻找机会，再突击至对方中路。中路追身球是削球运动员的共同弱点，他们在此失分较多。

to one side to force a returning chopping with weak spin, and then hit a smash to the middle. The bodyline ball in the middle is a traditional weakness of choppers. It often forces them to make many errors.

● 拉中路杀两角战术

先连续拉对方中路找机会，再杀两角得分。中路追身球不好削，因此突击的机会比较多。

● Corner smash after driving to the middle

Drive to one's middle, and then hit a smash wide to either corner. The bodyline ball in the middle is difficult to cut for the choppers. Therefore, you will seek many opportunities of smashing.

● 拉斜杀直

这是对付削球选手最常用的战术。因为拉斜线比较保险，杀直线突然性强、距离短、速度快。

● Sequences of crosscourt loops and then execute a powerful drive down the line

This tactic is mostly seen in games against the chopper. It is much safer to drive to the crosscourt and gets a shorter distance to execute a straight shot.

● 变化拉球的旋转，伺机突击

拉弧圈的选手，可拉出强烈的上旋球、侧旋和假弧圈三种不同的旋转。通过旋转的变化打乱削球选手的节奏，增加其削球的困难。

● Vary the spin in loop drives and then attack with a powerful drive

There are three types of loops that most loopers are able to create: heavy topspin, sidespin and light spin. The loopers can vary the spins to unsettle the opponent's chopping pace.

● 长拉短吊战术

采用长拉短吊战术有意识地调动对方。众所周知，步法问题是削球运动员存在的普遍问题，从远台削球迅速移动到近台回球对于他们来说有一定的难度。因此，我们对付削球时应利用好这个弱点。

● The rocking tactics

This tactic is to consciously play the shots with the combination of deep attack and short drop shot. As we know, footwork problems are common when switching from far chopping to short return. Therefore, we could utilize the weakness to make the chopper play our game.

● 稳健控制法

当对方稳削时，必须耐心等待机会，以稳为主，伺机进攻。

● Controlling

Sometimes when the chopper is defending well, you have to be patient to wait for an opportunity as well as keep the ball well.

四、搓攻战术

Ⅳ. Pushing Attack

搓攻是进攻型打法的辅助战术之一，又是防守型削球打法的主要战术之一。这种战术在业余选手中运用较多，可通过搓球的旋转和落点变化，为进攻创造机会。以下是搓攻战术的几种具体运用：

Pushing attack is mainly used by defensive choppers and also by offensive players as a supplementary tactic. This tactic is very popular among amateurs, who are expected to create the attacking opportunities by the variations of spin and placement of pushing. Strategies of pushing attack include:

● 先搓反手大角，再变直线，伺机进攻

这种战术主要用来对付不善于反手进攻的运动员，先逼住其反手大角，视其准备侧身进攻时或将注意力都放至反手后，就可以变线至正手，伺机进攻。

● Execute some pushes wide to his backhand corner and then change the direction to attack

This tactic is effective when the opponent is weak at backhand strokes. As the opponent intends to pivot attack or totally pay attention to his backhand side, you could change the direction of the ball rapidly and then execute an attacking drive.

● 以快搓（或摆短）短球为主，伺机进攻

在很多情况下，摆短，特别是加转短球，对方抢攻的难度很大。这种战术常用于对付攻击力很强的弧圈球运动员，而他们的普遍弱点在于处理不好短球。然而，当面对这类选手时，你必须控制好回球的落点和高度，避免

● Attack after a fast push (or drop shot) return

In most cases, the opponent would find it difficult to attack aggressively to the drop shot, especially the short spin push. This tactic is widely used to play against the power loopers who have a common weakness in short return. However, the depth and the

搓高,并且要树立搓一板即进攻的指导思想。

height of returns are critical in this tactic. Moreover, you should get prepared for attacking after each drop shot.

● 搓转与不转球后,伺机进攻

● Mix spin pushes and no-spin pushes before attacking

一般以先搓加转球至对方反手底线为主,然后用相似的动作搓不转球,使对方判断不清旋转而将球搓高,为自己进攻创造机会。在运用旋转变化时,最好与落点变化相结合,二者相辅相成。

Generally, execute some spin pushes to opponent's endline, and then return a no-spin push with a similar stroke motion. As the opponent fails to read the spin, he would be forced to make a weak return and provide an easy kill for you. This tactic is even more effective by varying the ball placement in addition to the mixed spins.

五、接发球战术

V. Tactics of Returning Serve

如果说发球是非常重要的技术,那么接发球战术也是同样重要的。否则,你就总是会输给那些发球好的对手。接发球技术与发球抢攻都属于前三板技术。你必须树立接发球战术非常明确的指导思想:

If the serve is the most important stroke, then receive of serve must be equally important, otherwise you will always lose to a player with good serves. Receiving and attack after serve are included in the tactics for the so-called "first three shots". We must establish a few clear cut directives of receiving:

➢ 学会三种接发球的方式以及专注于能把对方发球回接到对方球台的不同落点是很有必要的。

➢ It is essential to practice the three types of return and to concentrate on being able to return the serve to different places on the table.

➢ 力争积极主动,克服保守求稳的思想,能进攻时一定要进攻。特别是在 11 分制和无遮挡发球等一系列的乒乓球规则改革之后,更需要在接发球环节上大胆求变,积极突破。因

➢ Take initiatives. Player must try to snatch the offensive initiatives and overcome the conservatism. With a series of rule changes such as 11 points and no-hiding serve, it is essential to pay more attention to take initia-

此，要鼓励运动员在接发球时多侧身，增强用正手接发球的意识。

tives in receiving. Therefore, it is also encouraged for players to step around and to receive with forehand.

➢ 最大限度地控制对方的发球抢攻。在此基础上，应争取为第四板球的进攻创造机会。

➢ Try best to control the ball well to avoid opponent's attacking after serve. On this basis, you should take efforts to create opportunities for attacking at next shot (the fourth shot).

➢ 在接发球后，要有防御的准备。一旦被抢攻，应寻找机会进行反攻。

➢ Get ready to defend after receiving the serve. Even the opponent attacks after serve, keep looking for the opportunity to counterattack.

➢ 应尽量多进攻对方的半出台和出台了的发球，这将会迫使对方只能发短球，从而使你有可能在回接短球或长球时进行变化。

➢ You should always try to attack half long and long serves. This will often force your opponent to serve short, which gives you the possibility to vary between making short or long returns.

接发球战术的具体运用如下。

Several ways of receive attack as follows.

● 接发球抢攻

● Attack on receive

此为最具攻击力的接发球方法。当对方发短球时，你可以用正手挑打或反手拧拉技术进行还击。相反，在出现半出台球或长球时，你可以拉冲弧圈球。在练习中，你首先应该判断出球的旋转和落点，然后再迅速移动到位，这样才能在最佳的击球点和击球时间下挥拍击球。

It is the most offensive tactic of receiving the serve. Use fast flip or backhand twist-drive for short serve; conversely, use loop drive to return the middle-depth or deep serve. In practice, focus on reading the spin and placement of the ball, and then move quickly to hit the ball with proper hitting point and timing.

● 回接到对方的弱点处

● Return the weak side

用弹击、反手拨、推挡将球回至对方的弱点处，再应用其他你擅长的技术

Use flick, backhand drive, or block to return the serve to opponent's weak side to force him make a poor stroke, then show the

然而，你应注意要降低击球的弧线，控制好击球的落点，并保持一定的速度。

skill you are good at. Yet, it has to be kept in mind that lower the trajectory, control the placement of the ball well, and maintain the speed.

● 以快搓或摆短回接

● Execute fast push or drop shot to receive

用短球回接发球会使你的对手难以进攻，或较难为下一板球创造进攻机会。该战术主要用于对付凶狠型的弧圈球选手，他们普遍在回接短球时有较明显的漏洞。同样，该战术也可在回接强烈下旋球和侧下旋球时使用。

Return short will make it more difficult for the opponent to give an attacking drive or to create the attack opportunities for next shot. This tactic is widely used to play against the power loopers who share the common weakness in return short. Moreover, it can also be used to return the heavy backspin or side backspin serves.

● 稳健控制法

● Receive by controlling

该接发球方法主要用来对付削球运动员时使用，利用高吊弧圈球、推挡、搓或削球等技术接发球。虽然该方法较稳健，但是你仍然要在回接时加强对落点和弧线的控制。在回接时，要不断变化，也要避免给对方轻松进攻的机会。

This tactic can be used in games against the choppers. To execute this tactic, return the ball by using slow loop, blocking, pushing or chopping stroke. Although controlling is risk-free in most cases, it is still necessary to pay attention to the placement and trajectory of your receiving. Keep producing a lot of variation in returns. Avoid returning an easy kill for the opponent.

● 正手侧身接发球

● To step around and receive by the forehand

此为接发球战术中攻击性较强的方法之一。当接发球时，应尽可能地用正手技术回接发球。这有助于你在接下来的回合中争取主动。

It is one of the most offensive tactics of receiving. When receiving, use a forehand skill to return the ball as much as possible. This will also help you take initiatives for next shot.

第二节 基本打法

Section 2 Basic Playing Styles

一、快攻打法

采用快攻打法的运动员主要使用直握球拍法，在其正手贴用正胶胶皮；而少数使用横拍的快攻运动员在其反手面使用长贴胶皮。从 20 世纪 60 年代至 90 年代，中国的乒乓球世界冠军多采用快攻打法，如庄则栋、邓亚萍、刘国梁等。该打法至今仍很常见。快攻打法的运动员通常在球的高点期甚至上升期击球，其快速的进攻经常让对手猝不及防。正手攻球技术是该种打法运动员的主要得分手段，因此我们常看到快攻打法的运动员用正手击球技术进行全台进攻。总之，快攻打法的运动员应遵循“积极主动、快速进攻和快速多变”的指导思想。

● 传统优点

➢ 正手进攻凶狠；

➢ 处理短球能力较强；

➢ “前三板”技术突出；

➢ 反手位有一板加力推或弹击技术；

➢ 快速有力的进攻常使对方猝不及防；

➢ 击球变化多端。

I . Fast Attacker

Players who use this style of play mainly use the pen-hold grip with short pips-out rubber on the forehand side of the racket. Additionally, a few players use the shake-hands grip with long pips-out on the backhand. This style of play was made famous by many Chinese champions in the 1960 s through the 1990 s such as Zhuang Zedong, Deng Yaping, and Liu Guoliang; it is still common today. This style of players often hit the ball as early as possible either at the top of the bounce or as the ball is rising. This quick return of the ball takes away the opponent's time to react. It is a forehand-dominated style in which the player is expected to use the word, this style directive ideas of "taking initiatives, fast a attacking and change fast".

● Traditional strengths

➢ Strong forehand kills.

➢ Good short game.

➢ Excellent serve-return game.

➢ Punch block or trampoline from the backhand side.

➢ Very quick, off-the-bounce returns to give the opponent very time to react.

➢ Very variable on the strokes.

● 传统弱点

➢ 反手位防守弧圈球能力较弱;

➢ 中台相持能力一般;

➢ 被迫在正手位大角度击球后,运动员很难再返回其反手位进行进攻;

➢ 击球后还原较慢。

● Traditional weaknesses

➢ Weak defense against fast loops on the backhand side.

➢ Poor counterdrives from the middle court.

➢ When forced wide to the forehand, this style of player may have difficulty recovering and protecting the backhand side.

➢ Poor recovery.

二、两面弧圈球打法

采用两面弧圈球打法的运动员主要使用横拍,其两面均贴反胶胶皮,常在中台击球。欧洲运动员基本上都采用两面弧圈球打法,其代表运动员为迈克尔·赛弗、菲利普·盖亭和约格·罗斯科夫。他们的弧圈球技术力量大、旋转强、速度快,正反手都能进攻,这些运动员充分发挥了其身高臂长的优势,因此击球的范围较大。然而,40 mm“大球”的推出给两面弧圈球打法的运动员带来了前所未有的冲击。由于“大球”的旋转变弱,使得此类打法的运动员不得不变得更加凶狠,从而以力量取胜。两面弧圈球打法的指导思想是“强进攻、特长突出和快速转换”。

Ⅱ. Two-winged Looper

Players who use this style primarily use the shake-hands grip with inverted rubber on the both side and play at the mid-range from the table. This playing style is mostly used by European players such as Michel Saive, Philippe Gatien and Jorg Rosskopf. They use loop strokes that carry a lot of power, top-spin, and speed. They are equally strong with both forehand and backhand. These players can take full advantages of height and long reach to have a greater hitting space. However, the introduction of the 40-millimeter ball has had an unfavorable impact on this style of play. For the resulting loss of spin caused by the larger ball has forced this style of player to become more fit and powerful to survive. The directive ideas of this style of player can be summarized as: strong offense, sharp forte and forehand drive to attack on the full court. In a word, this style of player should build the directive ideas of "taking initiatives, fast smooth transition".

● 传统优点
➢ 正、反两面进攻能力强；
➢ 弧圈球速度快、力量大；
➢ 中台相持能力强；
➢ 攻防转换速度快。

● Traditional strengths
➢ Equal power from both sides.
➢ Very strong fast loop drives.
➢ Excellent counterdrives from the middle court.
➢ Smooth transition of attacking and defense.

● 传统弱点
➢ 稳定性较差；
➢ 处理短球能力较差；
➢ 前三板能力一般；
➢ 近台攻球实力一般。

● Traditional weaknesses
➢ Poor stability.
➢ Difficult in returning short balls.
➢ Weak serve-return game.
➢ Weak counterdrives when close to the table.

三、全面型打法

全面型打法是现代乒乓球发展中最新、最流行的打法之一。此类打法由横拍运动员首先采用，代表选手是马龙和简·诺瓦·瓦尔德内尔。全面型选手的正、反手位的基本功扎实，他们进入比赛状态快，能很快发现对方的弱点所在。另外，他们不仅自身发力好，而且借力击球的能力也较强。因此，全面型选手在比赛中就如一堵墙一样，扎实稳健。全面型选手的指导思想可被归纳为技术全面和攻守平衡。

Ⅲ. All-around Attacker

This is one of the newest and also the most popular styles in the evolution of the modern game. This playing style is firstly used by shake-hands grip players such as Ma Long and Jan-Ove Waldner. The all-around attacker is equipped with solid basic skill both on forehand and backhand sides. They also have the ability to adapt the game quickly and to attack the opponent's weakness. This all-around attacker is equally comfortable generating powerful strokes and relying on more energy of incoming ball. Therefore, this style of player is often referred to as a wall. The directive ideas of this style can be summarized as all-round skills and balanced offense and defense.

- ● 传统优点
- ➢ 很好的稳健性；
- ➢ 攻防转换速度快；
- ➢ 前三板技术优异；
- ➢ 进攻手段变化多端；
- ➢ 控球能力较强；
- ➢ 攻守平衡。
- ● 传统弱点
- ➢ 击球力量一般；
- ➢ 进攻得分手段较缺乏。

- ● Traditional strengths
- ➢ Good stability.
- ➢ Smooth transition of attacking and defense.
- ➢ Excellent serve-return game.
- ➢ Ability to produce a great deal of variation in attacks.
- ➢ Ability to control the ball well.
- ➢ Balanced offense and defense.
- ● Traditional weaknesses
- ➢ No real power.
- ➢ Often lacks a single, hard finishing shot.

四、攻削结合打法

攻削结合打法的运动员通常一面使用长胶，一面使用反胶。在比赛中转动球拍，从而在进攻和防守端制造出不同的旋转。朱世赫、范瑛和金暻娥就是这一打法类型的典型代表。削球又稳又转是该打法的最基本要求。攻削结合打法的运动员常通过削球的旋转和落点变化创造进攻机会。现代进攻型削球运动员都具有颇具威力的抢冲和反拉弧圈球的能力。由于40 mm“大球”的推出，攻削结合打法的运动员在击球时基本上形成了用正手攻球进攻、用反手削球防守的特点，并且他们的站位较之于以往更靠近球

Ⅳ. Attacking Chopper

Players of this style most often use long pips on one side of the racket and inverted rubber on the other and flip the racket to produce great variations in defense and attacking. Joo Se-Hyuk in the men’s game and Fan Ying and Kim Kyung-ah in the women’s game are icon players of this style of game style. Chopping with very steady and low returns is the basic requirement of this style of play. They are expected to create the attacking opportunities by the variations of spin and placement of chopping. Modern attacking choppers usually have powerful forehand loops and kills and a strong counterloops. Since the introduction of

台了。总的来说,他们的技术风格可以概括为转、稳、变、攻。

the 40-millimeter ball, the attacking chopper style has evolved into one in which almost every forehand return is attacked and backhand returns are chopped with very heavy-spin returns from a position a little closer to the table than in past years. Generally speaking, the directive ideas of this style of player can be summarized as spin, stability, variation and offensive.

● 传统优点
➢ 前三板技术优异;
➢ 第三板进攻威胁大;
➢ 旋转和落点变化多;
➢ 正、反手防守稳健;
➢ 削球下旋强烈。
● 传统弱点
➢ 反手进攻能力较差;
➢ 抵挡不住高压进攻;
➢ 大多数击球较为被动。

● Traditional strengths
➢ Good serve-return game.
➢ Strong third-ball attacks.
➢ Great variation of spin and placement.
➢ Excellent defense on both sides.
➢ Strong backspin in chopping returns.
● Traditional weaknesses
➢ Weak backhand attacks.
➢ The attacking chopper's defense cannot stand up under pressure.
➢ Most passive strokes.

第五章　乒乓球训练方法

Chapter 5　Training Methods of Table Tennis

第一节　技战术训练方法

Section 1　Training Methods for Techniques and Tactics

一、单线训练法

乒乓球基本击球线路有五条，分别为：左方直线、中路直线、右方直线、右方斜线和左方斜线。根据具体情况，运动员在五条基本击球线路的基础上进行单一线路的练习。以下是该训练的具体方法。

● 在单一线路进行单一技术的练习

例如，右方单线对攻和反手单线对搓练习。

● 在单一线路上进行两个或两个以上技术的练习

例如，推挡侧身练习。在进行该练习时，让你的同伴连续供球至你的反手位。你在反手位轮流用反手和正手攻一板斜线球。一组动作完成后重复此过程。

Ⅰ. One-Position Drills

There are five basic hitting paths: left down the line, middle down the line, right down the line, right crosscourt and left crosscourt. According to the specific situation, players can execute the one-position drills on the basis of the five hitting paths. Following are some methods of the drill.

● Execute a single skill drill on one position

For example, one-position forehand drives and one-position backhand pushes.

● Execute two or more skills drill on one position

For example, pivot drill. For this drill, have your partner send all balls to your backhand side. You alternatively execute a backhand counterattack and forehand counterattack diagonally from the backhand corner.

Repeat this pattern.

● 在单一线路上进行近台对中台的练习

例如，一名选手在近台拉弧圈球，另一名选手在中台削球。

● Short court to middle court drill on one position

For example, one player executes loop drives close to the table and the other executes chops far from the table.

● 在单一线路上进行中台练习

例如，在单一线路的中台正手对拉练习。

● Middle court drill on one position

For example, one-position forehand counterloops at the middle court.

● 注意事项

➢ 在击球时注意重心交换；

➢ 在击球时不能站立不动，在击一板球后应通过单步进行重心交换。

● Matters needing attention

➢ Pay attention to the weight transfer during the stroke.

➢ You can't be motionless during the stroke. Try to keep slightly adjusting your body position by single step after one shot.

二、复线训练法

Ⅱ. Multiple Position Drills

1. 两点打一点的练习

1. Two-position Against One-position Drill

方法：

● 在两点进行单一技术的练习

例如，正手两点攻练习。在进行该项目练习时，练习者轮流在正手大角和正手中路两点进行正手攻斜线球练习。

Methods:

● Execute a single skill drill from two positions

For example, forehand counterattack from two-points from forehand side. For this drill, the player alternatively executes the forehand counterattack from forehand corner diagonally and from the middle diagonally into forehand corner.

● 在两点进行两种或更多技术的练习

例如，反手搓后接正手位进攻。

● Execute two or more skills from two positions

For example, forehand attack after

backhand pushes.

● 有规律地变化左右半台落点练习

例如，左推右攻的练习。在练习时，让陪练者轮流送一板球至反手位，一板球至正手位。

● Regular placement changing on right and left half court

For example, backhand block with forehand attack. For this drill, have your practice partner alternate placing one ball on the right half and one ball on the left half of the table.

● 无规律地变化全台落点练习（无计划的正反手攻球练习）

在进行该项目练习时，让陪练方送球到你的全台任意落点。对正手位的来球，练习者用正手攻直线球；对反手位的来球，练习者用反手攻斜线球。

● Random placement changing on the full court

In this drill, have the practice partner send the ball to your full court without scheme. You execute the forehand counterattack on the whole forehand side down the line and the backhand counterattack on the whole backhand side diagonally.

● 半计划地变化左右半台落点练习

例如，练习者在反手对攻 1~3 个回合后，让陪练方变线至正手位，然后在正手位用正手直线击球一次。此后，重复该练习过程。

● Half-scheme placement changing on right and left half court

For example, backhand counterattack from backhand corner diagonally（1-3 rallies）and then have your practice partner change direction to the forehand corner, you execute a forehand counterattack from forehand corner down the line. Repeat this pattern.

● 注意事项

➢ 这些练习方法应从易到难、有序进行。考虑到无规律练习的难度，应在有规律落点练习的基础上再进行无规律落点的练习；

➢ 运用正确的步法并快速移动；

● Matters needing attention

➢ These drills should proceed in an orderly way and step by step. In consideration of its difficulty, random placement drill should be based on the regular placement drill.

➢ Use proper footwork and move quickly.

➢ 在移动时一定要注意保持平衡；

➢ 根据具体情况增大或减小训练的难度。

2. 两点对两点的练习

方法：

● 两斜线对两直线

规定一方只能轮流在正、反手位打两条斜线，另一方只能打两条直线（图 5.1.1）。

● 两斜对一斜一直

一方用反、正手各打两次斜线，另一方只能用正手走动攻，在反、正手位正手攻时都先击斜线球，再击直线球。具体练习方法如图 5.1.2 所示。另一种方法与此方法类似，叫两直对一直一斜，具体练习方法如图 5.1.3 所示。

● 无计划的正反手对攻练习

在进行该练习时，练习双方同时进行无计划的正反手对攻练习，运动

➢ Be sure to maintain your balance while moving.

➢ Increase or decrease difficulty in accordance with specific conditions.

2. Two-position Against Two-position Drill

Methods:

● Two-position return crosscourt against two-position return down the line

One player plays forehand and backhand counterattack diagonally and the other one plays forehand and backhand down the line. (Figure 5.1.1).

● Two-position return crosscourt against alternate one return crosscourt and one return down the line

One player alternates two balls from the backhand and two balls from the forehand to return crosscourt, the other player only uses his forehand drives from the backhand side and forehand side to first return crosscourt and then return down the line. The specific method is shown in Figure 5.1.2. The other similar method is two-position return down the line against alternate one return down the line and one return crosscourt. You can see the specific method in Figure 5.1.3.

● Backhand-forehand counterattack without scheme

In this drill, both players execute the backhand and forehand counterattack without

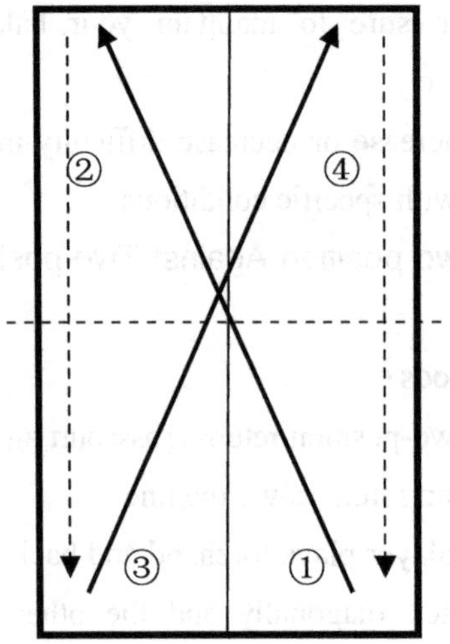

图 5.1.1　两斜线对两直线

Figure 5.1.1　Two-position return cross-court against two-position return down the line

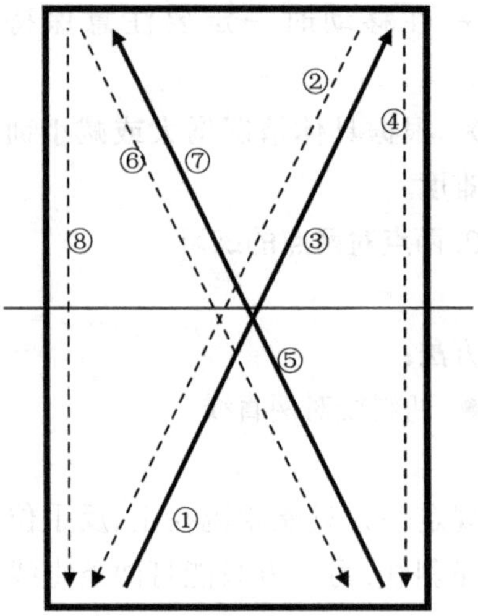

图 5.1.2　两斜对一斜一直

Figure 5.1.2　Two-position return crosscourt against alternate one return crosscourt and one return down the line

员可将球击到对方球台的任意落点。

scheme at the same time. The ball can be sent to any placement on the court.

- 注意事项

➢ 考虑到其难度,练习应从易到难,循序渐进;

➢ 两名运动员应互相配合。

- Matters needing attention

➢ In consideration of its difficulty, these drills should proceed step by step.

➢ Two players should work together in close cooperation.

3. 三点打一点的练习

3. Three-position Against One-position Drill

方法:

- 正手三点攻(图 5.1.4)

让陪练者给主练者供上旋球。轮流送球至主练的反手位、中路和正手位三点,主练皆用正手攻球回击。三板球后重复此过程。主练应每次将球

Methods:

- Three-position forehand drives (Figure 5.1.4)

Have your practice partner feed you topspin balls. Alternate the first ball to your backhand corner, the second ball to the middle of the table, and the third to your wide

回至对方的反手位。

forehand side. After three balls, repeat the drill. Return all balls using only your forehand drive. The target for your returns is the backhand side of your partner's table.

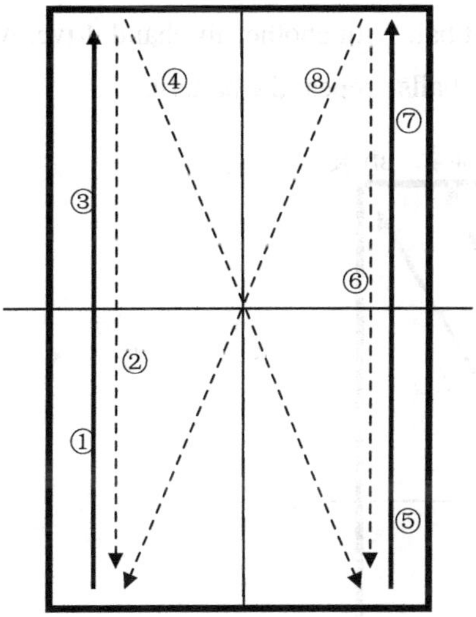

图 5.1.3 两直对一直一斜

Figure 5.1.3 Two-position return down the line and one return crosscourt

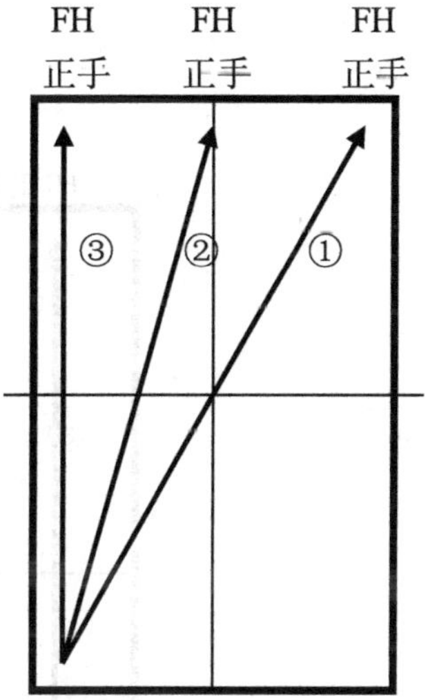

图 5.1.4 正手三点攻

Figure 5.1.4 Three-position forehand drives

● 推侧扑练习(图 5.1.5)

推侧扑练习是世界上最流行的练习方法之一。瑞典的一家乒乓球俱乐部将推侧扑练习推广开来,因此该方法也以该俱乐部的名称(法尔肯堡)来命名。推侧扑练习不仅包含了正、反手攻球,而且也是侧身步和交叉步的结合。

在进行该练习时,前两板球让陪练方均送至主练方的反手位,第三板

● Falkenberg drill with cross step (Figure 5.1.5)

This is one of the most popular drills worldwide. It is named after the Swedish table tennis club that popularized it. The Falkenberg drill combines both forehand and backhand drives along with pivot and cross step movements.

For this drill, have your practice partner send two balls to your backhand side and

球送至主练方的正手大角度。主练方第一板球先用反手攻,第二板球开始用侧身正手攻,第三板球用交叉步移动到正手位用正手攻回击。三板球后,继续重复此过程。

then one ball to your wide forehand. Use a backhand drive to return the first ball; then pivot into the backhand corner and return the second ball with a forehand drive. Move to your forehand using a cross step and return the third ball with another forehand drive. After three balls, repeat the pattern.

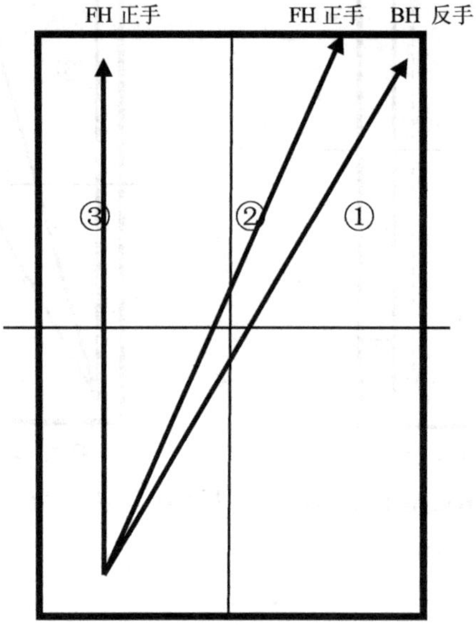

图 5.1.5 推侧扑练习

Figure 5.1.5 Falkenberg drill with cross step

● 注意事项

➢ 这些练习应由易到难,循序渐进;

➢ 根据具体情况增、减练习难度;

➢ 在练习过程中注意使用正确的步法并快速移动;

➢ 在移动时注意保持身体平衡。

● Matters needing attention

➢ These drills should proceed step by step.

➢ Increase or decrease difficulty in accordance with specific conditions.

➢ Focus on using the proper footwork and moving quickly.

➢ Be sure to maintain your balance while moving.

4. 三点打两点的练习

方法：

打三点者全部采用正手走动拉弧圈球的打法；打两点者，反手位来球用反手打，正手位来球用正手反拉弧圈球。双方击球具体线路如图 5.1.6 所示。

4. Three-position Against Two-position Drill

Method：

The three-position player returns all balls using only your forehand loop drives. The two-position player returns the ball on the backhand side using backhand drive, and execute counterloop on the forehand side. Figure 5.1.6 shows the path.

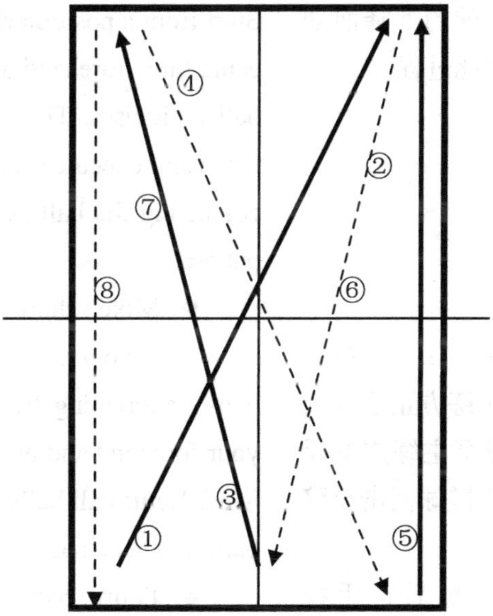

图 5.1.6 三点打两点的练习

Figure 5.1.6 Three-position Against Two-position Drill

注意事项：

➢ 在该练习的开始阶段，让你的陪练同伴减慢供球的速度并降低练习的难度。

Matters needing attention：

➢ Ask your practice partner to slow down the ball feeds and decrease the difficulty level at the beginning of this drill.

三、长短球训练法

Ⅲ. Mixed Short and Deep Ball Drills

方法：

● 前后正手攻球、拉球练习

练习者将轮流在正手的近台、中远台进行正手击球。让陪练者固定供球至你的正手位。你首先在近台打三板正手快攻，在球的上升期击球，然后退至中台拉弧圈球，在球的下降前期击球。之后的练习重复此过程。

● 长短搓球练习

陪练方用下旋球给主练方供球，先送一板下旋短球至主练方正手近网处，再送一板下旋长球至主练方的反手底线附近。主练方用搓球回击至陪练方反手位。

● 反手拧拉接发球后正手拉弧圈

主练方在接发球时，用反手拧拉技术回击近网来球。陪练方回接后，主练方在第四板侧身，用正手拉前冲弧圈球。

● 正手摆短接发球后正手拉弧圈

陪练方发下旋球至主练方的正手

Methods:

● In and out forehand drives or loop drives

For this drill, you will execute the forehand strokes from corner alternately close and far from the table. Have your partner feed topspin balls to one spot on your forehand side. Start from a position close to the table and execute three forehand drives, try to contact the ball as it rises. Then back up to middle distance and execute some forehand loop drives, contacting the ball as it descends. Repeat the pattern.

● Mixed short and long pushes

Have your practice partner feed backspin balls, alternating between one ball short to your forehand and one ball long to your backhand. Return all balls by using pushes to your partner's backhand.

● Fourth-ball attack with backhand twist-drive and forehand loop drive

Received the short ball by use a backhand twist-drive, and the fourth ball you step around and make a strong forehand loop drive.

● Fourth-ball attack with forehand drop shot and forehand loop drive

In this drill, have your partner send a

近网处。主练方用摆短回接发球至对方的反手位，然后陪练方反手搓斜线长球。最后，主练方侧身拉前冲弧圈球，争取得分。

short backspin serve to your forehand. Use a forehand drop shot to return the ball to your partner's backhand side. Then the feeder returns the third ball crosscourt by using a long push. Finally, you step around the table and make a strong forehand loop drive to try to win the point.

● 注意事项

➢ 在快速移动时注意运用正确的步法；

➢ 在前后移动时注意保持身体平衡和重心稳定；

➢ 要保证击球的质量。

● Matters needing attention

➢ Focus on using the proper footwork and moving quickly.

➢ Be sure to maintain your balance while stepping back or forward.

➢ Emphasize on the quality of your strokes.

四、快慢节奏训练法

Ⅳ. Mixed Slow and Fast Pace Drills

方法：

● 不同节奏的正手对攻练习

陪练方供上旋球至主练方的正手位。主练方先在近台用正手以较慢的节奏打一板球，然后下一板退到中台用正手扣杀以较快的节奏击球。之后继续重复该击球过程。

Methods：

● Forehand counter-attack with changing tempo

For this drill, have your partner feed topspin balls to one spot on your forehand side. Start from a position close to the table and execute a forehand drive with slow pace, and then back up to middle distance and execute a forehand smash with fast pace. Repeat the pattern.

● 两慢、一快正手弧圈球拉下旋练习

陪练方用多球连续送下旋球至主练方的正手位。主练方用正手弧圈球

● Two slow, one fast forehand topspins against backspin feed

For this drill, have your practice partner feed backspin balls to your forehand side

回击。回击时,前两板在球的下降期拉球,充分摩擦球;第三板球,在来球的高点拉球,使拉球速度加快。

using the multi-ball technique. Return all balls with forehand topspins. For the first two balls, hit the ball as it descends and create maximum spin. For the third ball, play the ball at the top of the ball with more speed.

● 两慢、一快反手弧圈球拉下旋练习

● Two slow, one fast backhand topspins against backspin feed

陪练方用多球连续送下旋球至主练方的反手位。你皆用反手弧圈球回击。回击时,前两板球在球的下降期拉球,充分摩擦球;第三板球,在来球的高点拉球,使拉球速度加快。

For this drill, have your practice partner use the multi-ball technique to feed backspin balls to your backhand side. Return all balls with backhand topspins. For the first two balls, hit the ball as it descends and create maximum spin. For the third ball, play the ball at the top of the ball with more speed.

● 注意事项

在拉前两板球时,拉球的摩擦力要大于撞击力;拉第三板球时,要打、摩结合。

● Matters needing attention

Be sure to contact the ball with maximum friction on the first two returns and with a mix of friction and force on the third ball (fast loop).

五、多球训练法

V. Multi-ball Drills

正如其名,多球练习法就是陪练方运用数量较多的乒乓球对主练方进行持续的供球。这是一种非常重要的乒乓球训练方法,因为多球训练不但可以用于基础技术的训练,而且可以解决很多特殊技术连接上的问题。多球训练法有以下优点:

As the name suggests, multi-ball drills are performed with a large amount of balls that are fed continuously by a feeder to the person doing a set drill. This is a very important training method, because the multi-ball drills are not only used for basic technical training, but also used to solve some special problems occurring in transitions between techniques. Multi-ball drills have the following advantages.

➢ 可以使练习者在短时间内获取较大的运动负荷；

➢ You can have more intense practice in a shorter amount of time.

➢ 节省了捡球时间，因此练习中击球时间较多；

➢ Because no time is wasted chasing balls, more strokes can be executed during practice.

➢ 在没有陪练者的条件下，练习者利用发球机也可以练习到不同的技术；

➢ By using the ball-throwing machines, you can practice varied skills without a skilled training partner.

➢ 可以提高练习者的有氧能力和身体素质。

➢ You can quickly increase aerobic and physical capacity.

方法：

Methods:

● 自供自练

● Individual multi-ball drill

在该项训练中，你可以自己练习发球或者进行自抛自打练习。

For this drill, you can practice serving by yourself, or hit the ball from your own throwing.

● 他人供多球练习

● Have your partner feed a large box of balls to you

陪练方按要求供球，主练方根据训练计划进行不同的练习。

Execute different drill in accordance with the training program.

● 发球机供球练习

● Ball-throwing machines

通过设定发球机的程序，你可以改变来球的旋转、速度和落点进行训练。

For this drill, you can change the spin, speed and location of the oncoming ball by setting the machine to get an actual point.

● 注意事项

● Matters needing attention

➢ 由于多球训练法不利于培养盯球的意识，所以应注意与单球训练结合；

➢ Given that the multi-ball drills probably undermine the development of the consciousness of watching the ball, so you should pay attention to combine it with the individual drills.

➢ 在训练中让供球者加快或减慢供球的速度和频率；

➢ Ask your practice partner to increase or decrease the frequency of the ball feeds.

➢ 在练习过程中注意使用正确的步法并迅速移动。

➢ Focus on using the proper footwork and moving quickly.

六、前三板训练法

Ⅵ. The First Three Shots Drills

1. 发球练习法

方法：

➢ 第一种方法是每名练习者一次性将一筐球连续发完，然后捡球后再继续练习。

➢ 另外一种方法是，练习者发球，另一方接发球；发球者可以通过对手的反馈了解自己发球的效果。

● 注意事项

➢ 练习时不要故步自封。一些运动员在练习发球时经常犯这样的错误：他们只发一种最为保险、练得最多的球，而不敢有所突破。因此，你必须迫使自己在练习发球时制造出更强烈的旋转和更有威胁的落点。

➢ 最佳的发球练习时间是在训练的中段。因为在这个时段，你身体已经充分活动开，手感也处于最佳状态，而且身体也不是很疲惫。

1. Serve Drill

Method:

➢ One way is to give each player a number of balls (a whole bucket if possible) and have them serve one at a time. Afterwards they pick up the balls and serve again.

➢ Another way is that you can have one player serve, the other player return the serve, and the server catch the ball and serve again. In this way, the server can ask his practice partner for feedback on his serve.

● Matters needing attention

➢ Practice above your level. A key mistake many people make when practicing serves is that they simply practice the same safe serve they've always used. You have to push yourself to create more spin and improve your placement.

➢ The best time to practice serving is in the middle of a training session. By that time you are warmed up and your hand skill are at their peak, but you are not physically tired.

2. 发球抢攻练习

在进行该练习时，发球者任意发球，陪练方回接发球后，发球者进行抢攻，两人再进入相持技术的练习。可采用以下具体的方式进行练习。

2. Attack After Serve Drill

In this drill, one player serves any serve and then the other returns the serve. The first player attacks and the two players play out the point like in a game. You can use the following patterns.

● 限定你陪练同伴接发球回球的落点和旋转

● Have your partner receive with a limitation of placement and type

例如，要求你的陪练同伴用搓接至你的反手位，然后你进行抢攻。

For example, have your partner receive by push return to your backhand corner. Then you execute a forehand attack.

● 不限制你陪练同伴接发球回球的落点和旋转

● Have your partner receive with no limitation of placement or type

在该练习中，让你的陪练同伴用各种不同的接法回接至全台不定点；然后你进行抢攻。

For this drill, ask your partner receive with any skill and send the ball to a random placement on full court. Then you try to attack the oncoming ball.

方法：

Methods:

● 发球后拉弧圈球抢攻

● Loop attack after serve

练习者发正手短球，对方搓长后，练习者以弧圈球技术进攻，形成相持后双方自由击球。

Short forehand serve → loop attack on deep backspin → free play.

● 发球后摆短并拉弧圈球进攻

● Loop drive after short-short-long

练习者发正手短球，对方回摆短，练习者继续回摆短，对方搓长后，练习者以弧圈球技术进攻，形成相持后双方自由击球。

Short forehand serve → short → short → long → loop drive → free play.

● 发球后摆短接挑打进攻

● Flip after short-short

练习者发正手短球，对方回摆短，练习者以挑打技术进攻，形成相持后双方自由击球。

Short forehand serve → short return → flip from the server → free play.

3. 接发球后抢攻练习

3. Attack After Receive Drill

方式：

Patterns:

● 限定你的陪练同伴发球的落点和旋转种类

● Have your partner serve with a limitation of placement and type

例如，让你的陪练同伴发左侧旋

For example, ask your partner execute

球至你的反手近网处。

left sidespin serve to your backhand net zone.

● 不限制你的陪练同伴发球的落点和旋转种类

在该项练习中，让你的陪练同伴发任何旋转和落点的球，而你进行回接时应注意提高回球质量。

● Have your partner serve with no limitation of placement or type

For this drill, ask your partner execute any type of serve and send the ball to a random position on full court. Try to avoid a passive return of your stroke.

方法：

● 拉弧圈球接抢对方长球

练习者用弧圈球技术接抢对方所发长球，形成相持后双方自由击球。

● 接发球摆短后拉弧圈球

练习者在接发球摆短后，对方搓球劈长，练习者用弧圈球技术进攻，形成相持后双方自由击球。

● 挑打或反手拧拉接发球

练习者用挑打或反手拧拉技术接对方发球，形成相持后双方自由击球。

● 接发球摆短后挑打或反手拧拉

练习者在接发球摆短后，对方继续回摆短球，练习者用挑打或反手拧拉技术进攻下旋短球，形成相持后双方自由击球。

Methods:

● Loop drive on long serve

Loop drive on long serve on whole table → free play.

● Loop drive after short return

Short return → long push → loop drive on long backspin → free play.

● Flip or backhand twist-drive on serve

Flip or a backhand twist-drive on short serve → free play.

● Flip or backhand twist-drive after short return

Short return → short push → flip or backhand twist-drive on short backspin → free play.

七、比赛训练法

方法：

● 发球抢攻比赛

发球抢攻者在第 5 板球内打死对方计 1 分。接发球者也应积极击球得分。发球抢攻者未在 5 板内打死对方

Ⅶ. Competition Training

Methods:

● Serve and attack games

In this drill, the server tries to win the point on the serve before the fifth-ball attack. The receiver also tries to win the point. Any

算接发球方得分。比赛采取 11 分制，不交换发球权，发球权都属一位运动员。一局之后互换角色。为了增加比赛难度，也可要求发球抢攻方在第三板内赢下这一分。

point lasting longer than five strokes belongs to the receiver. Play 11 points, with the server serving every point; then switch roles. To increase difficulty, the server must win the point by the third ball.

● 关键分比赛

在 8 平、8∶9、10 平后开始比赛，以提高运动员的心理素质和打制胜分的能力。

● Key point games

Begin a game with the point 8-8, 8-9, or 10-10. It is a good choice to improve your mentality in the competition and strengthen the ability of playing the winning point.

● 擂台赛

在该比赛训练法中，把运动员分为两个队，每个队大概 5~6 人。只比赛一局，且一局只打三分球。胜者继续比赛，负者下台等候轮转再战。输球的一方须接受如俯卧撑或跑圈之类的惩罚。

● Challenge matches

In this competition training, separate the team into two groups and five or six players work in one group. Only play 3 point each game. The winning player continues his match, while the loser is suspended until his next turn. The team losing the game should be punished to do some press-ups or running laps.

● 限定条件比赛

限定条件比赛是在运动员的训练比赛中加入一些约束性的规定。例如，要求运动员只能在球台某个固定的区域进行比赛，也可以要求运动员只能使用限定技术进行比赛，如正手攻球比赛。为了增加比赛的乐趣，提高运动员的比赛积极性，可以加入一些如仰卧起坐或跳跃训练等惩罚性措施。

● Conditional game

A conditional game is when the player has constraints imposed within a given practice situation. For example, only being able to play with a certain portion of the table, or only able to play forehand shots. To give the players a bit of fun and add some incentives, impose some penalties of several sit-ups or star-jumps if one side loses the game.

八、增、减难度训练法

方法：

● 击目标练习法

在你对手的台面上放置一些球或几片纸等目标物。你的目标是击球和发球必须击中某个目标物。该项练习能够提高你控制球的能力。

● 升降球网练习法

球网高度提升 1 cm，以增加击球的弧线。另外在搓球和削球练习时，可适当降低球网高度，以降低打出的弧线。

● 网上加线练习法

在球网上方约 5 cm 处系一条绳索，使其平行于球网。在击球时，使球从绳与网之间穿过。该练习通常用于搓球训练，以降低和控制击球的弧线。

● 加宽球台练习法

在该项练习中，将球台一方的台面面积扩大至原来的 2 倍，使球台加宽。此法多于改善步法训练和提高双打运动员的协调配合时使用。

Ⅷ. Increasing and Decreasing Difficulty Training Methods

Methods:

● Target hitting drill

Place some targets on your opponent's side of the table. Several balls or some pieces of papers can work fine. Your goal is to execute some strokes and serves to hit the target. This drill will improve your ability of controlling the ball.

● Raise and lower the net drill

Raise the height of the net about 1 cm to force you to increase the trajectory of your drives. Conversely, lowering the net slightly will help you to decrease the trajectory of your chopping or pushing.

● Under the rope drill

Attach a rope approximately 5 cm above and parallel to the top of the net. Guide your returns under the rope and into the side of your opponent's table. This drill is usually used for the push stroke to control the trajectory of your returns.

● Broaden the table drill

In this drill, we can double the size of the playing court to broaden the table. This drill is usually used for improving footwork training and enhancing the coordination of doubles' play.

● 降低球台练习法

由于儿童身材较矮,不适合在普通球台上开展练习,因此在训练儿童时可以将球台高度适当降低,使儿童能在自己的身高和能力范围内更好地掌握技术。

● Lower the table drill

The regulation table height is usually a bit too high for children. For this reason, we can lower the height of the table for the children to allow them to develop the skill of the game within their own heights and capabilities.

● 用加重拍进行练习

用铁制的加重球拍进行徒手挥拍练习。该练习增加了训练负荷,因此能有助于发展你执拍手的力量和耐力。

● Overloaded racket drill

Practice your shadow strike motions with an overloaded racket made of iron. The added weight and air resistance aid in developing strength and endurance in your hitting arm.

第二节 体能训练方法
Section 2 Physical Training Methods

成功的乒乓球运动员需要具备良好的身体素质。通常在一场乒乓球比赛中会有约 500 次的击球挥拍,并且要保持连续的快速移动。这样,运动员不仅要有很好的肌肉力量和肌肉快速工作的能力,而且要有较好的身体柔韧性和协调性。本节旨在向大家提供一些发展力量和速度的具体训练方法,并介绍关于柔韧性的一些重要概念和将这些训练方法应用于实践的一些技巧。

The game of table tennis has good physical demands and requirements for successful players. Usually, a table tennis match can contain nearly 500 strokes and keep players fast-moving. Therefore, it requires not only high levels of muscular strength and muscular working speed, but also the flexibility and harmonization of the body. The purpose of this section is to provide information regarding table tennis-specific training for strength and speed development as well as to introduce some important concepts of flexibility and actual tips for integrating these training methods into complete programs for players.

一、乒乓球运动员的力量训练

表 5.2.1 是一个力量训练计划的例子，每星期在健身房中进行 3 次练习：练习的第一天和第二天主要是力量、爆发力和稳定性的训练，第三天开始循环训练（全身肌肉和实心球训练）。该项训练对提高运动员躯干和腹部等核心区域的肌肉力量，以及维持身体稳定性有着较好的效果。

Ⅰ. Strength Training for Table Tennis Players

Table 5.2.1 shows a strength training program, which is performed three times per week in a gym, with days one and two in the strength training sequence are used primarily for strength, power and stability, with day three consist of circuit training (muscle complex and medicine ball). This is a good example to improve your core strength work for the trunk and abdomen and your body stability.

二、爆发力和速度训练

乒乓球运动员身体训练的主要目标之一是提高爆发力和速度素质。关于提高爆发力和速度的一个常见的错误说法是：单纯地只使用哑铃或力量器械以最快的速度来训练就可以达到目的。然而，这些传统的应用方法不仅不适合最快速度，而且也不安全。因此，教练员已经开发了一些专门的训练方法来提高速度和爆发力。

Ⅱ. Training for Explosive Power and Speed

One of the goals for training table tennis players includes the characteristics of explosive power and speed. One of the common mistakes about power and speed is the thought that using a dumbbell or weight machine at fast speeds is all that is required. However, these traditionally applied methods are not appropriate at fast speeds and also may not be as safe. Therefore, coaches have developed some special types of exercises to improve speed and power development.

1. 超等长训练法

超等长训练法是一种提高爆发力和速度的训练方法，已经在许多运动项目中应用了很多年。超等长训练法首先通过离心或伸长收缩来拉长肌肉

1. Plyometrics

Plyometrics is a type of training that has been used for years in many sports to obtain explosive power and speed development. Plyometric exercises begin with a stretch to

表 5.2.1 力量训练计划　　Table 5.2.1 Strength Training

第一天 **练习方法** 后深蹲 卧推 哑铃反向飞鸟 坐姿划船 哑铃肱三头肌伸展练习 **核心计划** 仰卧起坐 3 × 20 体侧屈 3 × 20 俯卧起 3 × 20 俯卧两头起 3 × 20	**Day 1** **Exercise** Back squat Bench press Dumbbell reverse fly Seated rows Dumbbell triceps extension **Core program** Sit-ups 3 × 20 Side bends 3 × 20 Reverse hypers 3 × 20 Reverse sit-ups 3 × 20
第二天 **练习方法** 侧弓箭步 肩外侧绕环 滑轮背部下拉（头后） 哑铃颈后臂屈伸 颈前深蹲推举 **核心计划** 仰卧起坐 3 × 20 体侧屈 3 × 20 俯卧起 3 × 20 俯卧两头起 3 × 20	**Day 2** **Exercise** Lateral lunges Shoulder external rotation Lat pull-downs（behind head） Dumbbell triceps kickbacks Front squats to a push-press **Core program** Sit-ups 3 × 20 Side bends 3 × 20 Reverse hypers 3 × 20 Reverse sit-ups 3 × 20
第三天 **练习方法** 屈臂提铃至胸 转动躯干 实心球对掷 实心球环绕 肌肉复合 **核心计划** 仰卧起坐 3 × 20 体侧屈 3 × 20 俯卧起 3 × 20 俯卧两头起 3 × 20	**Day 3** **Exercise** Bent-over rows Rotary torso Medicine-ball partner catches Medicine-ball circuit Muscle complex **Core program** Reverse hypers 3 × 20 Reverse sit-ups 3 × 20 Sit-ups 3 × 20 Side bends 3 × 20

长度，然后紧接着向心收缩或缩短收缩。与传统的单一向心收缩训练相比，超等长训练法先进行离心收缩可以增加随后向心收缩时的力量和爆发力，使向心收缩更快、更有力。

the muscles through an eccentric or lengthening contraction. This eccentric contraction immediately is followed by a concentric or shortening contraction. The eccentric contraction will increase the strength and power of the subsequent concentric contraction and produce stronger and more powerful concentric contractions when compared to traditional concentric-only training programs.

超等长训练法对乒乓球运动员非常有用，许多这样的肌肉动作模式可以在乒乓球运动中出现。

Plyometric training is very helpful for table tennis players and many types of muscular patterns are everywhere in table tennis play.

- 超等长训练法在下肢的应用

- Application of plyometrics to the lower body

典型的下肢超等长训练法是跳箱练习法。在这一练习方法中，运动员从 40~60 cm 高的木头或金属箱向下跳。在运动员落地时，股四头肌和小腿肌肉会产生离心收缩，然后运动员立即以最大力量向上跳，肌肉发生向心收缩。进行跳箱练习可有一些变化，可以将跳跃或往返跑结合起来模仿各种运动模式。

Typical lower-body plyometric drills is the box jumps. In this drill, players jump from wooden or metal boxes 40 cm to 60 cm high. Upon the player's landing from the box, the quadriceps and calf muscle undergo an eccentric contraction whereupon the player then immediately jumps up maximally performing a concentric contraction of the muscles. Many variations of these box-jump exercises have been used coupling the jump performance with a spirit or shuttle run to emulate various sport-specific movement patterns.

- 超等长训练法在躯干的应用

- Application of plyometrics to the trunk

躯干是乒乓球运动员肌肉力量发展不平衡和易受伤的主要部位。另外，正手攻球的力量多来自躯干的发

The trunk is an area in table tennis players where both muscular imbalances and injuries abound. Moreover, most force of a

力转动，而这其中腹肌主要起加速和稳定躯干的作用。运动员和教练员可以使用实心球来练习腹部肌肉。例如，在运动员训练计划中，实心球练习可以使运动员传统的仰卧起坐腹部练习增加一些额外的变化。

forehand stroke come from rotation of your trunk, whereas the abdominal muscles work to accelerate and stabilize the trunk during the forehand stroke. Players and coaches can use a medicine ball to train the abdominals. For example, medicine ball exercises can provide additional variety to the traditional sit up abdominal exercises in a player's program.

- 超等长训练法在上肢的应用

- Application of plyometrics to the upper extremities

对上肢的超等长训练可以用实心球来进行胸部传球和侧向传球。另外一个用于上肢的超等长训练方法就是推墙。这个训练方法需要同伴的配合。首先让一名队员在面对墙壁大约1 m的位置站立，并对墙伸出双臂使其与肩同高。同伴在后面朝墙推这名队员。在触及墙时，这名队员必须马上且快速地用手推墙还原，然后同伴再次将这名队员推向墙。重复该练习动作有助于增强运动员的上肢力量和爆发力，尤其是肩胛周围的肌肉、肱三头肌和屈腕肌的力量。

Plyometric exercises for the upper extremities, however, can be useful in the form of medicine ball chest passes and side throws. Another plyometric exercise that can be used for general upper extremities conditioning is the wall plyo. This partnered drill consists of one player standing about 1 m away from a wall with the arms outstretched at shoulder level. A partner from behind pushes the player toward the wall. Upon contacting the wall, the player immediately and rapidly push back away from the wall, and the partner again pushes the player's back toward the wall. This is repeated to promote upper extremities strength and power and especially helps to develop the muscles around the shoulder blade, triceps, and wrist flexors.

2. 阻力绳训练法

在该项训练中，将阻力绳绑在运动员的腰部，在场下进行速度和爆发力的训练。教练员抓住绳子的一端，

2. Resistance Cords Drills

In this drill, resistance cords can be secured around player's waist for off-court speed and power development. The coach

运动员以最快的速度、尽自己最大的努力来侧向移动。这时,绳子提供的阻力使肌肉组织超负荷工作,从而促进肌肉的速度和力量的发展。

holds one end of the cord while a player moves laterally at a maximum speed and with maximal effort. Resistance provided by the cord ensures that an overload is applied to the musculature that facilities the development of speed and power.

3. 等动训练法

另外一项经常用来恢复爆发力和速度的场下训练方法是等动训练法。这种训练使用等动练习器来进行,与其他的阻力训练设备不同,练习的速度保持不变,而阻力在变化。等动练习器可以使训练以更快、功能更佳的速度来进行,对发展高水平运动员的旋转肌群非常有效。

3. Isokinetic Training

Another off-court method used in training and often in rehabilitation for power and speed development is isokinetic training. This type of training utilizes an isokinetic machine that, unlike other resistance training equipment, sets and holds constant the speed of the exercise, not the resistance. The isokinetic machines offer training at faster, more functional speeds and have been particular effective in training the rotator cuff in elite-level table tennis players.

三、乒乓球运动员的柔韧性训练

Ⅲ. Flexibility Training for Table Tennis Player

从学术方面来讲,柔韧性是肌肉、肌腱和结缔组织围绕关节活动拉伸的能力。乒乓球运动员的训练主要有两种柔韧性练习:一种是静力性拉伸练习,另外一种是动力性拉伸练习。

Flexibility is described literally as the ability of the muscles, tendons, and connective tissue around joints to elongate to allow range of motion. There are two types of training methods that can be applied to enhance player's flexibility. One is the static stretching; the other is the dynamic stretching.

1. 静力性拉伸

静力性拉伸是指将一块肌肉或一部分肌肉群做最大限度的拉伸,并在

1. Static Stretching

Static stretching is a term that refers to the stretching of a muscle, or a group of

该拉伸位置保持静止不动一段时间。静力性拉伸有利于增加肌肉长度、预防损伤和提高身体的积极性。而且，其有助于增加关节活动的范围和降低训练后肌肉的僵硬程度。一般在比赛之后做静力性拉伸，或者至少在比赛之前 20~30 min 做。静力性拉伸有以下几种具体的训练方法：

muscles, to the farthest point and then holding the position for a specific amount of time. Static stretching is beneficial for increasing the length of the muscles, preventing injury and preparing the body for activity. Moreover, it can work on joint range of motion and help to decrease post-workout stiffness. Generally, static stretching is used after table tennis play, as well as at least 20 to 30 minutes before actually playing. There are some specific training methods as following.

- 手腕和前臂伸展；
- 肩后部伸展；
- 腿筋拉伸（压腿）；
- 腹股沟向右和向左拉伸；
- 右腿触胸或左腿触胸；
- 右小腿伸展或左小腿伸展。

- Wrist and forearm stretches each way with both arms.
- Posterior shoulder stretches.
- Hamstring stretch.
- Groin stretch to the right and left.
- Right leg to chest or left leg to chest.
- Right calf or left calf stretch.

2. 动力性拉伸

动力性拉伸是指将身体运动结合到拉伸过程中，通过一系列的位移动作积极地拉伸肌肉，与保持静止不动的静力性牵拉概念正好相反。动力性拉伸在体育活动之前尤为重要。因此，动力性拉伸常被用在比赛前的准备活动期间。以下是动力性拉伸的一些具体训练方法：

2. Dynamic Stretching

Dynamic stretching refers to stretching that incorporates body movement into the stretch. You stretch your muscles actively through a range of motion, which is opposite to standard static stretches that have no movement. It is particularly effective immediately before performing an activity. Therefore, dynamic stretching is always used at the warming-up period in prematch. Here are some training methods for dynamic stretching:

- 绕场地交叉步；
- 绕场地高抬腿走（最高点保持

- Cross step across court.
- Walking with high knees (hold at

一会儿)；

➢ 绕场地后踢走(最高点保持一会儿)；

➢ 绕场地直腿向上抬(右脚左手,左脚右手)；

➢ 绕场地转髋；

➢ 摆腿(10次/(腿·方向))。

以下为进行柔韧性训练的建议顺序：

(1)一般性热身(5~10 min),直到身体微微出汗；

(2)采用拉伸某一肌肉群的姿势进行静力性拉伸,每一姿势保持15~30 s,并重复2~3次；

(3)逐步增加动作的幅度和速度来进行动力性拉伸；

(4)乒乓球台上练习；

(5)整理活动采用静力性拉伸。

top) once across court.

➢ Walking with heel kicks (hold at top) once across court.

➢ Straight-leg front raises (right foot left hand, left foot right hand) once across court.

➢ Hip rotation once across court.

➢ Leg swinging (10 per direction each leg).

The following is a recommend sequence of flexible training.

(1)General body warm-up (5-10 minutes) until you achieve a light sweat.

(2)Perform static stretching of specific muscle groups using position that isolate that group; use 2-3 stretches holding each 15-30 seconds.

(3)Perform dynamic stretching with progressive increases in range and velocity of movements.

(4)Play table tennis.

(5)Execute static stretching during cool-down.

第三节　心理训练方法

Section 3　Psychological Training Methods

1. 放松训练法

虽然一些运动员的唤醒水平较低,但更严重的问题是处于高度焦虑

1. Relaxation Training

While some athletes may suffer from low levels of arousal, the more difficult prob-

和紧张中。放松训练可以有效地减轻运动过程中的紧张和焦虑。现今有三种比较流行的放松方式:自生训练法、沉思法和音乐放松法。这几种放松方式都有助于减少耗氧量、心跳变慢、呼吸减缓、骨骼肌活动性下降。

lems occur with athletes who experience very high levels of anxiety and tension. Relaxation training can effectively reduce tension and anxiety associated with sport. Three popular relaxation training can be adequately categorized under the board heading of relaxation. These are autogenic training, mediation and music relaxation. These methods help to decreasc in oxygen consumption, heart rate, respiration and skeletal muscle activity.

- 自生训练法

自生训练法依靠身体对四肢和肌肉的相关感觉来诱发放松反应。当你进行自生放松练习时,你必须找到一个安静的房间,并在一个舒服的地方坐下或躺下;然后,闭上你的双眼,慢慢地深呼吸来帮助你放松;开始进行以下六个自我暗示步骤:

(1)胳膊和腿发沉;
(2)胳膊和腿发暖;
(3)胸部发热,感觉心跳减慢;
(4)平静下来,放松呼吸;
(5)腹腔神经丛区域发暖;
(6)感觉前额有凉意。

- Autogenic training

Autogenic training relies on feelings associated with the limbs and muscles of the body to elicit the relaxation response. When you have the autogenic training, you must find a comfortable area in a quiet room where you can sit or lie down on your back. And then, close your eyes and practice some deep breathing to help you to relax. Begin with the following six self-statement steps.

(1)Heaviness in the arm and legs.
(2)Warmth in the arms and legs.
(3)Warmth in the chest and a perception of reduced heart rate.
(4)Calm and relaxed breathing.
(5)Warmth in the solar plexus area.
(6)Sensation of coolness on the forehead.

- 沉思训练法

沉思是一种放松方式。如果在一个安静的环境里进行沉思训练,同时

- Mediation training

Mediation, as a form of relaxation, will result in the relaxation response if practiced in

保持一种被动的态度,肌肉放松,就能引起放松反应。沉思法明显可以减轻焦虑、紧张和压力,这继而对焦虑型的运动员会有所帮助。在进行沉思法练习时,训练者采取舒服的姿势坐立,眼睛闭上,注意力集中在深呼吸上,同时默默地重复指示语。例如:“我感觉很平静”“我感觉很温暖、很放松”“我精神很舒适”。

a quiet environment that is associated with a passive attitude and decrease muscle tone. It is clear that mediation can reduce anxiety, tension and pressure to help the anxiety-prone athlete. In practice, the subject sits in a comfortable position with eyes closed. The subject concentrates on deep breathing while at the same time repeating the statements silently. For example, “I feel quiet” “I feel warm and relaxed” “My mind is at ease”.

2. 目标设置训练法

对每个人来说,设置好目标有助于人们朝着自己的理想前进,减少焦虑,并增强自信心。目标设置是一种动机理论,它可以有效地使运动员增加活力,变得更加成功。在你准备设定目标之前,一定要阅读以下原则:

2. Goal Setting Training

On a personal level, setting goals helps people work towards their own objectives, reduce anxiety, as well as build their confidence. Goal setting is a cognitive theory of motivation which effectively energizes athletes to become more productive. Read the following principles before you prepare to set some goals.

➢ 目标的设置应具体、可测量、行动导向、现实以及适时;

➢ Goals should be specific, measurable, action-oriented, realistic and timely.

➢ 具体目标要优于一般目标;

➢ Specific goals are better than general goals.

➢ 有难度的目标要优于较容易的目标;

➢ Difficult goals are better than easy goals.

➢ 利用短期目标去实现长期目标;

➢ Use short term goals to achieve long term goals.

➢ 用表现目标代替结果目标;

➢ Set performance goals instead of outcome goals.

➢ 把目标写下来并定期检查以保证其激励作用;

➢ Goals should be written down and closely monitored to maintain their motivational value.

➢ 目标的设置是因人而异的。

➢ Setting goals differs from man to man.

3. 注意力训练

注意力训练包括注意力集中和注意力转移。运动员在比赛中的注意力是否集中,会很明显地影响技术的发挥。然而,具有讽刺意味的是,在比赛比分相近时,你越注意动作,在压力下你就越不可能做好。这种情况在运动员身上很常见。短暂的注意力集中和注意力转移在比赛时也非常重要。总是注意已错过的机会球或裁判的误判只会完全破坏击球动作。现在需要做的就是注意此时的情况,一次只注意一个方面。比赛时,这种短暂的注意有助于动作自动化地发生。运动员们通常说当动作自动化时,他们就会有很好的表现。在心理上注意盯球或快速移动有助于动作自动化。

3. Attention Training

Attention training includes attention concentrated and attention transferred. The athletes' focus of attention during competitive play clearly affects mechanics. However, it is ironical that the more you focus on mechanics between and during points, the less likely you are to execute properly under pressure. This situation is all too familiar to players. Temporal focus and attention transferred also are important in competition. Frequently focus on the past such as missed opportunities or erroneous judgment can completely derail stroke production. The specific competency required here is the ability to maintain a present focus, to essentially focus on only one point at a time. A present moment-to-moment focus during points facilitates a highly instinctive style of play. Players consistently report they perform best when stroke production is essentially on automatic pilot. Mentally focusing on watching the ball or "fast feet" facilitates the desired automatic effect.

4. 自我谈话

对于许多运动员而言,积极的和鼓励性的自我谈话会增强个人对压力的控制。相反,消极的自我谈话会起到相反的作用。责备自己、不断地发

4. Self talk

Positive and encouraging self-talk serves to enhance personal control of the stress response for many players, and the opposite is true in the case of negative self-talk. Berating

现自己错的地方和自己的处理方法会增强负面的唤醒，在高压的情况下严重影响动作的准确性。在比赛中常用的自我谈话的规则是：无论你说什么，越少越好，并尽量是积极的和鼓励性的话。

yourself, and constantly finding fault with what you do and how you do it, increasing negative arousal and can severely compromise your mechanical precision in high-stress situations. The general rule regarding self-talk in competitions is simply this: say as little as possible and whatever is said, make it positive and encouraging.

5. 想象

运动员们经常会提及，他们在每一分的开始前想象一下发球和接发球的动作有助于动作的完成。在比赛中运用想象纠正错误对动作完成的准确性有着积极的作用，也有助于本能的发生和动作的自动化。在下一分开始之前，简单地“感觉”正确的击球动作或从心理上和身体上演练一下具体的纠正方法有助于建立信心和积极的回应。例如，在比赛之前，运动员应制定好比赛策略，而且要非常清楚在压力的情况下如何打；在比赛中，运动员可以在发球和接发球之前想象一下，来帮助你“预想”一下这一分应如何来打。

5. Visualization

Players consistently report that visualizing the serve or serve return before the start of the point facilitates execution. Using visualization to correct mistakes during play can have a very positive effect on mechanical precision. It also facilitates instinctive and automatic play. Simply “feeling” the correct stroke or mentally and physically rehearsing the specific correction before the next point builds confidence and positive response expectancy. For example, before the match, athletes should plan your play and have a crystal clear idea of exactly how you want to play in pressure situations; during the competition, players can use visualization before serving or receiving to help you “see” how you want the point to develop.

6. 情绪控制能力

运动员一旦具备了身体能力，而后就要做出相应的正确的情绪反应。动作的准确性要求情绪反应具有准确性。情绪控制来源于自我意识。所谓

6. Emotional Competencies

Once the physical competencies are in place, the foundation is set for mobilizing the right emotional response. Mechanical precision requires emotional precision. Emotional

意识就是你知道和注意到正在发生什么。例如,运动员在打关键分时就会感觉到手和手臂的紧张感增加,或者随着比赛的进行,挫败感和暴躁程度又会影响动作完成的能力。意识对情绪控制能力是极其重要的。在比赛中,不能控制好情绪的运动员在压力情况下,动作的准确性就会出现很大的问题。

control begins with self-awareness. Awareness means to be tuned in and conscious of what's happening. For example, a player immediately senses how the increase in tension in the muscles of his hands and arms at a critical point or his increasing frustration and irritability as the match progresses is compromising his ability to perform optimally. Awareness is the most essential emotional competency. Players who are obvious to their feelings or who argue that feelings are irrelevant and unrelated to competitive success have created a substantial barrier to mechanical precision under pressure.

另外,我们要学习运用呼吸来控制自己的情绪。比赛时和比分之间的呼吸节奏很明显地会影响动作的生物力学机制。击球时,吸气或屏住呼吸会使肌肉变紧,这会影响挥拍的速度和精细动作的控制。由于吸气有利于肌肉放松,当击球点和呼吸协调得很好时,动作就会非常流畅和稳定。有一些运动员在击球时会采取发出声音的方式来吸气和呼气。在比分之间,有节奏的、胸式呼吸有助于生理和心理的调节。腹式呼吸可以降低心率和血压,保持头脑清醒,降低不稳定情绪的强度,如生气和害怕。

Additionally, we can learn how to use breath to control our emotion. The rhythm of one's breath both during and between points clearly affects bio-mechanics. Breathing in or breath holding during a stroke causes muscles to tighten, affecting racket acceleration and fine-motor control. Because exhaling stimulates muscle relaxation, strokes tend to be more fluid and smooth when contact point and our-breaths are coordinate. For some players, this takes the form of grunting. Between points, rhythmic, diaphragmatic breathing facilitates recovery, both physiological and psychological. Diaphragmatic breathing lowers heart rate and blood pressure, improves mental clarity, and reduces the intensity of disruptive emotions such as anger and fear.

第四节 乒乓球训练理论

Section 4 Table Tennis Training Theory

一、一般原则

➢ 训练应培养和提高运动员身体和心理素质。

➢ 运动员应该及时地开始训练；训练应该将多方面的内容整合在一起进行。

➢ 教练员和运动员应该有计划、长期地组织安排训练。

➢ 训练过程中的负荷由运动员的年龄和训练现状、训练准备状态和训练可能性共同决定。

为了使运动员有更真实的体验，可以组织测试或者比赛。通过一系列合适的训练措施可以实现好的训练状况。您务必记住：只要训练给您带来乐趣，那么训练原则上就是顺利的。

I. General Principles of Training

➢ Training should develop and improve the physical and mental qualities of athletes.

➢ Athletes should start training in a timely manner; training should integrate various aspects together.

➢ Coaches and athletes should organize training in a planned and long-term manner.

➢ The load during training is determined by the age of the athlete and the current state of training, the state of training readiness and training possibilities.

In order to obtain an actual state of training, you can organize tests or competitions. A good training status can be achieved by a series of suitable training measures. You must remember: as long as the training provides athletes with pleasure, the training is in principle effective.

二、训练组织

为了能够使运动员带着乐趣参加训练，以及看到他们刻苦训练的成果，教练员必须采用有针对性的措施有计划、有意义地组织训练。

II. Organization of Training

In order to enable athletes to train with pleasure and to see the results of their hard work, coaches must use targeted measures to organize training in a planned and meaningful way.

主要有两个基本构成要素决定了训练组织情况：

（1）训练时间的分配；

（2）训练周期化。

然而，为了从总体上能够开始训练工作，一个训练先决条件的"详细目录"是不可缺少的。以下内容就属于这个"详细目录"：

- 每周训练时数；
- 训练助手；
- 训练器材和场地可能性；
- 参加训练人数和人员结构；
- 参加训练运动员的能力现状。

There are two main basic components that determine the organization of training:

(1)Allocation of training time.

(2)Periodic training.

However, in order to be able to start training in general, a "detailed list" as training prerequisites must not be missing. The following elements belong to this "detailed list".

- Number of training hours per week.
- Training assistants.
- Training equipment and space.
- Number of participants and structure of personnel.
- The current state of the athletes' abilities.

三、训练时间分配

Ⅲ. Allocation of Training Time

每次训练时间或者更准确地说每个训练单元应该由以下三部分组成：

- 开始部分；
- 主体部分；
- 结束部分。

Each training session or, more precisely, each training unit should consist of three parts.

- The beginning section.
- The main section.
- The ending section.

1. 开始部分

1. The Beginning Section

目标：热身，或者说是对训练单元中将要实施的负荷进行准备和统一认识。

Objective: warm-up, or get athletes prepared and unified athletes' understanding of the loads that will be implemented in the training.

练习：始终以慢跑开始，然后进行跑步和跳跃练习、体操和拉伸练习、反

Exercises: the training can be always started with a jog, followed by running and

应练习，最后安排几次冲刺跑。

时间：总时间的10%。

2. 主体部分

目标：为乒乓球比赛改进和提高运动员的技术和战术能力。

练习：乒乓球的训练和比赛形式。

时间：总时间的70%。

3. 结束部分

目标：和谐的结尾，当然也为改善和增强一般体能服务。

练习：所有团队体育运动项目(足球和篮球)，但是也可以组织循环训练或者放松练习，例如拉伸练习等。

时间：总时间的20%。

四、周期训练

对于休闲娱乐乒乓球领域而言，当然不要求在训练组织方面有清晰的概念，但也应该在“缩小的”范围内接受这些训练的措施。对于竞技乒乓球运动员而言，训练必须如此有计划地进行，才能在大型比赛中获得理想的竞技能力。

对于俱乐部和协会的竞技体育项目而言，将全年的训练安排分成不同的周期是必不可少的一种基本做法。对于乒乓球运动而言，将全年的训练

jumping exercises, gymnastics and stretching exercises, reaction exercises, and finally a few sprint runs can be scheduled.

Time: 10% of the total time.

2. The Main Section

Objective: improving and enhancing the technical and tactical skills of the athletes for the game of table tennis.

Exercises: training and game of table tennis.

Time: 70% of the total time.

3. The Ending Section

Objective: Harmonious ending, improving and enhancing athletes' physical fitness.

Exercises: all team sports (soccer and basketball), but also circuit training or relaxation exercises, such as stretching exercises.

Time: 20% of the total time.

IV. Periodic Training

For table tennis training for recreational purposes, a clear training organization is not required, however, training should also be done within a “reduced” scope. For competitive table tennis players, training must be planned in order to achieve the desired ability in major competitions.

For competitive sports organized by club and association, it is essential to divide the training schedule into several part throughout the year as a basic practice. For table tennis,

安排分成三个周期证明是可取的：

- 准备期；
- 比赛期；
- 过渡期。

准备期的训练以明显强调体能领域的训练为特点，而比赛期的训练则对技术和战术的训练给予特别的重视。过渡期的训练应该通过其他的体育运动项目随之安排一个“轻松的”训练结尾部分。

如果运动员无法得到周期性的训练，那么运动员就会有过度训练的危险。其状况以无精打采、缺乏训练投入和对所有训练失去兴趣为特征。在这种情况下必须减少和降低训练的量和强度。

dividing the training schedule into three cycles throughout the year has proven to be desirable and effective.

- Preparation period.
- Competition period.
- Transition period.

The preparation period is characterized by an emphasis on physical fitness training, while the training in the competition period is characterized by technical and tactical training. Training in the transition period should be followed by a "easier" training end using other sports.

If the athlete doesn't receive periodic training, then the athlete is in danger of overtraining. The state of the athlete is characterized by lethargy, lack of training commitment and loss of interesting. In such cases the volume and intensity of training must be reduced and decreased.

五、训练负荷

对于制订训练计划而言，一个非常重要的因素就是训练负荷的正确的量和强度的安排。训练负荷的量和强度包括以下一些指标：

- 年龄，性别；
- 训练和健康现状；
- 休闲选手还是竞技体育运动员；

V. Training Load

A very important factor in developing training plan is the correct amount and intensity of the training load. The amount and intensity of the training load contains some of the following indicators.

- Age, gender.
- Training and health status.
- Recreational or competitive athletes.

➢ 气候,时间。

● 在训练过程中负荷太大以下列情况为特征:

➢ 脉搏次数只是慢慢下降;

➢ 脸色非常红或者非常苍白。

● 在训练之后可能会出现以下负面的反应:

➢ 疲劳;

➢ 无精打采;

➢ 虚弱。

当这些负面反应出现时则必须在今后的训练中在更低的训练负荷范围内安排训练。

➢ Climate, time.

● Too much load during training is characterized by the following conditions.

➢ Pulse count decreasing slowly.

➢ Very red or very pale face.

● After training the following negative reactions may occur.

➢ Fatigue.

➢ Lethargy.

➢ Weakness.

When negative reactions showed up, you must schedule future training with a lower training load.

六、初学者训练

1. 无球台练习

根据"由易到难"的基本原则,可以安排初学者进行熟悉乒乓球器材的练习。

(1)综合练习:颠球,拍球,平衡。

目标:熟悉球拍和球。

● 练习1:在球拍上颠球。

● 练习2:用球拍在地面上拍球,进行正手和反手球性适应练习。

● 练习3:在走和跑的过程中用正手和反手在球拍上掌握球的平衡。

VI. Beginner Training

1. Practice Without Table

According to the basic principle of "from easy to difficult", we can arrange exercises for beginners to familiarize themselves with the table tennis equipment.

(1)Comprehensive exercises: ball bouncing, ball tapping, balancing.

Objective: To become familiar with the racket and the ball.

● Exercise 1: Bouncing the ball over using the racket.

● Exercise 2: Acclimatization exercises that tapping the ball on the ground by forehand and backhand.

● Exercise 3: Balancing the ball on the racket with the forehand and backhand during

● 练习 4:练习 1~3 的变化可能性:

➢ 柔和和用力地颠球或者拍球。

➢ 交替进行颠球和拍球。

➢ 交替使用正手和反手击球等。

(2)综合练习:对墙击球。

目标:基本姿势和触球稳定性训练。

● 练习 1:使用正手或者反手对墙、门等击球,让球飞回后落地反弹一次。

● 练习 2:其余要求同上,但是击球超过墙上标记的高度(高度为 1 m)。

● 练习 3:不让飞回的球利落地反弹,而是在空中直接(截击)击球。

● 练习 4:在墙上标记出一块区域(3 m×3 m),然后完成练习 1 和练习 2。

(3)综合练习:击球越过绳子、长凳或者乒乓球挡板。

目标:掌握乒乓球运动的大体形式。

● 练习 1:使用正手或者反手击球。

walking and running.

● Exercise 4: Possibility of variations of Exercises 1 to 3:

➢ Soft and hard bouncing the ball using racket.

➢ Alternating bouncing and tapping.

➢ Alternating forehand and backhand.

(2)General Exercise: Hitting the ball against the wall.

Objective: Basic posture and touch stability training.

● Exercise 1: Using the forehand or backhand to hit the ball against the wall. Let the ball fly back and bounce once on the ground.

● Exercise 2: The rest of the requirements are the same as above, but hitting the ball over the height marked on the wall (1 meter in height).

● Exercise 3: Instead of letting the ball bounce back sharply, hitting the ball directly in the air (interception).

● Exercise 4: Mark an area on the wall (3 m×3 m) and complete Exercises 1 and 2.

(3)Integrated exercise: hitting the ball over a rope, bench or table tennis stopper.

Objective: To master the general form of the table tennis game.

● Exercise 1: Hitting the ball with the forehand or backhand.

● 练习 2:不让飞回的球落地反弹,而是在空中直接(截击)击球。

● Exercise 2: Not letting the ball fly back to the ground and bounce, but hitting the ball directly in the air (interception).

● 练习 3:练习 1 和练习 2 的变化可能性:

➢ 4 人一组练习(双打比赛);

➢ 只击打直线球或者斜线球;

➢ 交替使用反手和正手击球;

➢ 柔和和有力地击球;

➢ 每隔一次击球时不让球落地反弹,而在空中直接击球。

● Exercise 3: Possibility of variations of Exercises 1 and 2:

➢ Practice in groups of 4 (doubles matches).

➢ Hit only straight or diagonal balls.

➢ Alternating backhand and forehand strokes.

➢ Soft and hard strokes.

➢ Don't let the ball bounce on the ground every other stroke but hit it directly in the air.

2. 有球台练习

● 要点

在刚开始进行有球台练习时,应该不安装球网。这样的话练习者就能够更长时间地处于击球练习状态。

● 练习举例

(1)挥拍动作抓球练习。练习者将乒乓球弹在本方球台的底线区域,在球的最高点时,按照正手徒手挥拍的方式挥臂并用手抓住弹起的球。

(2)尽量使用正手或者反手击球过网,尽可能朝对方半台的中间击球。目标:触球和击球过网。

2. Practice with a Table

● Key Points:

When you first start practicing with a table, you should not install a net. This way the ball can be in practice for a longer period of time.

● Examples of exercises:

(1) Swinging racket while catching the ball practice: The player bounces the ball on the table and swings his arm with a forehand style; finally grabs the bouncing ball with his hands at the highest point of the ball.

(2) Try to hit the ball over the net using forehand or backhand, as far as possible towards the middle of the opponent's court. Goal: touching and hitting the ball over the net.

第五节 营养训练
Section 5 Nutritional Training

运动员在进行乒乓球训练和比赛时都需要身体热量，以提供最佳表现所需的能量。营养训练对提供训练课程和比赛所需的能量至关重要。人体必须适时获得足够的热量，以提供所需的能量。

Both training and match-play need fuelling in order to provide the energy required to perform at your best. Nutritional training is vital to make sure enough of the right time to provide the energy needed for training sessions and competitive play. It is essential that the body receives the correct fuel at the correct time to supply the energy needed.

然而，通过训练自己在正确的时间吃正确的食物，你可以在训练和比赛中取得更好的成绩。适合你的“正确”食物可能与其他人的食物大不相同，因此你需要记录你在比赛和训练的不同阶段吃了什么以及感觉如何，以便为自己找到“正确”的饮食计划。

By training yourself to eat the right foods at the right time, however, you can achieve better performances both in training sessions and competition. The “right” foods for you may be very different from those for anyone else, so you will need to keep a record of what you eat and how you feel at different stages of a competition and training session in order to find the “right” eating programme for yourself.

参加乒乓球正式比赛，你需要了解自己吃什么食物以及什么时候就餐：即赛前、比赛中和赛后。就餐时间和内容将根据你自己的要求和那些不同情况下的食物耐受性而定。因此，在全天的训练课程中进行实验是很重要的，首先要找出在不同时间最适合你的饮食计划，然后在一次比赛中进行尝试。以下有一些一般性的指导方

Competition requires you to find out about what and when to eat: pre-competition, during an event and post-competition. The timing and content will be individual to your own requirements and food tolerances in these different situations. It is therefore important to experiment during full-day training sessions, first to find out what suits you best at different times and then to try this out at an event.

针可以帮助你做出这些决定，但是运动营养师可以提供比这更详细的建议，并可以为你设计一个个人计划。

There are some general guidelines to help you make these decisions but a sports nutritionist will be able to advise you in more detail than is possible here, and devise an individual programme for you.

一、比赛前饮食

在比赛前的一周，应确保摄入大量的复合碳水化合物。在两餐之间，可食用包括基于碳水化合物的零食，其示例见表 5.5.1。比赛前一天也要多喝些水。赛前当晚饮食的重点仍然是摄入足够的碳水化合物，确保体内肝糖原的储备达到最大量。

I. Pre-competition

In the week leading up to an event ensure a high intake of complex carbohydrates. In between meals include a carbohydrate-based snack, examples of which are given in Table 5.5.1. Also drink plenty of water the day before an event. On the night before the game, the focus of diet is still to eat enough carbohydrates to ensure that the liver glycogen reserve in the body reaches the maximum.

表 5.5.1 适宜的富含碳水化合物的零食　　Table 5.5.1 Suitable Carbo-rich Snacks

小罐头水果	Small cans of fruit
香蕉	Bananas
水果面包	Fruit bread
低脂谷物棒	Low-fat cereal bars
普通饼干或薄脆饼干	Plain biscuit or crackers
米糕（上面有果酱、蜂蜜或香蕉）	Rice cakes (topped with jam, honey or banana)
新鲜沙拉	Fresh salad
果酱或蜂蜜三明治	Jam or honey sandwiches
米饭	Rice
燕麦粥	Oatmeal porridge
无糖果汁，低脂酸奶或牛奶	Sugar free juice, low-fat yogurt or milk
水果干	Dried fruit

二、比赛期间饮食

在第一场比赛前 2~3 h 吃顿饭，以便在休息一晚后补充血糖水平。这顿饭不应该吃太多，应该富含复合碳水化合物，而脂肪含量较低，因为脂肪会加速消化，你将无法在足够长的时间内保持这些脂肪。补充水分也很重要，所以要在比赛前 2 h 喝两杯水，在第一场比赛前 15~30 min 再喝一杯。在持续 20 min 以上的比赛中，多喝水是很重要的。

II. During an Event

Take a meal about 2-3 hours before your first match in order to top up blood glucose levels after a night's rest. The meal should not be too large and should be high in complex carbohydrates and low in fat, because fat speeds up digestion and you will not sustain the benefits long enough into the event. It is also important to take on fluids, so drink two cups of water 2 hours before and another one about 15-30 minutes before your first match. In matches lasting more than 20 minutes it is important to take on more fluid.

少食多餐通常是最好的方法，因为吃得太多会让你感到沉重和昏昏欲睡。所以，如果比赛间隔不到 1 h，只需补充液体，但如果有更多的时间，则可以在比赛间隙吃点儿零食。比赛间歇时的零食应在 1~2 h 的休息时间内食用，表 5.5.1 中列出的富含碳水化合物的零食就是最合适的。试着在训练期或比赛时随身携带这些食品，因为这些食品可能在比赛场地内不可用。

Little and often is the best approach as eating too much can make you feel heavy and lethargic. So if there is less than an hour between matches replace fluids only, but if there is more time eat an in-between snack. In-between snacks should be eaten during any break of 1-2 hours and the carbo-rich snacks listed in Table 5.5.1 are most suitable. Try to take a supply of these with you to a training session or competition, as they may not be available at the venue.

三、比赛后饮食

这一时期的饮食是非常重要的，其目标是补充肝糖原和肌糖原，提供蛋白质，修复和生长适应肌肉细胞，并通过补充因出汗而流失的水分和电解质来重新补充身体水分。

Ⅲ. Post-competition

This period is very important and the goals are to refuel liver and muscle glycogen stores, provide protein to repair and grow the adapting muscle cells and re-hydrate the body by replacing the water and electrolytes lost

食用富含碳水化合物的零食能够保持糖原储存水平，如果与含有蛋白质的零食结合食用，将促进肌肉蛋白质的合成，促进肌肉细胞的生长和修复。

在比赛或训练之前和之后记录你的体重，可以显示你已经失去了多少水分，需要补充多少水分。每损失1 kg体重，就应饮用1 L水。

仅通过饮水可能不足以使身体重新补充水分，因为还必须考虑电解质（盐）平衡。当今，运动饮料不断被开发，其含有钠、其他电解质和/或葡萄糖聚合物，这些物质易于消化，有助于延缓糖原消耗。运动饮料有三种类型：低渗、等渗和高渗。它们的主要区别在于溶液中溶质的浓度不同。在乒乓球比赛中，几乎所有的比赛都会持续不到一个小时，所以最合适的运动饮料应该是低渗饮料。这种类型的溶质浓度最低，水也同样合适（尽管有些运动员可能更喜欢运动饮料的味道）。然而，训练时间比比赛时间要长得多，含有较高浓度溶质的运动饮料可能更有益。

through sweating.

The consumption of a carbo-rich snack will store the glycogen levels and if this is combined with a snack containing protein, muscle protein synthesis will be promoted for the growth and repair of muscle cells.

Recording your weight before and after competition or a training session will give an indication of how much water has been lost and how much needs to be replaced. For every 1 kg lost, 1 litre of water should be drunk.

Drinking water alone may not be enough to re-hydrate the body, as the elecrolyte (salt) balance must also be considered. Nowadays sport drinks are continually being developed, and contain sodium, other electrolytes and/or glucose polymer, which is easily digested and can help to delay glycogen depletion. There are three types of sports drinks: hypotonic, isotonic and hypertonic, and they differ in the concentration of solutes in the solution. In table tennis nearly all matches will last less than an hour so the most appropriate sports drink would be a hypotonic one. This type has the lowest concentration of solutes and water is just as suitable (although some players may prefer the taste of a sport drink). However, training sessions last much longer than a match and a sports drink containing a higher concentration of solutes may be more beneficial.

提示：

适当的恢复零食：

- 500 mL 低脂奶昔；
- 200 g 低脂酸奶和一根麦片棒或香蕉或一杯水果沙拉；
- 用瘦肉（火腿、鸡肉或牛肉）或奶酪填充的三明治。

Tips:

Appropriate Recover Snacks:

- 500 mL of a low-fat milkshake.
- 200 g of low-fat yogurt and a cereal bar or banana or cup of fruit salad.
- A sandwich with lean meat (ham, beef or chicken) or cheese filling.

第六章　乒乓球教学计划

Chapter 6　Planning for Teaching Table Tennis

第一节　学期教学计划

Section 1　Semester Plan

在这一节里，将介绍教师怎样制订学期教学计划。学期教学计划是一个学期训练的框架。一份组织缜密、科学的教学计划，有助于提高教学效率，可使整个学期的教学、训练工作有条不紊、循序渐进。

In this section, you will learn how to create your semester plan, which is a framework for the practices that make up your semester. A well-articulated and scientific plan helps to improve the teaching efficiency and makes your teaching and training proceed in an orderly way.

在大部分学校中，每学期会安排12~16周的乒乓球课。以下是一个学期、包含32节课的教学计划样式，适用于中学或大学的乒乓球课。在教学期间，如果有学生跟不上某项技术的学习进度或者教师的时间和课程规划有冲突，都需要对教学计划进行调整。在每节课的训练开始前，教师必须带领学生做热身运动，并在下课之前进行放松活动。

Most school table tennis semesters vary in length from 12 to 16 weeks. Shown below is a sample one-semester, 32-Lesson plan for students in a middle school or a university. If a student is not capable of doing a specific drill, change to a simpler drill. If you run into time problems, change the schedule. You may want to start each session with a warming-up exercise and end up with a cooling down exercise.

第一课

(1)介绍乒乓球

➢ 概况；

Lesson 1

(1)Introduction to table tennis

➢ General introduction.

➢ 乒乓球简要规则；
➢ Rules.

➢ 乒乓球器材。
➢ Equipment.

(2)握拍法
(2)Grip

➢ 示范直握球拍和横握球拍法；
➢ Demonstrate shake-hands and pen hold grips.

➢ 让学生进行模仿握拍练习。
➢ Have students demonstrate grips.

(3)颠球练习
(3)Ball bouncing

➢ 示范颠球练习；
➢ Demonstration.

➢ 让学生进行模仿颠球练习；
➢ Have students practice.

➢ 计连续颠球次数。
➢ See how many they can do in a row.

(4)自由练习或颠球接力
(4)Free play or relay races

第二课
Lesson 2

(1)复习颠球练习
(1)Review the ball bouncing practice

(2)颠球游戏
(2)Ball bouncing game

(3)学习正手攻球技术
(3)Study the forehand drive

➢ 教师示范正手攻球动作；
➢ Forehand demonstration.

➢ 学生正手攻球徒手挥拍练习；
➢ Class shadow-strokes forehand together.

➢ 多球练习正手攻球。
➢ Forehand practice by multi-ball drills.

(4)正手攻球接力
(4)Forehand drive rally

第三课
Lesson 3

(1)复习正手攻球
(1)Review the forehand drive

➢ 正手攻球徒手挥拍练习；
➢ Class shadow-strokes forehand together.

➢ 正手攻打多球练习；
➢ Forehand practice by using multi-ball drills.

➢ 老师供球，和学生一对一正手攻球练习。
➢ Instructor feed the ball to the student. He should move from table to table and try to work with each player individually.

（2）正手攻球接力

（3）示范发球

➢ 正手发上旋球；

➢ 正手发下旋球；

➢ 学生发球练习。

第四课

（1）正手徒手挥拍练习

（2）正手攻球练习

➢ 老师一对一供球；

➢ 学生正手对攻练习。

（3）学生正手对正手比赛

第五课

（1）学习反手攻球技术

➢ 反手攻球动作示范；

➢ 反手徒手挥拍练习；

➢ 反手攻打多球练习。

（2）学生正手对攻练习

（3）力量素质训练

第六课

（1）复习反手攻球

➢ 反手攻球徒手挥拍练习；

➢ 反手攻打多球练习；

➢ 老师供球，和学生一对一反手攻球练习。

（2）示范反手发球

➢ 反手发上旋球；

（2）Forehand drive rally

（3）Serve demonstration

➢ Forehand topspin serve.

➢ Forehand backspin serve.

➢ Serve practice.

Lesson 4

（1）Class shadow-strokes forehand together

（2）Forehand practice

➢ Instructor feed the ball to the student.

➢ Forehand to forehand practice.

（3）Forehand to forehand match

Lesson 5

（1）Study the backhand drive

➢ Backhand demonstration.

➢ Class shadow-strokes backhand together.

➢ Backhand practice by using multi-ball drills.

（2）Forehand to forehand practice

（3）Strength training

Lesson 6

（1）Review the backhand drive

➢ Class shadow-strokes backhand together.

➢ Backhand practice by using multi-ball drills.

➢ Instructor feed the ball to the student and try to work with each player individually.

（2）Backhand serve demonstration

➢ Forehand topspin.

➢ 反手发下旋球。

(3)学生发球练习

第七课

(1)正手对攻练习

(2)反手攻球练习

➢ 老师一对一供球;

➢ 学生反手对攻练习。

(3)学生反手对反手比赛

第八课

(1)乒乓球理论教学

➢ 乒乓球运动发展史。

第九课

(1)学习步法

➢ 老师做单步、并步、侧身步和交叉步的动作示范;

➢ 学生进行步法的模仿练习。

(2)用并步做左推右攻的练习

(3)用侧身步做推挡侧身的练习

第十课

(1)复习所学步法

(2)复习左推右攻练习

(3)复习推挡侧身练习

(4)学习用交叉步做推侧扑练习

➢ Forehand backspin.

(3)Serve practice

Lesson 7

(1)Forehand to forehand practice

(2)Backhand practice

➢ Instructor feed the ball to the student.

➢ Backhand to backhand practice.

(3)Backhand to backhand match

Lesson 8

(1)Table tennis theory

➢ The Evolutionary History of Table Tennis.

Lesson 9

(1)Study the footwork

➢ Demonstrate single step, level step, pivot step, and cross step.

➢ Have students practice.

(2)Backhand block with forehand attack by using level step

(3)Have a pivot drill by using pivot step

Lesson 10

(1)Review the footwork

(2)Review the backhand block with forehand attack drill

(3)Review the pivot drill

(4)Learn the Falkenberg drill with cross step

第十一课

(1)复习推挡侧身扑正手

(2)学习搓球技术

➢ 正手和反手搓球动作示范;

➢ 学生搓球徒手挥拍练习;

➢ 多球练习搓球技术;

➢ 老师供球,和学生一对一搓球练习。

(3)力量素质训练

Lesson 11

(1)Review the Falkenberg drill with cross step

(2)Study the push stroke

➢ Forehand and backhand demonstration.

➢ Class shadow-strokes forehand and backhand together.

➢ Push practice by using multi-ball drills.

➢ Instructor feed the ball to the student.

(3)Strength training

第十二课

(1)复习搓球技术

➢ 反手对搓练习;

➢ 正手对搓练习;

➢ 全台搓。

(2)擂台赛

Lesson 12

(1)Review the push stroke

➢ Backhand to backhand practice.

➢ Forehand to forehand practice.

➢ Push strokes on the full court.

(2)Challenge matches

第十三课

(1)复习正手攻球技术

(2)复习反手攻球技术

(3)学习正手扣杀技术

➢ 正手扣杀动作示范;

➢ 徒手挥拍练习;

➢ 正手扣杀多球练习。

Lesson 13

(1)Review the forehand drive

(2)Review the backhand drive

(3)Introduce the forehand smash

➢ Forehand smash demonstration.

➢ Class shadow-strokes forehand smash together.

➢ Forehand smash practice by using multi-ball drills.

第十四课

(1)正手扣杀练习

➢ 连续几板正手击上旋球后接

Lesson 14

(1)Forehand smash practice

➢ Forehand smash after sequences of

正手扣杀；

➢ 发不转球后正手扣杀。

（2）学习正手侧旋发球

➢ 发球示范；

➢ 发球练习。

（3）学习反手侧旋发球

➢ 发球示范；

➢ 发球练习。

（4）学习接发球

（5）发侧旋球抢攻比赛

第十五课

（1）发侧旋球练习

➢ 正手侧旋发球；

➢ 反手侧旋发球。

（2）接发球练习

➢ 摆短；

➢ 劈长；

➢ 挑打。

（3）速度素质训练

第十六课

（1）乒乓球理论教学

➢ 乒乓球竞赛规则和国际比赛竞赛规程。

（2）通知学期期中比赛事宜，并宣布比赛规则

第十七课

（1）组织学期中期比赛

（2）记录比赛成绩并排名

topspin drives.

➢ Forehand smash after little spin serve.

(2)Introduce the forehand sidespin serve

➢ Serve demonstration.

➢ Serve practice.

(3)Introduce the backhand sidespin serve

➢ Serve demonstration.

➢ Serve practice.

(4)Introducc thc receive

(5)Sidespin serve and attack games

Lesson 15

(1)Review the sidespin serve

➢ Forehand sidespin serve.

➢ Backhand sidespin serve.

(2)Receive practice

➢ Drop shot.

➢ Long push.

➢ Flip.

(3)Speed training

Lesson 16

(1)Tablc tcnnis theory teaching

➢ The basic laws and regulations for international competitions.

(2)Give a notice of the midterm competition and introduce the rules

Lesson 17

(1)Organizc the midterm game

(2)Record and rank

第十八课

(1)正手对攻练习

(2)左推右攻练习

(3)学习正手高吊弧圈球技术

➢ 正手高吊弧圈球动作示范;

➢ 徒手挥拍练习;

➢ 正手拉高吊弧圈球多球练习。

Lesson 18

(1)Forehand drive practice

(2)Backhand block with forehand attack drill

(3)Introduce the forehand high-spin loop

➢ Forehand high-spin loop demonstration.

➢ Class shadow-strokes forehand high-spin loop together.

➢ Forehand high-spin loop practice by using multi-ball drills.

第十九课

(1)正手高吊弧圈球练习

➢ 搓后拉高吊弧圈球;

➢ 发下旋球后抢拉高吊弧圈球。

(2)学习高抛发球和下蹲发球

➢ 发球动作示范;

➢ 学生练习。

(3)发球抢攻比赛

Lesson 19

(1)Forehand high-spin loop practice

➢ Forehand high-spin loop after sequences of push strokes.

➢ Forehand high-spin loop after backspin serve.

(2)Introduce the high-toss serve and squatting serve

➢ Serve demonstration.

➢ Serve practice.

(3)Serve and attack game

第二十课

(1)学习正手前冲弧圈球技术

➢ 正手前冲弧圈球动作示范。

(2)正手前冲弧圈球练习

➢ 正手前冲弧圈球多球练习;

➢ 正手连续攻打上旋球后接正手前冲弧圈球;

Lesson 20

(1)Introduce the forehand fast loop

➢ Forehand fast loop demonstration.

(2)Forehand fast loop practice

➢ Forehand fast loop practice by using multi-ball drills.

➢ Forehand fast loop after sequences of topspin drives.

➢ 搓后抢冲弧圈球。

➢ Forehand fast loop after sequences of push strokes.

(3)速度素质训练

(3)Speed training

第二十一天

Lesson 21

(1)推挡侧身练习

(1)Backhand with pivot attack drill

(2)正手前冲弧圈球练习

(2)Forehand fast loop practice

➢ 在反手位拉冲上旋球练习;

➢ Forehand fast loop against topspin feed on the backhand side.

➢ 在反手位拉冲下旋球练习;

➢ Fast forehand loop drive against backspin feed on the backhand side.

➢ 发球抢冲练习。

➢ Forehand fast loop after serve practice.

第二十二课

Lesson 22

(1)乒乓球理论教学

(1)Table tennis theory teaching

➢ 乒乓球基本理论知识。

➢ The basic theory of table tennis.

第二十三课

Lesson 23

(1)反手中台对攻练习

(1)Backhand to backhand practice at the mid-range from the table

(2)学习反手高吊弧圈球技术

(2)Introduce the backhand high-spin loop

➢ 反手拉高吊弧圈球动作示范;

➢ Backhand high spin loop demonstration.

➢ 徒手挥拍练习;

➢ Class shadow-strokes backhand high-spin loop together.

➢ 反手拉高吊弧圈球多球练习。

➢ Backhand high-spin loop practice by using multi-ball drills.

(3)柔韧性训练

(3)Flexibility training

第二十四课

Lesson 24

(1)反手拉高吊弧圈球练习

(1)Backhand high-spin loop practice

➢ 搓后拉高吊弧圈球;

➢ Backhand high-spin loop after sequences of push strokes.

➢ 发下旋球后拉高吊弧圈球。

➢ Backhand high-spin loop after backspin serve.

(2)学习反手前冲弧圈球技术

(2)Introduce the backhand fast loop

➢ 反手前冲弧圈球动作示范。

➢ Backhand fast loop demonstration.

(3)反手前冲弧圈球练习

(3)Backhand fast loop practice

➢ 反手前冲弧圈球多球练习。

➢ Backhand fast loop practice by using multi-ball drills.

➢ 反手连续攻打上旋球后接正手前冲弧圈球。

➢ Backhand fast loop after sequences of topspin drives.

第二十五课

Lesson 25

(1)反手前冲弧圈球练习

(1)Backhand fast loop practice

➢ 拉冲上旋球练习；

➢ Backhand fast loop against topspin feed.

➢ 拉冲下旋球练习；

➢ Fast backhand loop drive against backspin feed.

➢ 发球抢冲练习。

➢ Backhand fast loop after serve practice.

(2)关键分比赛

(2)Key point games

第二十六课

Lesson 26

(1)学习进攻战术

(1)Introduce the offensive tactics

➢ 对攻战术；

➢ Counter attack.

➢ 搓攻战术。

➢ Pushing attack.

(2)进攻战术的演练

(2)Offensive tactics practices

(3)擂台赛

(3)Challenge match

第二十七课

Lesson 27

(1)学习双打比赛规则

(1)Introduce the rules for doubles play

(2)学习双打比赛站位

(2)Introduce the formations for doubles play

(3)学习双打步法移动

(3)Introduce the movement patterns

(4)双打练习

(4)Doubles' practice

➢ 多球练习；

➢ Multi-ball drills.

➢ 双打选手打教师供球练习。

➢ Instructor feed the ball to the double.

第二十八课

Lesson 28

(1)双打练习

(1)Doubles' practice

➢ 多球练习；

➢ Multi-ball drills.

➢ 双打选手打教师供球练习。

➢ Instructor feed the ball to the double.

(2)双打比赛

(2)Doubles' game

(3)柔韧性训练

(3)Flexibility training

第二十九课

Lesson 29

(1)乒乓球理论教学

(1)Table tennis theory teaching

➢ 乒乓球基本战术与打法。

➢ The tactics and playing styles of table tennis.

(2)通知举行期末比赛,并宣布比赛规则

(2)Give a notice of the terminal competition and introduce the rules

(3)比赛抽签

(3)Draw for the game

第三十课

Lesson 30

(1)组织比赛

(1)Organize the final game

(2)记录比赛成绩并排名

(2)Record and rank

第三十一课

Lesson 31

(1)介绍考试内容

(1)Introduce the test content

(2)学生复习考试内容

(2)Students review the test content

第三十二课

Lesson 32

(1)考试

(1)Administer test

(2)老师对整个学期进行评价与总结

(2)Coach's evaluation and summarizations of the term

第二节　课时教学计划

Section 2　Lesson Plan

在完成学期教学计划的制订后，教师必须对每一堂训练课做更深入、

After you have created your semester plan, you have to take it a step further and

更翔实的规划。课时教学计划就能很好地发挥作用。对教师来说，制订一份详细的课时教学计划是很有必要的，从而对每堂训练课进行描述。课时教学计划应包括以下内容：

- 练习的日期和时间，课时长度；
- 练习目标；
- 所需器材；
- 准备活动；
- 复习所学技术；
- 教授新技术；
- 放松活动；
- 教师讲评。

应根据学期教学计划，按以上内容编写课时教学计划。表 6.2.1 为课时教学计划的模板格式。

specify in detail what you will be doing at every practice. The lesson plan can play this role. For the teacher, it is necessary to develop a specific lesson plan, which outlines how you will approach each practice.Every lesson plan should include the following.

- Date, time of practice, and length of practice session.
- Practice objective.
- Equipment needed.
- Warm-up.
- Practicing previously taught skills.
- Teaching and practicing new skills.
- Cool-down.
- Coaches' comments and evaluation of practice.

Using these elements, you can develop a lesson practice plan based on the semester plan. Table 6.2.1 shows a sample lesson plan.

表 6.2.1 课时教学计划

练习时间:9 月 7 日,星期一
练习开始时间:8:00 a.m.
练习时长:90 min
练习目标:正手对攻和反手攻球
练习器材:乒乓球、球拍

时间	活动名称	教学内容	教学要求
上午 8:00—8:05	练习前的讲评	学生迅速整队集合,教师介绍本节课的学习任务	
上午 8:05—8:15	热身运动	学生通过慢跑和一些伸直运动进行热身	➢ 保持运动 ➢ 把肌肉充分活动开
上午 8:15—8:35	复习:正手攻球技术	学生正手对攻练习	➢ 失误较少 ➢ 击球前合理引拍 ➢ 击球点较固定
上午 8:35—9:10	学习新技术:反手攻球技术	教师介绍并示范反手攻球动作。之后,学生进行反攻球的徒手挥拍练习和多球练习。教师注意纠正学生的错误动作	➢ 引拍 ➢ 击球点 ➢ 落点 ➢ 肌肉不要紧张
上午 9:10—9:25	比赛:限定条件比赛	比赛为三局两胜,学生只能用反手攻球技术进行比赛。输球的一方接受惩罚	➢ 控制好落点 ➢ 击球命中率高 ➢ 击球后迅速还原
上午 9:25—9:30	教师讲评	学生迅速整队集合,教师对本次训练进行回顾和总结,并对下节课进行预告	

Table 6.2.1 Lesson Plan

Date: Monday, September 7

Practice Start Time: 8:00 a.m.

Length of Practice: 90 minutes

Practice Objectives: To practice rally skill using forehand and backhand drives.

Equipment: Balls, rackets.

Time	Name of activity	Description	Key teaching point
8:00-8:05 a.m.	Prepractice meeting	Students assemble quickly and coach introduces the learning task	
8:05-8:15 a.m.	Warm-up	Students warm up by light jogging and some stretching movements	➢ Keep moving ➢ Stretching out your muscle.
8:15-8:35 a.m.	Skill review: Forehand drive	Two students forehand to forehand practice	➢ Few errors ➢ Good backswing for shots ➢ Good contact point on every shot
8:35-9:10 a.m.	New skill: Backhand drive	The coach introduces and demonstrates the backhand drive. Students practice the skill by performing the following: shadow-strokes, and multi-ball drills. The coach should pay attention to students' mistakes	➢ Backswing ➢ Contact point ➢ Placement ➢ Don't be tense
9:10-9:25 a.m.	Game: Conditional game	Players are only able to play with backhand shots. Best of three games. The losers receive punishment	➢ Control ➢ Consistency ➢ Recover quickly
9:25-9:30 a.m.	Coach's comments	Students assemble quickly, while coach reviews this practice and announces the topic for next practice	

第七章 乒乓球课程思政教学

Chapter 7 Ideological and Political Education of Table Tennis

中国教育部指出，课程思政建设要在全国所有高校、所有学科专业全面推进，并打造一批有特色的体育、美育类课程。课程思政是指高校的所有课程都要发挥思想政治教育作用，其实质是将高校思想政治教育融入课程教学和改革的各环节、各方面。乒乓球是一门在我国高校开课率和普及率很高的体育课程。乒乓球运动的自身特点和作为中国“国球”在国际上取得的辉煌成就（图 7.1.1），使其在课堂教

图 7.1.1 容国团（中国第一个世界冠军运动员）

Figure 7.1.1 Rong Guotuan (The First World Champion Player in China)

The Ministry of Education of People's Republic of China pointed out that the ideological and political education in courses should be comprehensively promoted in all universities and disciplines across China, and a number of distinctive sports and aesthetic courses should be established accordingly. Ideological and Political Education in courses requires that all courses in universities should educate students with ideological and political knowledges, which in essence is to integrate ideological and political education into all sections and aspects of courses teaching and reform in higher education. Table tennis course is a physical education course that enjoys great popularity in China's universities. The characteristics of table tennis, as well as China's glorious international achievements in table tennis as Chinese 'national ball' (Figure 7.1.1) add the sport with unique advantages to take the lead in carrying out ideological and political education in courses. The course can help students strengthen their

学中开展“课程思政”发挥“价值引领”方面具备独特的优势。乒乓球教学过程既可帮助学生增强体质、健全人格、锤炼意志,又有助于激发学生的爱国主义情怀和创新精神。

physical fitness, personality and will, as well as enhance their patriotism and innovative spirit.

第一节　思政课程教学案例

Section 1　Teaching Cases of Ideological and Political Education

一、教学案例1:乒乓外交

1971年,世乒赛在日本名古屋市举行,此前中国因众所周知的原因连续缺席了两届世乒赛。时任日本乒协主席的后藤钾二不顾日本国内右翼分子的威胁,力排众议,亲自赴北京力邀中国乒乓球队赴日参赛,促成中国队出现在了名古屋世乒赛赛场上。正是在名古屋世乒赛上,中美“乒乓外交”也拉开了序幕。之后,中、美乒乓球队互访推动了中、美关系正常化,对日后中、日邦交正常化也带来了积极的影响,被誉为“小球推动大球”的“乒乓外交”。

Ⅰ. Teaching Case 1: Ping-pong Diplomacy (Table Tennis Diplomacy)

In 1971, the World Table Tennis Championships were held in Nagoya, Japan. Before that, China had been absent for two consecutive world Table Tennis Championships due to well-known reasons. Goto, then president of Japan Table Tennis Association, disregarding the threat from the right-wing people in Japan, defied the public opinion and went to Beijing to invite the Chinese table tennis team to play in Japan, which promoted the Chinese team to appear in the Nagoya World Table Tennis Championships. It was at the Nagoya World Table Tennis Championships that the “Ping-pong diplomacy” between China and the United States began. After that, the mutual visits of the Chinese and American table tennis teams promoted the normalization of Sino-US relations and had a positive impact on the normalization of Sino-Japanese relations in the future. It was known as "Ping-pong diplomacy" of "small ball pushing big ball".

1971年，在中、美领导人的直接推动下，两国乒乓球队实现了互访（图7.1.2），从而结束了长期互相隔绝的状态，揭开了中美关系新的序幕，被称为"小球转动了地球"。原国际奥委会主席萨马兰奇在一次贺电中说："20世纪70年代初促使中美两国关系发展的'乒乓外交'，生动地展示了体育在促进世界和平、增进各国人民之间的友谊和互相了解方面，起到了多么积极的作用！"而"乒乓外交"的成功又大大提高了中国乒乓球队的社会声望。他们的声名在全中国、全世界广为传扬。这一方面促使他们从思想上、组织上和道德作风上更加高标准地严格要求自己，努力维护自己的公众形象；另一方面也为乒乓球运动的发展创造了更加良好的外部环境。

In 1971, under the direct promotion of the leaders of China and the United States, the table tennis teams of the two countries realized the exchange of visits (Figure 7.1.2), thus ending the long-term isolation from each other and opening a new prelude to Sino-US relations, which is called "small ball turns the earth". In a congratulatory message, former IOC President Juan Antonio Samaranch said, "The 'Ping-pong diplomacy' that promoted the development of Sino-US relations in the early 1970s vividly demonstrated the positive role sports played in promoting world peace and enhancing friendship and mutual understanding between people of all countries!" The success of "ping-pong diplomacy" greatly enhanced the social prestige of the Chinese ping-pong team. Their fame spread throughout China and the world. On the one hand, it urges them to be stricter with themselves in terms of ideology, organization and moral style, and strive to maintain their own public image. On the other hand, it also creates a better external environment for the development of table tennis.

图 7.1.2　美国乒乓球队访华并与中国队比赛

Figure 7.1.2　The American Table Tennis Team Visited China and Played Against the Chinese Team

二、教学案例 2:创新精神使国乒长盛不衰并引领世界乒乓球运动的发展

Ⅱ.Teaching Case 2: The spirit of innovation makes China Table Tennis prosperous and leads the development of table tennis in the world

国乒长盛不衰的秘诀之一就是依靠技术创新勇站潮头,中国乒乓队鼓励技术上的“百花齐放”和学术上的“百家争鸣”。乒乓球队倡导创新,支持探索新的技术和打法。

One of the secrets of the everlasting prosperity of the Chinese table tennis is to rely on technological innovation to bravely stand on the trend. The Chinese table tennis team encourages technical “a hundred flowers bloom” and academic “a hundred schools of thought contend”. The table tennis team advocates innovation and supports the exploration of new techniques and styles of play.

中国乒乓球运动员努力求新求

Chinese players strive for novelty and

变,并善于从偶然中捕捉必然。高抛发球的创新发明,是有人在偶然中发现球从高处落下,加上手臂和腕部的发力能增强旋转。许绍发刻意去练习,后来终于在世界大赛上立下奇功。这种发球,至今仍被各国选手使用。到了 20 世纪 80 年代后期,我国直拍近台快攻反手的弱点越来越明显,面对欧洲选手凶狠的两面拉弧圈球进攻常处于被动地位。要想摆脱困境,必须创新。教练员与科研人员经过精心试验和论证,终于推出“直板横打”的新技术。刘国梁、王皓等人率先苦练新打法,从不习惯到运用自如,最终在比赛中见到成效。“直拍横打”的新技术现在已被许多直拍运动员包括一些亚洲选手掌握和运用,同时还派生出一些新的打法。技术创新不仅使我国形成了传统的直拍正胶、反胶快攻,还形成了具有中国特色的横拍快攻结合弧圈和防守结合进攻等打法,例如张继科的特色横拍反手拧拉技术。中国队在打法品类方面做到了“外国有的我们有,外国没有的我们也有”。

change, and are good at catching the inevitable from the accidental. The high toss was invented by someone who accidentally discovered that the spin of the ball would be enhanced by the power of the arm and wrist as it fell from above. The Chinese table tennis player Xu Shaofa practiced high toss specifically, and then finally made an important contribution in the world table tennis games. This kind of serve is still used by players of all countries. In the late 1980s, the weakness of backhand of China's pen-hold grips close to table fast attack became more and more obvious. Facing European players' fierce double-sided topspin offense, it was often in a passive position. If you want to get out of the predicament, you must innovate. After careful experimentation and demonstration by coaches and scientific researchers, the new technology of "pen-hold reverse backhand stroke" was finally launched. Liu Guoliang, Wang Hao and others took the lead in practicing the new techniques, and realized the process from never getting used to mastering them more freely to using them effectively in the competition. This style of play has been mastered and used by many pen-grip players and some new strokes have been derived. Technological innovation has not only formed the traditional pen-hold fast break with short pips-out rubber or inverted rubber, but also formed the shake-hands fast break combined with looping and defense combined with attack with Chinese characteristics. For example, Zhang Jike has a special shake-hands backhand twist-drive. The Chinese team achieved "we have what foreign countries have, and we also have what foreign countries do not have" in terms of playing styles.

中国运动员利用各种打法夺得世界冠军。据统计，截至 2001 年，在世界乒乓球运动的百年历程中，共有 46 项技术和打法的创新，其中 27 项属于中国健儿，占总数的 58.7%。技术创新推动着中国队长期处于国际乒坛的领先地位。要使学生认识到发展才是硬道理，科学之路上“唯有创新才有生命力”，做学问要有与时俱进、大胆实践的优秀品质。

Chinese players can win the world championship using various styles of play. According to statistics, as of 2001, in the century of world table tennis, there were 46 innovations in technology and play style, 27 of which belonged to Chinese athletes, accounting for 58.7% of the total. Technological innovation has promoted the Chinese team's long-term leading position in the international table tennis world. We must make students realize that development is the last word, "Only innovation can have vitality" on the road of science, and learning must have the excellent qualities of advancing with the times and boldly practicing.

三、教学案例 3：刘国正挽救七个赛点，率领中国队绝境反击

Ⅲ. Teaching Case 3: Liu Guozheng saved seven match points and led the Chinese team to fight back in desperation

2001 年世乒赛男子团体半决赛，中国队和韩国队狭路相逢。前四盘双方战成 2∶2 平，刘国正对金泽洙的比

In the men's team semifinals of the 2001 World Table Tennis Championships, the Chinese and South Korean teams came into an in-

赛是中韩男团半决赛的决胜盘比赛（图 7.1.3）。第二和第三局中，金泽洙共得到 7 个赛点，刘国正只要再输 1 分，全场比赛就宣告结束，如是，韩国人将是第一次有机会在最高级别的比赛中赢中国队。但是，年轻的刘国正凭着钢铁般的意志，成功地遏制了韩国人的胜利势头，他在中国队最困难、最艰难的时刻挽救了中国队。刘国正的精神，代表了中国人民不屈不挠、顽强拼搏的精神，体现了运动员们对祖国、人民的高度责任感。教师要教育学生像国乒队员一样磨炼自己强大的内心，培养学生在比赛中追求卓越、胜不骄败不馁的精神。

图 7.1.3　刘国正对金泽洙

Figure 7.1.3　Liu Guozheng vs Kim Taek Soo

evitable confrontation. In the first four sets, the two sides drew 2 : 2. The match between Liu Guozheng and Kim Taek-soo was the deciding set of the semi-finals of the Chinese and Korean men's teams(Figure 7.1.3). In the second and third rounds, Kim Taek Soo scored a total of 7 match points. As long as Liu Guozheng loses another point, the game will be over. If so, the Koreans will have the first chance to win China in the highest level of competition. However, the young Liu Guozheng succeeded in containing the momentum of victory of the Koreans with the will of steel. He saved the Chinese team at the most difficult time of the Chinese team. The spirit of Liu Guozheng represents the indomitable and tenacious spirit of the Chinese people, and embodies the athletes' high sense of responsibility to the motherland and people. Educate students to hone their strong heart like a national table tennis team, and cultivate students' spirit of pursuing excellence in the game and "not being arrogant and not discouraged".

四、教学案例 4:“公正”让我别无选择

在 2005 年上海世乒赛中,有一场令人难忘的淘汰赛,由中国选手刘国正对阵德国选手波尔(图 7.1.4)。前六局比赛双方比分为 3∶3,在决胜局中,刘国正 12∶13 落后,最后一球刘国正回球出界了。波尔的教练起立狂欢,准备冲进场内拥抱自己的弟子。就在这一瞬间,波尔却优雅地伸手示意,指向台边——这是个擦边球,应该是刘国正得分。就这样,刘国正被对手从悬崖边“救”了回来,最终反败为胜。

这是一场足以震撼世人的经典之战!不仅因为双方选手的高超球技和刘国正在绝境中的毅力,更因为波尔那个优雅的手势。对于波尔,夺取世界冠军一直是他的夙愿,但他却屡屡与冠军失之交臂。这一次,他如此接近自己的梦想,只要赢下那一分,就可顺利晋级。最后一球是否擦边或许只在 0.01 cm 之间,观众看不到,对手看不太清楚,裁判也可能错判。但是,波尔却毫不犹豫地选择了主动示意。波

Ⅳ. Teaching Case 4: “Justice” left me no choice

In the 2005 Shanghai World Table Tennis Championships, there was an unforgettable match between Chinese player Liu Guozheng and German player Tim Boll(Figure 7.1.4). The score between the two sides in the first six games was 3∶3. In the deciding game, Liu Guozheng fell behind by 12 to 13 and he returned the last ball out of table. Boll’s coach immediately stood up to celebrate and was ready to rush into the arena to embrace his disciple. At this moment, Boll stretched out his hand gracefully, pointing to the edge of the table— “this is a side ball, it should be Liu Guozheng scoring”. In this way, Liu Guozheng was saved back from the cliff by his opponent, and finally turned defeat into victory.

It’s a classic battle that can shock the world. Not only because of the superb skills of the players on both sides and Liu Guozheng’s perseverance in a desperate situation, but also because of Boll’s elegant gestures. For Boll, winning the world championship is his long-cherished wish, but he has repeatedly missed it. This time, he was so close to his dream that as long as he wins the last score, he can be promoted smoothly. Whether or not the ball is rubbed may only be

尔失利了，却赢得了观众雷鸣般的掌声。赛后，记者们追问他为何要这么做。他只是轻描淡写地说了句：“公正让我别无选择。”波尔不假思索地做出的那个动作，说明诚实已成为他的一种下意识的举动。将诚实变成一种习惯，这位赛场上的失败者给我们上了一堂生动的人生之课。

between 0.01 centimeters, the audience can't see it, the opponent can't see it clearly, and even the referee may make a wrong judgment. However, Boll did not hesitate to take the initiative to signal. Boll lost the game but won applause from audiences. After the game, reporters asked him why he did this. He just said lightly that "Justice left me no choice." The action Boll made almost without thinking is subconscious action originates from his honesty. Making being honest one's habit, the loser on the field taught us a vivid life lesson.

图 7.1.4　刘国正与蒂姆·波尔

Figure 7.1.4　Liu Guozheng and Timo Boll

人生就如一场比赛，只有拥有良好的品德，严格遵守赛场规则，才能真真正正地在比赛中获胜；失掉了品德，

Life is like a game. Only with good morals and strict compliance with the rules of the game can you truly win the game. If you lose

就注定将成为人生赛场上的一名败将。

your morals, you will be doomed to become a loser in the game of life.

五、教学案例5：体育的力量

V. Teaching Case 5: The power of sports

（1）体育不仅能壮筋骨，还能调感情、强意志，是人格教育的最好方式。人的全面发展从体育运动开始。运动员在赛场上奋力拼搏，是对卓越和荣誉的追求；为此艰苦训练，不断付出，考验的是敬业精神和意志力；最后在公平竞争中收获尊重和友谊，完成自我实现和超越。

(1)Sports can not only strengthen the body, but also regulate emotions and strengthen will. It is the best way of personality education. The all-round development of people begins with sports. When athletes struggle hard on the field, it is the pursuit of excellence and honor; the hard training that athletes pay for the competition tests professionalism and willpower; athletes finally gain respect and friendship in fair competition, complete self-realization and transcendence.

（2）体育教会我们要公平公正，遵守规则，体面并且有尊严地输；必须懂得尊重别人，包括尊重对手，尊重教练和尊重队友。

(2)Sports teaches us to be fair and just, obey the rules, lose with dignity and dignity. People must know how to respect others, opponents, coaches, and teammates.

（3）多从自己身上找问题。成功永远不会有捷径。任何成功的运动员，依靠的都是在训练场不断地挥洒着自己的汗水，注重身体素质的锻炼以及心理素质的提升。

(3)Look for problems more from yourself. There is never a shortcut to success. Any successful athlete depends on constantly swaying his sweat on the training ground, training his physical fitness and improving his mental quality.

（4）永远要向前看。球王贝利一生进球无数，但他总说自己打进的最精彩的球是下一个。人生有时就是在纠结中消耗、虚度，过去的一切都无法改变，着眼未来才是关键。

(4)Always look forward. Pele has scored countless goals throughout his life, but he always said that the most exciting goal he scored was the next one. Life is sometimes consumed and wasted in entanglement. Everything in the past cannot be changed. Focusing on the future is the key.

第二节　思政课程教学设计样例

Section 2　Example of Instructional Design of Ideological and Political Education

一、教学目标

➢ 知识目标:掌握正手攻球和正手发下旋球技术理论;了解发球的规则要求。

➢ 能力目标:掌握正手攻球和正手发下旋球技术动作方法,提高专项技能,增强身体素质。

➢ 价值目标:激发学生爱国热情和民族自豪感;启发学生在逆境中磨炼自己坚忍不拔的心理素质和意志品质,培养学生遵规守法意识。

Ⅰ. Teaching Objectives

➢ Knowledge Objectives: Students will master the technical theory of forehand attack and forehand backspin serve; Students will understand the rules of serve.

➢ Ability Objectives: Students will master the forehand attacking shot and forehand backspin shot, improve special skills, and enhance physical fitness.

➢ Value Objectives: The curriculum shall arouse students' patriotism and national pride, inspire students to temper their perseverance and will in adversity, and cultivate students' awareness of compliance and law-abiding.

二、乒乓球思政课程教学设计内容

1. 课前

教师结合中国乒乓球运动员的比赛照片和视频,引导学生们对国乒队员的优良传统和精神面貌进行了解和学习,激发他们的学习兴趣,帮助他们树立崇高的理想信念;同时,让学生欣

Ⅱ.Contents of Instructional Design of Ideological and Political Education in Table Tennis Curriculum

1. Before the Curriculum

The teacher will guide students to understand and learn the fine tradition and spiritual outlook of the Chinese table tennis players using photos and videos of the Chinese table tennis players, stimulate their interests in

赏乒乓球竞技运动中的击球速度、旋转和弧线的精妙之处,从而增强他们的审美意识。

learning, and help them establish lofty ideals and beliefs. Students will appreciate the subtleties of speed, rotation and trajectory in table tennis, thereby enhancing students' aesthetic awareness.

2. 课中

2. In the Curriculum

1)介绍本堂课的主要学习内容

1)Introduce the main content of the curriculum

乒乓球正手攻球技术的特点、作用和种类。

The teacher will introduce the main content of the curriculum: the technical characteristics, functions and types of table tennis forehand attacking technique.

2)切入国乒经典比赛案例——刘国正力挽狂澜七个赛点

2)Introduce the classic game of Chinese table tennis—Liu guozheng saved the game by saving seven match points

介绍国乒世界冠军刘国正在中国队和韩国队的世乒赛决胜盘当中,面临对手七个赛点时临危不乱,利用正手抢攻技术为中国队力挽狂澜的案例,既为学生直观地体现了正手攻球技术的重要性,又启发学生在逆境中磨炼自己坚忍不拔的心理素质,面对困难时要永不放弃。

The teacher will introduce the case that Liu guozheng, the Chinese table tennis world champion, saved the game using forehand attack technique when facing difficulties that his opponents had seven game points in the defining set of finals of World Table Tennis competition between China and Korea. The case shows students clearly the importance of forehand attack technique and inspires students to temper their mental quality of perseverance in adversity, and never give up when facing difficulties.

3）从乒乓球课程思政案例导入乒乓球专项技术教学——正手攻球技术学习

通过学习，让学生高度重视正手攻球技术的练习；让学生在练习中互相配合，提高团结协作的能力；教育学生从基础开始做起，练好基本功，做到从量变到质变。

● 教法

问题导向法，直观教学法，纠错法，体验感悟式、渗透式、启发式、互动式。

● 教学组织

（1）重复讲解正手攻球技术特点、作用和动作要领，再通过观看2001世乒赛刘国正比赛视频，讲解正手攻球的重要性，并培养学生敢于面对困难并迎难而上的顽强的意志品质。

（2）教师边讲解边做动作示范。

（3）徒手挥拍练习。

（4）自抛自打。

3）Combine the teaching of table tennis techniques with the ideological and political education in the lesson—forehand attack techniques

The teacher will make students attach great importance to the study of forehand attacking techniques. The teacher shall encourage students cooperate with each other in practice, improve the ability of unity and cooperation; teach them to start from the foundation and practice basic skills, so as to change from quantity to quality.

● Teaching method

problem-oriented, intuitive teaching method, error correction, experience perception, penetration, heuristic and interactive.

● Organization of teaching

（1）The teacher should repeatedly explain the technical characteristics, functions and action essentials of forehand attacking ball, and then explain the importance of forehand attacking ball by watching the video of Liu Guozheng's match in the 2001 World Table Tennis Championships, and train students to have the courage to face difficulties and grasp the nettle.

（2）The teacher demonstrates the techniques while explaining.

（3）Free hand swing practice.

（4）Students practice individually.

(5)和发球机练习。

(5)Students practice with the ball machine.

(6)教师进行个别指导。

(6)Individual instruction by teachers.

● 练习中的问题

● Questions in the practicing

(1)为什么正手攻球时球总是出左侧边线?

(1)Why does the ball go out of the left sideline when hit by forehand?

(2)为什么攻球不是下网就是出界?

(2)Why is the attacking ball either in the net or out of bounds?

(3)为什么攻球时感觉发不出力?

(3)Why do you feel unable to exert force when attacking the ball?

4)学习发球技术及发球规则

4)Study the techniques and rules of serve

结合乒乓球竞赛规则学习,讲述乒乓球经典比赛案例“公正让我别无选择”,培养学生高尚的道德品质,教育学生通过遵守运动规则,形成自觉遵纪守法意识,尊重对手和队友,服从集体安排。

In combination with the rules of table tennis competition, the teacher tells the classic case of table tennis competition “Justice leaves me no choice”, so as to cultivate students’ noble moral quality, educate students to form the consciousness of observing laws and regulations consciously, respect their opponents and teammates, and obey the collective arrangement by obeying the rules of sports.

● 教学组织

● Organization of teaching

(1)教师讲解规则的概念,切入乒乓球比赛经典案例“公正让我别无选择”。

(1)The teacher explained the concept of rules and cut into the classic case of table tennis “Justice leaves me no choice”.

(2)讲解发球规则。

(2)The teacher explains the serve rules.

(3)合法发球和各种不合法发球示范,给学生直观感受。

(3)The teacher demonstrates the legal serve and all kinds of illegal serve, giving students intuitive feelings.

(4)讲解下旋球的性质、特点。

(4)The teacher explains the nature and

characteristics of backspin.

(5)讲解和示范发正手下旋球的动作要领。

(5)The teacher explains and demonstrate the essentials of backspin forehand serve.

(6)学生徒手模仿练习发下旋球的技术动作。

(6)Students imitate and practice backspin technique with bare hands.

(7)一发一接,发10个球后交换,教师巡视指导。

(7)One serve and one catch, exchange after serving 10 balls, and the teacher will patrol and guide.

● 练习中的问题

● Questions during exercises

(1)为什么发出的球总是出左侧边线?

(1)Why does the ball always go out of the left sideline?

(2)为什么发出的球总是不过网?

(2)Why does the ball always go under the net?

(3)为什么发出的球不转?

(3)Why does the ball not spin?

3. 课后

3. After the Curriculum

教师通过专项技术、竞赛规则的教学和分组教学比赛过程反馈的学习状态进行总结,总结和检验学生的学习状态和学习效果。从课程思政出发引导学生反思自己是否完成教学目标,提升学生在乒乓球思政课上的获得感。

The teacher summarizes and tests students' learning status by the teaching of special techniques, competition rules and with feedback in the process of teaching competition in groups. The teacher guides students to reflect on whether they have fulfilled their learning objectives from the perspective of ideological and political education, help students to improve their sense of gain in ideological and political education in table tennis curriculum.

第八章　乒乓球竞赛规则

Chapter 8　Competition Rules of Table Tennis

第一节　基本规则

Section 1　Basic Rules

一、乒乓球比赛的物质条件

1. 球台

球台的上层表面，叫比赛台面。比赛台面应为与水平面平行的长方形，球桌长 2.74 m，宽 1.525 m，离地高 76 cm。比赛台面不包括球台台面的垂直侧面。

2. 球网装置

球网装置包括球网、悬网绳、网柱和夹钳部分。球网顶端距离比赛台面 15.25 cm。

3. 球

直径为 40 mm 的球体，重 2.7 g。球应由赛璐珞或类似的塑料制成，颜色为白色或橙色，无光泽。

Ⅰ. The Material Conditions of Table Tennis

1. The table

The upper surface of the table, known as the playing surface, shall be rectangular, 2.74 m long and 1.525 m wide, and shall lie in a horizontal plane 76 cm above the floor. The playing surface shall not include the vertical sides of the tabletop.

2. The net assemble

The net assemble shall consist of the net, its suspension and the supporting posts, and the clamps attaching them to the table. The top of the net, along its whole length, shall be 15.25 cm above the playing surface.

3. The ball

The ball shall be spherical, with a diameter of 40 mm. The ball shall weigh 2.7 g. The ball shall be made of celluloid or similar plastics material and shall be white or orange, and matt.

4. 球拍

球拍大小、形状和质量不限,但底板应平整、坚硬。底板的85%应由天然木材制成。加强底板的黏合层可用诸如碳纤维、玻璃纤维或压缩纸等纤维材料,每层黏合层不超过底板总厚度的7.5%或0.35 mm。用来击球的拍面应用一层颗粒朝外的普通颗粒胶覆盖,连同黏合剂,厚度不超过2 mm;或用颗粒向内或向外的海绵胶覆盖,连同黏合剂,厚度不超过4 mm。

球拍两面无论是否有覆盖物,必须无光泽,且一面为鲜红色,另一面为黑色。

4. The racket

The racket may be of any size, shape or weight but the blade shall be flat and rigid. At least 85% of the blade by thickness shall be of natural wood; and adhesive layer within the blade may be reinforced with fibrous material such as carbon fiber, glass fiber or compressed paper, but shall not be thicker than 7.5% of the total thickness or 0.35 mm, whichever is the smaller. A side of the blade used for striking the ball shall be covered with either ordinary pimpled rubber, with pimples outwards having a total thickness including adhesive of not more than 2 mm, or sandwich rubber, with pimple inwards or outwards, having a total thickness including adhesive of not more than 4 mm.

The surface of the covering material on a side of the blade, or of a side of the blade if it is left uncovered, shall be matt, bright red on one side and black on the other.

二、定义

➢ 回合:球处于比赛状态的一段时间。

➢ 球处于比赛状态:从发球时球被有意向上抛起前静止在不执拍手掌上的最后一瞬间开始,直到该回合被判得分或重发球。

Ⅱ. Basic Definitions

➢ A rally is the period during which the ball is in play.

➢ The ball in play is from the last moment at which the ball is stationary before it is intentionally projected in serve until the rally is decided as a let or a point.

➢ 重发球:不予判分的回合。

➢ A let is a rally of which the result is not scored.

➢ 一分:判分的回合。

➢ A point is a rally of which the result is scored.

➢ 执拍手:正握着球拍的手。比赛中运动员可以用左右手交替执拍击球,而正握着球拍的手就是"执拍手"。但是,运动员不能左右手各拿一个球拍进行比赛。

➢ The racket hand is the hand carrying the racket. A player can strike the ball with either left hand or right hand alternately in the match, for the hand carrying the ball is the racket hand. The player, however, cannot take a racket in each hand.

➢ 非执拍手:未握着球拍的手。

➢ The free hand is the hand not carrying the racket.

➢ 击球:用握在手中的球拍或执拍手手腕以下部分击球。在比赛中,如果运动员的球拍掉落,他企图用刚才握着球拍的手击球将是不合法的。

➢ Striking the ball is a player strike the ball if he touches it in play with his racket, held in the hand, or with his racket hand below the wrist. If the racket falls in the match, it is illegal for the player try to strike the ball with the hand carrying the racket before.

➢ 阻挡:对方击球后,在比赛台面上方或向比赛台面方向运动的球,在没有触及本方台区、也未越过端线之前即触及本方运动员或其穿戴的任何物品。

➢ A player obstructs the ball if he, or anything he wears or carries, touches it in play when it is above or travelling towards the playing surface and has not passed beyond his end line, not having touched his court since last being struck by his opponent.

➢ 发球员:在一个回合中,首先击球的运动员。

➢ The server is the player due to strike the ball first in a rally.

➢ 接发球员:在一个回合中,第二个击球的运动员。

➢ The receiver is the player due to strike the ball second in a rally.

➢ "穿或带"的物品:运动员在一个回合开始时穿或带的任何物品,但不包括比赛用球。

➢ Anything that a player wears or carries includes anything that he was wearing or carrying, other than the ball, at the start of a rally.

➢ 越过或绕过球网装置：除球从球网和比赛台面之间通过以及从球网和网柱之间通过的情况外，球均应被视为已越过或绕过球网装置。

➢ The ball shall be regarded as passing over or around the net assembly if it passes anywhere other than between the net and the net post or between the net and the playing surface.

➢ 球台的端线：包括球台端线以及端线两端的无限延长线。

➢ The end line shall be regarded as extending indefinitely in both directions.

三、合法发球

Ⅲ. A Good Serve

➢ 发球开始时，球自然地放置在非执拍手的手掌上，手掌张开，保持静止。

➢ Serve shall start with the ball resting freely on the open palm of the server's stationary free hand.

➢ 发球员须用手将球几乎垂直地向上抛起，不得使球旋转，并使球在离开不执拍手的手掌之后上升不少于16 cm，球下降至被击出前不能触碰任何物体。

➢ The server shall then project the ball near vertically upwards, without imparting spin, so that it rises at least 16 cm after leaving the palm of the free hand and then falls without touching anything before being struck.

➢ 当球从抛起的最高点下降时，发球员方可击球，使球首先触及本方台区，然后越过或绕过球网装置，再触及接发球员的台区。在双打比赛中，球应先后触及发球员和接发球员的右半区。

➢ As the ball is falling the server shall strike it so that it touches first his court and then, after passing over or around the net assembly, touches directly the receiver's court; in doubles, the ball shall touch successively the right half court of server and receiver.

➢ 从发球开始到球被击出，球始终要高于比赛台面和在发球员的端线以外；而且不能被发球员及其双打同伴的身体或衣服的任何部位挡住。球一旦被抛起，发球员的不执拍手应立即从发球员的身体和球网之间的区域

➢ From the start of serve until it is struck, the ball shall be above the level of the playing surface and behind the server's end line, and it shall not be hidden from the receiver by any part of the body or clothing of the server or his doubles partner; as soon as

移开。

the ball has been projected, the server's free arm shall be removed from the space between the server's body and the net.

➢ 运动员发球时,应让裁判员或副裁判员看清自己是否按照合法发球的规定发球。

➢ It is the responsibility of the player to serve so that the umpire or assistant umpire can see that he complies with the requirements for a good serve.

➢ 如果裁判员对运动员的发球合法性有怀疑,在一场比赛中第一次出现时,可判重发球,并警告发球方。

➢ If the umpire is doubtful of the legality of a serve he may, on the first occasion in a match, declare a let and warn the server.

➢ 此后裁判员对该运动员或其双打同伴发球动作的合法性再次怀疑,将判接发球方得 1 分。

➢ Any subsequent serve of doubtful legality of that player or his double partner will result in a point to the receiver.

➢ 无论是否第一次或任何时候,只要发球员明显没有按照合法发球的规定发球,无须警告,应判接发球方得 1 分。

➢ Wherever there is a clear failure to comply with the requirements for a good serve, no warning shall be given and the receiver shall score a point.

➢ 运动员因身体伤病而不能严格遵守合法发球的某些规定时,可由裁判员做出决定免于执行。

➢ Exceptionally, the umpire may relax the requirements for a good serve where he is satisfied that compliance is prevented by physical disability.

四、合法还击

Ⅳ. A Good Return

对方发球或还击后,本方运动员必须击球,使球直接越过或绕过球网装置,或触及球网装置后,再触及对方台区。

The ball, having been served or returned shall be struck so that it passed over or around the net assembly and touches the opponent's court, either directly or after touching the net assembly.

五、1 分

Ⅴ. A Point

除被判重发球的回合,下列情况

Unless the rally is let, a player shall

运动员得1分：

➢ 对方运动员未能合法发球；

➢ 对方运动员未能合法还击；

➢ 运动员在合法发球或合法还击后，对方运动员在击球前，球触及了除球网装置以外的任何东西；

➢ 对方击球后，该球没有触及本方台区而越过本方端线；

➢ 对方阻挡；

➢ 对方连击；

➢ 对方运动员或他穿戴的任何东西使球台移动；

➢ 对方运动员不执拍手触及比赛台面；

➢ 双打时，对方运动员击球次序错误；

➢ 实行轮换发球法时，包括接发球，接发球方连续13次合法还击。

score a point:

➢ If his opponent fails to make a good serve;

➢ If his opponent fails to make a good return;

➢ If, after he has made a good return, the ball touches anything other than the net assembly before being struck by his opponent;

➢ If the ball passes beyond his end line without touching his court, after being struck by his opponent;

➢ If his opponent obstructs the ball;

➢ If his opponent strikes the ball twice successively;

➢ If his opponent, or anything his wears or carries, moves the playing surface;

➢ If his opponent's free hand touches the playing surface;

➢ If a double opponent strikes the ball out of the sequence established by the first server and first receiver;

➢ As provided under the expedite system, the receiver makes 13 good returns, including the receiving.

六、一局比赛和一场比赛

➢ 在一局比赛中，先得11分的一方为胜方。10平后，先多得2分的一方为胜方。

Ⅵ. A Game and a Match

➢ A game shall be won by the player or pair first scoring 11 points unless both players and pairs score 10 points, when the game shall won by the first player or pair subsequently gaining a lead of 2 points.

➢ 一场比赛由奇数局组成。

➢ A match shall consist of the best of any odd number of games.

七、重发球

Ⅶ. A Let

回合出现下列情况应判重发球：

➢ 如果发球员发出的球，在越过或绕过球网装置时触及球网装置，此后成为合法发球或被接发球员或其同伴阻挡；

➢ 如果接发球员或接发球方未准备好时，球已发出，而且接发球员或接发球方没有企图击球；

➢ 由于发生了运动员无法控制的干扰，而使运动员未能合法发球、合法还击或遵守规则；

➢ 裁判员或副裁判员暂停比赛。

可以在下列情况下暂停比赛：

➢ 由于要纠正发球、接发球次序或方位错误；

➢ 由于要实行轮换发球法；

➢ 由于警告或处罚运动员；

➢ 由于比赛环境受到干扰，以致该回合结果可能受到影响。

The rally shall be a let：

➢ If in serve the ball，in passing over or around the net assembly，touches it，provided the serve is otherwise good or the ball is obstructed by the receiver or his partner.

➢ If the serve is delivered when the receiving player or pair is not ready，provided that neither the receiver nor his partner attempts to strike the ball.

➢ If failure to make a good serve or a good return or otherwise to comply with the laws is due to a disturbance outside the control of the player.

➢ If play is interrupted by the umpire or assistant umpire.

Play may be interrupted：

➢ To correct an error in the order of serving，receiving or ends；

➢ To introduce the expedite system；

➢ To warn or penalize a player；

➢ Because the conditions of play are disturbed in a way which could affect the outcome of the rally.

八、比赛次序

Ⅷ. The Order of Play

➢ 选择发球、接发球和方位的权

➢ The right to choose the initial order

利应由抽签来决定。中签者可以选择先发球或先接发球,或选择先在某一方位。当一方运动员选择了先发球或先接发球,或选择了先在某一方位后,另一方运动员则接受另一种选择。

serving, receiving and ends shall be decided by lot and the winner may choose to serve or to receive first or to start at a particular end. When one player or pair has chosen to serve or to receive first or to start at a particular ends, the other player or pair shall have the other choice.

➢ 在单打中,首先由发球员合法发球,再由接发球员合法还击,然后两者交替合法还击。

➢ In singles, the server shall first make a good servc, the receiver shall then make a good return and thereafter server and receiver alternately shall each make a good return.

➢ 在双打中,首先由发球员合法发球,再由接发球员合法还击,然后由发球员的同伴合法还击,再由接发球员的同伴合法还击,此后,运动员按此次序轮流合法还击。

➢ In doubles, the server shall first make a good serve, the receiver shall then make a good return, the partner of the receiver shall then make a good return, the partner of the server shall then make a good return and there after each player in turn in that sequence shall make a good return.

➢ 在获得每 2 分之后,接发球方即成为发球方。依此类推,直至该局比赛结束,或者自至双方比分都达到 10 分或实行轮换发球法,这时,发球和接发球次序依然不变,但每人只轮发 1 分球。

➢ After a each 2 points have been scored, the receiving player or pair shall become thc serving player of pair until the end of the game, unless both players or pairs score 10 points or the expedite system is in operation, when the sequences of serving and receiving shall be the game but each player shall serve for only 1 point in turn.

➢ 在双打的第一局比赛中,先发球方确定第一发球员,再由先接发球方确定第一接发球员。在以后各局比赛中,第一发球员确定后,第一接发球员应是前一局发球给他的运动员。

➢ In each game of a double match, the pair having the right to serve first shall choose which of them will do so and in the first game of a match the receiving pair shall decide which of them will receive first; in subsequent games of the match, the first server having been chosen, the first receiver shall be the player who served to him in the preceding game.

➢ 在双打中,每次换发球时,前面的接发球员应成为发球员,前面的发球员的同伴应成为接发球员。

➢ In doubles, at each change of serve the previous receiver shall become the server and the partner of the previous server shall become the receiver.

➢ 一局中首先发球的一方,在该场下一局应首先接发球。在双打决胜局中,当一方先得5分时,接发球方应交换接发球次序。

➢ The player or pair serving first in a game shall receive first in the next game of the match and in the last possible game of a doubles match the pair due to receive next shall change their order of receiving when first one pair scores 5 points.

➢ 一局中,在某一方位比赛的一方,在该场下一局应换到另一方位。在决胜局中,一方先得5分时,双方应交换方位。

➢ The player or pair starting at one end in a game shall start at the other end in the next game of the match and in the last possible game of a match the player s or pairs shall change ends when first one player or pair scores 5 points.

九、纠正错误

Ⅸ. To Correct the Errors

➢ 裁判员一旦发现发球、接发球次序错误,应立即暂停比赛,并按该场比赛开始时确立的次序,按场上比分由应该发球或接发球的运动员发球或接发球;在双打中,则按发现错误时那一局首先有发球权的一方所确立的次序进行纠正,再继续比赛。

➢ If a player serves or receives out of turn, play shall be interrupted by the umpire as soon as the error is discovered and shall resume with those players serving and receiving who should be server and receiver respectively at the score that has been reached, according to the sequence established at the beginning of the match and, in doubles, to the order of serving chosen by the pair having the right to serve first in the game during which the error is discovered.

➢ 裁判员一旦发现运动员应交换方位而未交换，应立即暂停比赛，并按该场比赛开始时所确立的次序，按场上比分运动员应站的正确方位进行纠正，再继续比赛。

➢ If the players have not changed ends when they should have done so, play should be interrupted by the umpire as soon as the error is discovered and shall resume with the players at the ends at which they should be at the score that has been reached, according to the sequence established at the beginning of the match.

➢ 在任何情况下，发现错误之前的所有得分均有效。

➢ In any circumstance, all points scored before the discovery of an error shall be reckoned.

十、轮换发球法

X. The Expedite System

➢ 如果一局比赛进行到 10 分钟仍未结束，双方都已获得至少 9 分时除外，或者在此之前任何时间应双方运动员要求，应实行轮换发球法。

➢ Except where both players or pairs have scored at least 9 points, the expedite system shall come into operation if a game is unfinished after 10 minutes' play or at any earlier time at the request of both players or pairs.

➢ 当时限已到，球仍处于比赛状态，裁判员应立即叫停比赛，由被暂停回合的发球员发球，继续比赛。

➢ If the ball is in play when the time limit is reached, play shall be interrupted by the umpire and shall resume with serve by the player who served in the rally that was interrupted.

➢ 当时限已到，球未处于比赛状态，应由前一回合的接发球员发球，继续比赛。

➢ If the ball is not in play when the time limit is reached, play shall resume with serve by the player who received in the immediately preceding rally.

➢ 此后，每位运动员都轮换一个

➢ Thereafter, each player shall serve

发球，直至该局结束。如果接发球方进行了13次合法还击，则判接发球方得1分。

for 1 point turn until the end of the game and if the receiving player or pair makes 13 good returns the receiver shall score a point.

➢ 轮换发球法一经实行，将一直使用到该场比赛结束。

➢ Once introduced, the expedite system shall remain in operation until the end of the match.

第二节 国际竞赛规程

Section 2 Regulations for International Competitions

一、简介

Ⅰ. Brief Introduction

1. 器材和比赛条件

1. Equipment and Playing Conditions

➢ 球拍击球拍面的覆盖物应是国际乒联现行许可的品牌和型号，在其边缘必须附有清晰可见的商标型号及国际乒联（ITTF）的标记。

➢ The covering materials on a side of the blade used for striking the ball shall be of a brand and type currently authorized by the ITTF and shall be attached to the blade so that the brand and the ITTF logo are clearly visible near the edge of the striking surface.

➢ 赛区空间应不小于14 m长、7 m宽、5 m高。

➢ The playing space shall not be less than 14 m long, 7 m wide and 5 m high.

2. 比赛官员

2. Match Officials

● 裁判长

● Referee

➢ 每次竞赛应指派一名裁判长，其身份和工作地点应告知所有参赛者和队长。

➢ For each competition as a whole a referee shall be appointed and his identity and location shall be made known to the participants and, where appropriate, to the team captains.

（1）裁判长应对以下事项负责：

(1)The referee shall be responsible for:

➢ 主持抽签；

➢ The conduct of the draw;

➢ 编排比赛日程；

➢ The scheduling of matches by time and table;

➢ 主持裁判人员的赛前短会；

➢ Conducting a pre-tournament briefing for match officials;

➢ 审查运动员的参赛资格；

➢ Checking the eligibility of players;

➢ 决定在紧急时刻是否中断比赛；

➢ Deciding whether play may be suspended in an emergency;

➢ 决定在一场比赛中运动员是否可以离开赛区；

➢ Deciding whether players may leave the playing area during a match;

➢ 决定是否可以延长法定练习时间；

➢ Deciding whether statutory practice periods may be extended;

➢ 决定在一场比赛中运动员能否穿长运动服；

➢ Deciding whether players may wear track suits during a match;

➢ 对解释规则和规程的任何问题做出决定，包括服装、比赛器材和比赛条件的可接受性；

➢ Deciding any question of interpretation of Laws of Regulations, including the acceptability of clothing, playing equipment and playing conditions;

➢ 决定在比赛紧急中断时，运动员能否练习，以及练习地点；

➢ Deciding whether, and where, players may practice during an emergency suspension of play;

➢ 对于不良行为及其他违反规程的行为采取纪律行动。

➢ Taking disciplinary action for misbehavior or other breaches of regulations.

（2）经竞赛管理委员会的同意，当裁判长的任何职责托付给一些其他人员时，这些人员的每个人的特殊职责和工作地点应告知参赛者和队长。

（2）Where, with the agreement of the competition management committee, any of the duties of the referee are delegated to other persons, the specific responsibilities and locations of each of these persons shall be made known to the participants and, where appropriate, to the team captains.

（3）裁判长或在其缺席时负责代理的副裁判长，在比赛过程中自始至

（3）The referee, or a responsible deputy appointed to exercise authority in his absence,

终应亲临比赛场地。

shall be present at all times during play.

（4）如果裁判长认为有必要，可在任何时间更换裁判人员，但不得更改被更换者在其职权范围内就事实问题做出的判定。

（4）Where the referee is satisfied that it is necessary to do so he may replace a match official with another at any time, but he may not alter a decision already made by the replaced official on a question of fact within his jurisdiction.

（5）从抵达比赛场地开始至离开比赛场地，运动员应处于裁判长的管辖之下。

（5）Player shall be under the jurisdiction of the referee from the time at which they arrive at the playing venue until they leave it.

● 裁判员

● Umpire

（1）每场比赛均应指派1名裁判员和1名副裁判员。

（1）An umpire and an assistant umpire shall be appointed for each match.

（2）裁判员应坐在或站在球台一侧，与球网成一条直线。副裁判员应面对裁判员坐在球台另一侧。

（2）The umpire shall sit or stand in line with the net and the assistant umpire shall sit directly facing him, at the other side of the table.

（3）裁判员应对下列事项负责：

（3）The umpire shall be responsible for:

➢ 检查比赛器材和比赛条件的可接受性，如有问题向裁判长报告；

➢ Checking the acceptability of equipment and playing conditions and reporting any deficiency to the referee;

➢ 需要时指定比赛用球；

➢ Taking the specified ball for the competition;

➢ 主持抽签确定发球、接发球和方位；

➢ Conducting the draw for the choice of serving, receiving and ends;

➢ 决定是否由于运动员身体伤病而放宽合法发球的某些规定；

➢ Deciding whether the requirements of the serve law may be relaxed for a player with physical disability

➢ 控制方位和发球、接发球次序，纠正上述有关方面出现的错误；

➢ Controlling the order of serving, receiving and ends and correcting any errors therein;

➢ 决定每一回合得1分或重发球；

➢ 根据规定的程序报分；

➢ 在适当的时间执行轮换发球法；

➢ 保持比赛的连续性；

➢ 对违反场外指导或行为等规定者采取行动。

(4)副裁判员决定处于比赛状态的球是否触及距离他最近的比赛台面的上边缘。

(5)裁判员和副裁判员均可判决：

➢ 运动员发球动作不合法；

➢ 合法发球在球越过或绕过球网装置时，是否触及球网装置；

➢ 运动员阻挡球；

➢ 比赛环境受到意外干扰，该回合结果可能受到影响；

➢ 练习时间、比赛时间及间隔时间；

➢ 裁判员不得否决副裁判员对时间问题和计数员对接球员击球板数问题所做出的决定；

➢ 从抵达比赛区域开始至离开

➢ Deciding each rally as a point or a let;

➢ Calling the score, in accordance with specified procedure;

➢ Introducing the expedite system at the appropriate time;

➢ Maintaining the continuity of play;

➢ Taking action for breaches of the advice or behavior regulations.

(4)The assistant umpire shall decide whether or not the ball in play touches the edge of the playing surface at the side of the table nearest to him.

(5)Either the umpire or the assistant umpire may

➢ decide that a player's serve action is illegal;

➢ decide that, in an otherwise good serve, the ball touches the net assembly while passing over or around it;

➢ decide that a player obstructs the ball;

➢ decide that the conditions of play are disturbed in a way that may affect the outcome of the rally;

➢ time the duration of the practice period, of play and of intervals.

➢ A decision made by assistant umpire or stroke counter within his jurisdiction may not be overruled by the umpire.

➢ Player shall be under the jurisdiction

比赛区域,运动员应处于裁判员的管辖之下。

of the umpire from the time at which they arrive at the playing area until they leave it.

3. 比赛的管理

3. Match Conduct

● 报分

● Score indication

当球一结束比赛状态,裁判员应立即报分。

The umpire shall call the score as soon as the ball is out of play.

➢ 报分时,裁判员应首先报下一回合即将发球一方的分数,然后报另一方的分数。

➢ In calling the score during a game, umpire shall call first the number of points scored by the player or pair due to serve in the next rally of the game and then the number of the points scored by the opposing player or pair.

➢ 一局比赛开始时或交换发球时,裁判员的手势指向即将发起者,也可在报完分后,报出下一回合发球员的名字。

➢ At the beginning of a game and when a change of server is due, the umpire shall point to the next server, and may also follow the score call with the next server's name.

➢ 一局比赛结束后,裁判员应先报胜方运动员的姓名,然后报胜方的分数,再报负方的分数。

➢ At the end of a game, the umpire shall name the winning player or pair and shall then call the number of points scored by the winning player or pair followed by the number of points scored by the losing player or pair.

● 间歇

● Intervals

➢ 在局与局之间,有不超过 1 分钟的休息时间。

➢ An interval of up to 1 minute between successive games of a match.

➢ 一名或一对双打运动员可在一场比赛中要求一次暂停,时间不超过 1 分钟。

➢ A player or pair may claim one time-out period of up to 1 minute during a match.

➢ 在单项比赛中,暂停应由运动员或指定的场外指导提出;在团体比赛中,应由该队队长提出。

➢ In an individual event the request for time-out may be made by the player or pair or by the designated adviser; in a team event, it may be made by the team captain.

➢ 如果一名运动员或一对运动员与其指导者或教练员对是否暂停有不同意见时，在单项比赛中决定权属于这名或这对运动员，在团体比赛中决定权属于指导者或教练员。

➢ If a player or pair and an advisor or captain disagree whether a time-out is to be taken, the final decision shall be made by the player or pair in an individual event and by the captain in a team event.

➢ 请求暂停只有在球未处于比赛状态时做出，应用双手做"T"形表示。

➢ The request for a time-out, which may be made only when the ball is out of play, shall be indicated by making a "T" sign with the hands.

➢ 在一方获得合理的暂停要求后，裁判员应暂停比赛并出示白牌放在提出暂停一方运动员的台区上。

➢ On receiving a valid request for a time-out, the umpire shall suspend play and hold up a white card, he shall then place the card on the table of the player or pair making the request.

➢ 当提出暂停一方的运动员准备继续比赛或1分钟暂停时间已到时（以时间较短的为准），白牌应被拿走并立即恢复比赛。

➢ The white card shall be moved and play resumed as soon as the player or pair making the request is ready to continue or at the end of 1 minute, whichever is to the sooner.

➢ 如果比赛双方运动员或是他们的代表同时提出要求暂停，应在双方运动员准备恢复比赛或暂停时间满1分钟时继续比赛。在这场单项比赛中，双方运动员不再有暂停的权利。

➢ If a valid request for a time-out is made simultaneously by or on behalf of both players and pairs, play will resume when both players and pairs are ready or at the end of 1 minute, whichever is the sooner, and neither player nor pair shall be entitled to another time-out during that individual match.

➢ 每局比赛中，打到6的倍数时，或决胜局交换方位时，双方运动员可用短暂的时间擦汗。

➢ Brief intervals for toweling after every 6 points from the start of each game and at the change of ends in the last possible game of a match.

● 换拍

➢ 在一场单项比赛中，不允许更换球拍，除非球拍意外严重损坏到不能使用。如果运动员在比赛中损坏了球拍，应立即替换随身带来的另一个球拍，或场外递进的球拍。

➢ 运动员在比赛间歇时，应将球拍留在比赛台面上，得到裁判员的特殊许可除外。

● 练习

➢ 在一场比赛开始前，运动员有权在比赛球台上练习不超过 2 min，正常间歇时不能练习。

➢ 在紧急中断比赛时，裁判长可允许运动员在任何球台上练习，包括比赛用的球台。

➢ 运动员应有合理的机会检查和熟悉将要使用的器材，在替换破损球或损坏的球拍以后，运动员可练习少数几个回合，然后继续比赛。

● To change the racket

➢ A racket shall not be replaced during an individual match unless it is accidently damaged so badly that it cannot be used; if this happens the damaged racket shall be replaced immediately by another which the player has brought with him to the playing area or one which is handed to him in the playing area.

➢ Unless otherwise authorized by the referee, players shall leave their rackets on the table during intervals.

● Practice

➢ Players are entitled to practice on the match table for up to 2 minutes immediately before the start of a match but not during normal intervals.

➢ During an emergency suspension of play, the referee may allow players to practice on any table, including the match table.

➢ Players shall be given reasonable opportunity to check and to familiar themselves with any equipment which they are to use, but this shall not automatically entitled them to more than a few practice rallies before resuming play after the replacement of a damaged ball or racket.

参 考 文 献
References

[1] 苏丕仁. 乒乓球运动教程[M] . 北京：高等教育出版社，2004.

[2] MC AFEE R. Table tennis：steps to success[M]. [S.l.] Human Kinetics，2009.

[3] 中国乒乓球协会. 乒乓球竞赛规则[M]. 北京：人民体育出版社，2017.

[4] 李晓东. 现代乒乓制胜之道（下）[J]. 乒乓世界，2010（2）：114-117.

[5] 保罗·勒特尔. 世界一流网球技术[M]. 刘文娟，译. 北京：北京体育大学出版社，2007.

[6] HEATON J. Table tennis：skills · techniques · tactics [M]. Ramsbury：the Crowood Press Ltd.，2012.

[7] 拉尔夫·米歇利思，马丁·斯柯罗茨. 乒乓球：从入门到实战[M]. 花勇民，葛艳芳，译. 北京：北京体育大学出版社，2008.

附录1 乒乓球词汇

Appendix 1 Glossary of Table Tennis

防护圈胶皮：一种用来对付对方的旋转和速度的胶皮。

Anti-spin: a rubber type that counters spin and speed.

下旋：通过球拍向下摩擦球使球能向回旋转。

Backspin: produced by brushing the ball downwards so that the ball rotates backwards.

底板：主要以木材制成的且没有覆盖物的球拍部分。

Blade: the part of the racket made mainly of wood without the covering.

推挡：一种以拍面前倾的方式用于控制来球旋转和速度的击球技术。

Block: a stroke used to control spin and speed using a closed bat angle.

削球：一种运动员在远台采用的下旋击球技术。

Chop: a backspin stroke played away from the table.

放松练习：在训练或比赛之后的一个短期训练，旨在防止疼痛和伤病。

Cool down: a short session following training or competition aimed at preventing soreness and injury.

上旋对拉：一种用弧圈球回击对方弧圈球的击球技术。

Counter-spin: a stroke in which topspin is returned using topspin.

斜线球：从一个角斜线击打到另一个角的球。

Cross-court: a ball which is hit diagonally from corner to corner.

交叉步：一种用于快速回击远距离球的步法。

Crossover: a style of footwork used to cover large distance quickly.

远台球：回球不会在对手一侧的台子上弹起两次。

Deep: a ball that would not bounce twice on the opponent's side of the table.

平分：当比分为 10：10 平时，每

Deuce: when the score is 10-all and

一分轮换一次发球，直到比赛一方先领先对方 2 分时才为赢下这一局比赛。

serve changes every point until one player is two points clear of his/her opponent and has won the game.

两跳：在某一方回击前，球在同一侧比赛台面弹击了两次，即该方输掉这 1 分。

Double bounce: a ball hits the same side of the table twice before being returned. The person on that side loses the point.

双打：乒乓球比赛的一种形式，两个人在桌子的两边成对打球，且每人必须轮流击球。

Doubles: a format in table tennis where two people play as a pair on each side of the table and must alternate at striking the ball.

直线球：回球平行于边线。

Down the line: a ball hits parallel to the side line.

攻球：以一种拍面前倾的拍型击球的中后部。

Drive: a stroke played with a closed bat angle hitting the back.

摆短：以一种拍面前倾且向上的挥拍方向击打球的背面的技术。

Drop shot: a stroke played with a closed bat angle hitting the back of the ball in an upward direction.

轮换发球制：一场比赛超过比赛时限后，如果接发球方连续 13 次成功回击球，他/她将赢得该分。

Expedite time: after a time limit has expired during a game the receiver wins the point if he/she returns the ball successfully 13 times in a row.

拧拉（挑打）：一种用于回击短球的手腕快速向上的击球技术。

Flick: a stroke played against a short serve using a fast wrist action in an upward direction.

步法：乒乓球运动员通过移动进行击球的方式。

Footwork: how the player moves into position to play a stroke.

正手和反手：乒乓球正手和反手是以人的位置为参考的。如果惯用手是右手，右手边就是正手位，中间偏左手边就是反手位。如果惯用手是左手，左手边就是正手位，中间偏右手边就是反手位。

Forehand and backhand: the division of forehand and backhand in table tennis is based on the position of the person. If a player's dominant hand is right hand, the player uses forehand when the ball is in the right side of his or her body while uses backhand when the ball is in the center and left side of his or her body. If a player's dominant hand is left hand, the player uses forehand when the ball is in the left side of his or her body while uses backhand when the ball is in the center and right side of his or her body.

非执拍手：没有握着球拍的那只手，用于在击球时保持平衡。

Free hand: the hand not holding the bat and which is important in balance.

一局比赛：通常是首先获得 11 分的选手为胜方。除非已经达到 10 比 10 平局，在这种情况下，直到一方运动员领先对手 2 分，一局比赛才结束。

Game: is usually the first player to reach 11 points unless deuce has been reached in which case it is not over until one player is two points clear of their opponent.

硬胶皮：一种不含有海绵层的球拍覆盖物。

Hard rubber: a type of racket covering without a sponge layer.

国际乒联：乒乓球运动的世界管理部门，总部设置在瑞士洛桑。

International Table Tennis Federation: the world governing body for the sport, based in Lausanne, Switzerland.

重发球：由于发球击中网并越过或由于场外干扰而导致的比赛中断。

Let: a stoppage of play as a result of the serve hitting the net and going over or as a result of interference from outside the court.

放高球：通常为高的上旋球回球在球台底线处，容易被扣杀进攻。

Lob: a high topspin return played well back from the table usually in response to a smash.

长颗粒胶：表面由若干个长颗粒组成的胶皮，能产生让人捉摸不透的旋转。

Long pimples: a rubber whose surface consists of fairly long pimples which produces unpredictable spin.

弧圈球：一种产生强烈上旋的进攻性技术。

Loop: an attacking stroke used to produce a lot of topspin.

弧圈球打法：一种主要使用弧圈球技术作为击球方式的乒乓球打法。

Looper: a style of play in which the main stroke used is the loop.

一场比赛：一场比赛由奇数局组

Match: consists of the best of any odd

成,通常是三局两胜、五局三胜或七局四胜。

number of games, usually best of 3, 5 or 7.

直拍:一种主要在亚洲普遍使用的握拍法,该握拍法像握笔或拿筷子一样。

Penhold: a type of grip used mainly in Asia where the bat is held like a pen of chopsticks.

比赛台面:球台的顶层面,包括了球台的上边缘,球台颜色可为任意深色、哑光色,但最多的球台颜色为绿色和蓝色。

Playing surface: the top of the table, including the edges, which can be any dark, matt color but the most commonly used colors are green and blue.

得分:当对手未能将球击过或绕过球网,并使其落在桌面上方或边缘时,即得1分。

Point: is won when an opponent fails to hit the ball over or round the net so that it lands on the top or edge, on your side of table.

搓球:一项用于控制球的技术,击球时常通过后仰的拍型来进行使用。

Push: a stroke used for control, which is produced using an open bat angle.

球拍:乒乓球板的另一种正确的名称。

Racket: the alternative and correct name for the bat.

执拍手:用于握着球拍的手。

Racket hand: the hand that is used to hold the racket.

回合:比赛双方来回击球,从发球开始,到得分为结束。

Rally: the hitting of the ball back and forth, starting with a serve and ending when the point is won.

积分:在第一次比赛后指定给运动员的数字,选手积分越高表明其越优秀。

Rating: a number assigned to a player after their first tournament. The higher the rating a player has the better the player should be.

接发球:对发球的还击。

Receive: the return of the serve.

直板反面拉(直板横拉):直板选手采用的一项反手弧圈球技术,由直板选手使用握拍的反面而不是正常的一面来制造弧圈球进攻技术。

Reverse backhand topspin: a topspin stroke played by penhold players where the reverse side of the grip is used rather than the normal side to produce a topspin attacking stroke.

胶皮:乒乓球底板上的覆盖物,常有一层海绵覆盖在胶皮下面。

发球方:先击球开始一个回合的运动员。

发球:一个回合的开始,开始发球击球时,运动员先将球从非执拍手的手掌上向上抛起,然后将球发到本方球台一侧。

横板:乒乓球握拍法的一种,横握球拍时中指、无名指和小指缠绕握住拍柄,食指放置在球拍的背面。

短球:一次击球或发球至少会在对方球台台面弹击两次。

侧旋:一种通过从右向左或从左向右摩擦球所产生的旋转,并产生侧向的转动。

侧滑步:乒乓球最常用的步法,特别是在近台使用得多。

扣杀:一种用于高球的进攻性技术,在击打时高速向下挥拍击球。

旋转:球在击出后转动的方向。

海绵:附在橡胶背面的弹性材料层。海绵的使用在20世纪50年代结束了硬胶皮时代,海绵和胶皮的使用使得比赛速度更快,并能更多地制造

Rubber: the covering put onto the blade usually with a layer of sponge underneath it.

Server: the player who starts a rally.

Serve: the beginning of a rally where one player strikes the ball onto his/her own side of the table first after the ball has been thrown upwards from the palm of the free hand.

Shake hands: a type of grip where the racket is held with the middle, ring and little finger wrapped around the handle and the first finger resting on the back of the racket.

Short: a stroke or serve that would bounce at least twice on the opponent's side of the table.

Sidespin: a type of spin produced by brushing the ball from right to left or left to right producing a sideways rotation.

Sidestepping: the most commonly used footwork in table tennis, particularly when closed to the table.

Smash: an attacking stroke used against a high bouncing ball and struck downwards at high speed.

Spin: the direction the ball rotates after contact the bat.

Sponge: the layer of bouncy material attached to the back of the rubber. The use of sponge ended the hard rubber age in the 1950s and both made the game faster and allowed a

旋转。

greater use of spin.

击球:球员用球拍击球的方法,包括发球。

Stroke: the method by which the ball is struck by a player with the racket, including the serve.

上旋:一种以前倾的拍形并通过向上摩擦球所产生的旋转。

Topspin: a type of spin produced by brushing the ball upwards using a closed bat angle.

裁判:在比赛中负责计分和执行比赛规则的官员。

Umpire: the official who keeps score and enforces the rules during the match.

阻挡:在球在你方球台上弹起之前击球,则为阻挡,失1分。

Volley: to hit the ball before it bounces on your side of the table, which will result in you losing the point.

热身:训练或比赛之前的部分,热身的目的是让运动员的身体和心理状态做好准备。

Warm up: the session prior to training or competition, which is aimed at preparing the player both physically and mentally.

附录 2　乒乓球裁判员实用英语 100 句

Appendix 2　Practical English 100 Sentences for Umpires of Table Tennis

序号	中文术语	英文术语
1	你是日本队的 401 号运动员吗?	Are you No.401 from Japan?
2	你叫什么名字?	What is your name?
3	队长,请来挑边。	Captain, come and toss, please.
4	你要哪一边,红的还是蓝的?	Which side do you prefer, red or blue?
5	你猜中了。	You are right.(You won the toss.)
6	你要 ABC 还是 XYZ ?	Which one do you prefer, A; B; C or X; Y; Z?
7	请填写排名表。	Fill in the list, please.
8	请把排名表交给我。	Hand me the list, please.
9	请看一下对方的排名表。	Take a look at the list of your opponent.
10	你选什么? 发球还是接发球? 这边还是那边?	Which one is your choice? Serving or receiving? This end or that end?
11	你的号码是多少? 让我看一下你的号码布。	What is your number? Let me have a look.
12	你应该穿短衣短裤。	You should wear shorts.
13	同队服装应一致。	Players of the same team should be dressed uniformly.
14	你们双方服装的颜色应不同。	The color of your clothing should be different.
15	让我检查一下你的球拍。	Let me check your racket.
16	请挑两只比赛用球。	Please choose two balls.
17	这一只,你同意吗?	Is this one, OK?
18	请跟我入场,你走在他后面。	Follow me, please. You go behind him.
19	请带好毛巾。	Take care of the towel, please.
20	练习 2 分钟。	Practice for two minutes.
21	停止练习。	Stop practicing.
22	谁先发球? 谁先接发球?	Who will serve first? Who will receive first?

续表

序号	中文术语	英文术语
23	比赛开始，准备——发球，0 : 0。	Begin playing, ready-serve, love all.
24	现在开始实行轮换发球法。	Expedite system begins now.
25	犯规。	Fault.
26	暂停，重发球。	Let.
27	发球擦网。	Net.
28	侧面。	Side.
29	停。	Stop.
30	时间到。	Time.
31	暂停。	Time out.
32	交换发球。	Change service.
33	交换方位。	Change ends.
34	手掌未伸平。	The palm was not flat.
35	未静止。	Not stationary.
36	未近乎垂直。	Not near vertical.
37	低于 16 cm。	Less than 16 cm.(centimeter)
38	端线内发球。	Inside the end line.
39	超过最远点。	Beyond the farthest back.
40	擦边球。	Edge ball.
41	不执拍手低于台面。	The free hand was below the playing surface.
42	阻挡。	Obstruction.
43	触网。	Touched net.
44	手扶台面。	Hand on table.
45	台面移动。	Table moved.
46	连击。	Double hit.
47	两跳。	Double bounce.
48	出界。	Outside.
49	发(接)球员错误。	Wrong player.
50	次序错误。	Wrong order.
51	方位错误。	Wrong ends.
52	比分错误。	Wrong score.

续表

序号	中文术语	英文术语
53	纠正错误。	Correct a mistake.
54	处罚 1 分。	Penalize one point.
55	发球擦网。	Net service.
56	未准备好。	Not ready.
57	外界球进入场地。	Intrusion of a ball.
58	球破裂。	Broken ball.
59	意外事故。	Accident.
60	轮换发球法。	Expedite system.
61	请勿指导。	Do not advice.
62	请勿擦汗。	Do not towelling.
63	不能再休息了。	No long breaks.
64	继续比赛。	Continue playing.
65	请不要离开赛区。	Do not leave the playing area.
66	停止冒犯行为。	Stop the offending behavior.
67	不要拖延比赛。	Do not delay the game.
68	不能使用有毒胶水。	Do not use the toxic glues.
69	1,2,3,4,5,6,7,8,9,10,11,12,13,14,15,16,17,18,19,20,21。	One, Two, Three, Four, Five, Six, Seven, Eight, Nine, Ten, Eleven, Twelve, Thirteen, Fourteen, Fifteen, Sixteen, Seventeen, Eighteen, Nineteen, Twenty, Twenty-one.
70	第一(二、三、四、五)局。	First(Second, Third, Fourth, Fifth) game.
71	马琳对波尔。	Ma Lin versus Boll.
72	第一局比赛,马琳发球,0 ： 0。	First game Ma Lin to serve, love all.
73	第一局比赛结束,马琳胜。	First game to Ma Lin.
74	第二局比赛,波尔发球,0 ： 0。	Second game, Boll to serve, love all.
75	第五局,马琳胜。	Fifth game to Ma Lin.
76	马琳 3 : 2 获胜。	Match to Ma Lin 3 games to 2.
77	请等一下,我去报告裁判长。	Just a moment, I'll report to the referee.
78	请你签名。	Sign your name, please.
79	给你一份记分表。	Here you go the details of the match.
80	单项记分单。	Individual Event Score Sheet.
81	胜方签字。	Signature Winner(s).

续表

序号	中文术语	英文术语
82	负方签字。	Signature Loser(s).
83	裁判员签字。	Signature Umpires.
84	如有书面报告请在此标记。	If written report attached please mark here.
85	五局三胜制。	Best of five games.
86	第一阶段。	First stage.
87	A 组。	Group A.
88	第一轮。	Round 1.
89	3 号台。	Table No 3.
90	运动员姓名（协会）。	Player's name (Association).
91	运动员位置号。	Player's Position.
92	国际乒联竞赛经理。	ITTF Competition Manager.
93	国际级裁判长。	International Referee (IR).
94	国际级蓝牌裁判员。	International Blue Badge Umpire (IU BB).
95	国际级白牌裁判员。	International White Badge Umpire (IU WB).
96	国际级裁判员。	International Umpire (IU).
97	国家级裁判员。	National Umpire (NU).
98	志愿者。	Volunteer.
99	球拍检测组。	Racket Control Center (RCC).
100	成绩公告（编排组）。	Results Processing.

附录 3　国际乒联会员名缩写

Appendix 3　ITTF Members' Name Abbreviation

序号	Country and Region	缩写	国家和地区
1	AFGHANISTAN	AFG	阿富汗
2	ANGUILLA	AIA	安圭拉
3	ALBANIA	ALB	阿尔巴尼亚
4	ALGERIA	ALG	阿尔及利亚
5	ANDORRA	AND	安道尔
6	ANGOLA	ANG	安哥拉
7	ANTIGUA AND BARBUDA	ANT	安提瓜和巴布达
8	ARGENTINA	ARG	阿根廷
9	ARMENIA	ARM	亚美尼亚
10	ARUBA	ARU	阿鲁巴
11	AMERICAN SAMOA	ASA	美属萨摩亚群岛
12	AUSTRALIA	AUS	澳大利亚
13	AUSTRIA	AUT	奥地利
14	AZERBAIJAN	AZE	阿塞拜疆
15	BAHAMAS	BAH	巴哈马
16	BANGLADESH	BAN	孟加拉国
17	BARBADOS	BAR	巴巴多斯岛
18	BURUNDI	BDI	布隆迪
19	BELGIUM	BEL	比利时
20	BENIN	BEN	贝宁
21	BERMUDA	BER	百慕大群岛
22	BONAIRE	BES	博内尔岛
23	BHUTAN	BHU	不丹

续表

序号	Country	缩写	国家和地区
24	BOSNIA-HERZEGOVINA	BIH	波斯尼亚—黑塞哥维那
25	BELIZE	BIZ	伯利兹
26	BELARUS	BLR	白俄罗斯
27	BOLIVIA	BOL	玻利维亚
28	BOTSWANA	BOT	博茨瓦纳
29	BRAZIL	BRA	巴西
30	BAHRAIN	BRN	巴林
31	BRUNEI	BRU	文莱
32	BULGARIA	BUL	保加利亚
33	BUKINA FASO	BUR	布基纳法索
34	CENTRAL AFRICA	CAF	中非
35	CAMBODIA	CAM	柬埔寨
36	CANADA	CAN	加拿大
37	CAYMAN ISLANDS	CAY	开曼群岛
38	CONGO BRAZZAVILLE	CGO	刚果（布）
39	CHAD	CHA	乍得
40	CHILE	CHI	智利
41	CHINA	CHN	中国
42	COTE D'LVOIRE	CIV	科特迪瓦
43	CAMEROON	CMR	喀麦隆
44	CONGO DEMOCRATIC	COD	刚果（金）
45	COOK ISLANDS	COK	库克群岛
46	COLOMBIA	COL	哥伦比亚
47	COMOROS	COM	科摩罗
48	CAPE VERDE	CPV	佛得角
49	COSTA RICA	CRC	哥斯达黎加
50	CROATIA	CRO	克罗地亚
51	CUBA	CUB	古巴
52	CURACAO	CUW	库拉索岛
53	CYPRUS	CYP	塞浦路斯

续表

序号	Country	缩写	国家和地区
54	CZECH REPUBLIC	CZE	捷克
55	DENMARK	DEN	丹麦
56	DJIBOUTI	DJI	吉布提
57	DOMINICA W.I.	DMA	多米尼克
58	DOMINICAN REPUBLIC	DOM	多米尼加共和国
59	ECUADOR	ECU	厄瓜多尔
60	EGYPT	EGY	埃及
61	ENGLAND	ENG	英格兰
62	ERITREA	ERI	厄立特里亚
63	EL SALVADOR	ESA	萨尔瓦多
64	SPAIN	ESP	西班牙
65	ESTONIA	EST	爱沙尼亚
66	ETHIOPIA	ETH	埃塞俄比亚
67	FIJI	FIJ	斐济
68	FINLAND	FIN	芬兰
69	FRANCE	FRA	法国
70	FAROE ISLANDS	FRO	法罗群岛
71	MICRONESIA	FSM	密克罗尼西亚
72	GABON	GAB	加蓬
73	GAMBIA	GAM	冈比亚
74	GUINEA-BISSAU	GBS	几内亚比绍
75	GEORGIA	GEO	格鲁吉亚
76	EQUATORIAL GUINEA	GEQ	赤道几内亚
77	GERMANY	GER	德国
78	GUERNSEY C.I.	GGY	格恩西 C.I.
79	GHANA	GHA	加纳
80	GIBRALTAR	BIG	直布罗陀
81	GREECE	GRE	希腊
82	GREENLAND	GRL	格陵兰
83	GRENADA	GRN	格林纳达

续表

序号	Country	缩写	国家和地区
84	GUATEMALA	GUA	危地马拉
85	GUINEA	GUI	几内亚
86	GUAM	GUM	关岛
87	GUYANA	GUY	圭亚那
88	HAITI	HAI	海地
89	HONG KONG，CHINA	HKG	中国香港
90	HONDURAS	HON	洪都拉斯
91	HUNGARY	HUN	匈牙利
92	ISLE OF MAN	IMN	马恩岛
93	INDONESIA	INA	印度尼西亚
94	INDIA	IND	印度
95	IRAN	IRI	伊朗
96	IRELAND	IRL	爱尔兰
97	IRAQ	IRQ	伊拉克
98	ICELAND	ISL	冰岛
99	ISRAEL	ISR	以色列
100	US VIRGIN ISLANDS	ISU	美属维尔京群岛
101	ITALY	ITA	意大利
102	BRITISH VIRGIN ISLANDS	IVB	英属维尔京群岛
103	JAMAICA	JAM	牙买加
104	JERSEY	JEY	泽西岛
105	JORDAN	JOR	约旦
106	JAPAN	JPN	日本
107	KAZAKHSTAN	KAZ	哈萨克斯坦
108	KENYA	KEN	肯尼亚
109	KYRGYZSTAN	KGZ	吉尔吉斯斯坦
110	KIRIBATI	KIR	基里巴斯
111	KOREA REPUBLIC	KOR	韩国
112	KOSOVO	KOS	科索沃
113	SAUDI ARABIA	KSA	沙特阿拉伯

续表

序号	Country	缩写	国家和地区
114	KUWAIT	KUW	科威特
115	LAOS	LAO	老挝
116	LATVIA	LAT	拉脱维亚
117	LIBYA	LBA	利比亚
118	LEBANON	LIB	黎巴嫩
119	LIBERIA	LBR	利比里亚
120	ST. LUCIA	LCA	圣卢西亚
121	LESOTHO	LES	莱索托
122	LIECHTENSTEIN	LIE	列支敦士登
123	LITHUANIA	LTU	立陶宛
124	LUXEMBOURG	LUX	卢森堡
125	MACAO，CHINA	MAC	中国澳门
126	MADAGASCAR	MAD	马达加斯加
127	ST. MAARTEN	MAF	圣马丁岛
128	MOROCCO	MAR	摩洛哥
129	MALAYSIA	MAS	马来西亚
130	MALAWI	MAW	马拉维
131	MOLDOVA	MDA	摩尔多瓦
132	MALDIVES	MDV	马尔代夫
133	MEXICO	MEX	墨西哥
134	MONGOLIA	MGL	蒙古
135	MARSHALL ISLANDS	MHL	马绍尔群岛
136	NORTH MACEDONIA	MKD	北马其顿
137	MALI	MLI	马里
138	MALTA	MLT	马耳他
139	MONTENEGRO	MNE	黑山
140	NORTHERN MARIANA ISLANDS	MNP	北马里亚纳群岛
141	MONACO	MON	摩纳哥
142	MOZAMBIQUE	MOZ	莫桑比克
143	MAURITIUS	MRI	毛里求斯

续表

序号	Country	缩写	国家和地区
144	MAURITANIA	MTN	毛里塔尼亚
145	MYANMAR	MYA	缅甸
146	NAMIBIA	NAM	纳米比亚
147	NICARAGUA	NCA	尼加拉瓜
148	NEW CALEDONIA	NCL	新喀里多尼亚
149	NETHERLANDS	NED	荷兰
150	NEPAL	NEP	尼泊尔
151	NORFOLK ISLAND	NFK	诺福克岛
152	NIGERIA	NGR	尼日利亚
153	NIGER	NIG	尼日尔
154	NIUE	NIU	纽埃
155	NORWAY	NOR	挪威
156	NAURU	NRU	瑙鲁
157	NEW ZEALAND	NZL	新西兰
158	OMAN	OMA	阿曼
159	PAKISTAN	PAK	巴基斯坦
160	PANAMA	PAN	巴拿马
161	PARAGUAY	PAR	巴拉圭
162	PERU	PER	秘鲁
163	PHILIPPINES	PHI	菲律宾
164	PALESTINE	PLE	巴勒斯坦
165	PALAU	PLW	帕劳
166	PAPUA NEW GUINEA	PNG	巴布亚新几内亚
167	POLAND	POL	波兰
168	PORTUGAL	POR	葡萄牙
169	KOREA DPR	PRK	朝鲜
170	PUERTO RICO	PUR	波多黎各
171	TAHITI	PYF	塔希提岛
172	QATAR	QAT	卡塔尔
173	ROMANIA	ROU	罗马尼亚

续表

序号	Country	缩写	国家和地区
174	SOUTH AFRICA	RSA	南非
175	RUSSIA	RUS	俄罗斯
176	RWANDA	RWA	卢旺达
177	SAMOA	SAM	萨摩亚
178	SCOTLAND	SCO	苏格兰
179	SENEGAL	SEN	塞内加尔
180	SEYCHELLES	SEY	塞舌尔
181	SINGAPORE	SIN	新加坡
182	SAINT KITTS AND NEVIS	SKN	圣基茨和尼维斯
183	SIERRA LEONE	SLE	塞拉利昂
184	SLOVENIA	SLO	斯洛文尼亚
185	SAN MARINO	SMR	圣马力诺
186	SOLOMON ISLANDS	SOL	所罗门群岛
187	SOMALIA	SOM	索马里
188	SERBIA	SRB	塞尔维亚
189	SRI LANKA	SRI	斯里兰卡
190	SOUTH SUDAN	SSD	南苏丹
191	SAO TOME AND PRINCIPE	STP	圣多美和普林西比
192	SUDAN	SUD	苏丹
193	SWITZERLAND	SUI	瑞士
194	SURINAME	SUR	苏里南
195	SLOVAK REPUBLIC	SVK	斯洛伐克
196	SWEDEN	SWE	瑞典
197	SWAZILAND	SWZ	斯威士兰
198	SYRIA	SYR	叙利亚
199	TANZANIA	TAN	坦桑尼亚
200	TONGA	TGA	汤加
201	THAILAND	THA	泰国
202	TAJIKISTAN	TJK	塔吉克斯坦
203	TOKELAU	TKL	托克劳

续表

序号	Country	缩写	国家和地区
204	TURKMENISTAN	TKM	土库曼斯坦
205	EAST TIMOR	TLS	东帝汶
206	TOGO	TOG	多哥
207	CHINESE TAIPEI	TPE	中国台北
208	TRINIDAD AND TOBAGO	TRI	特立尼达和多巴哥
209	TUNISIA	TUN	突尼斯
210	TURKEY	TUR	土耳其
211	TUVALU	TUV	图瓦卢
212	UNITED ARAB EMIRATES	UAE	阿拉伯联合酋长国
213	UGANDA	UGA	乌干达
214	UKRAINE	UKR	乌克兰
215	URUGUAY	URU	乌拉圭
216	USA	USA	美国
217	UZBEKISTAN	UZB	乌兹别克斯坦
218	VANUATU	VAN	瓦努阿图
219	VENEZUELA	VEN	委内瑞拉
220	VIETNAM	VIE	越南
221	ST. VINCENT	VIN	圣文森特
222	WALES	WAL	威尔士
223	WALLIS AND FUTUNA	WLF	瓦利斯和富图纳群岛
224	YEMEN	YEM	也门
225	ZAMBIA	ZAM	赞比亚
226	ZIMBABWE	ZIM	津巴布韦